THE EMERGING BUSINESS

MANAGING FOR GROWTH

SEYMOUR JONES

M. BRUCE COHEN

COOPERS & LYBRAND

THE EMERGING BUSINESS

MANAGING FOR GROWTH

A Ronald Press Publication

JOHN WILEY & SONS

New York • Chichester • Brisbane • Toronto • Singapore

This publication is designed to provide accurate and
authoritative information in regard to the subject
matter covered. It is sold with the understanding that
the publisher is not engaged in rendering legal, accounting,
or other professional service. If legal advice or other
expert assistance is required, the services of a competent
professional person should be sought. *From a Declaration
of Principles jointly adopted by a Committee of the
American Bar Association and a Committee of Publishers.*

Library of Congress Cataloging in Publication Data:

Jones, Seymour, 1931-
  The emerging business.

  "A Ronald Press publication."

  1. Small business—Management.   I. Cohen, M. Bruce.
II. Title
HD62.7.J66   1983   658'.022   82-17650
ISBN 0-471-09800-0

Printed in the United States of America
10 9 8 7 6 5 4

CONTRIBUTORS

The range of business interests in this book called for contributions by a number of Coopers & Lybrand professionals who could bring a depth of experience to each of the areas covered. Because of the size of our organization and our long involvement with middle-market business, we were able to bring together our practitioners from various sections of the country to provide a balanced, comprehensive work. The contributors are:

Charles Bodo, Philadelphia
Michael Borsuk, Huntington, New York
Gordon Budke, Spokane
David Carpenter, Philadelphia
Richard Cummins, New York
Louis Donnini, Philadelphia
Frederick Haas, Philadelphia
Richard Kaye, Detroit
James Lafond, Springfield, Massachusetts
Norman Milefsky, New York
Charles Porter, Atlanta
Raymond Tasch, Chicago
Michael Tashjian, Washington, D. C.
Alan Vituli, New York

PREFACE

This book has grown out of a need that Coopers & Lybrand, as a national accounting and business advisory firm, perceived many years ago—a need arising from the encroachment of financial pressures, whether they be high interest rates, inflation, taxation or regulations, upon the profitability and potential of American enterprise.

We believe that the potential for growth is still here, that the marketplace is not only viable but also dynamic. But the business, whether it is relatively young or rich in tradition, and whether it is owner–manager operated or has a full financial staff, must accept the challenge of the contemporary economic environment.

This book is designed not only to help emerging business to meet that challenge but also to provide a multitude of ideas, systems, suggestions, and plans to enhance profitability and real growth. It has been written by the undersigned and other partners and staff of Coopers & Lybrand. All are practicing professionals who have dedicated their careers to working with businesspersons in the "middle market"—a term we use here to describe what is probably over 90 percent of American business: those organizations that are operated by their owners rather than by professional managers. The middle market includes most closely held and many small public companies that encompass almost every type of enterprise, from service-oriented to manufacturing.

The reader will find in this book coverage of many basic elements that may be critical to his or her success: business planning, reporting systems, sources of financing and utilization of credit, forms of doing business, and asset management. There are also more specialized areas covered, such as effective use of small computers, doing business with government (even for smaller businesses), and evaluating your business. On a personal note and to protect the fruits and rewards of a successful operation, such areas as estate and personal financial planning are included. Finally, the gamut of subjects extends from buying and selling your business to considerations in going public. This list merely suggests the range of topics—all or at least many of which will be important to businesses seeking not merely to stay afloat but also to overcome the pressures of the current environment and to prosper.

In writing this book, we had the assistance and support of many Coopers & Lybrand people beyond those mentioned in the contributor list preceding this preface. The contributions of Warren Wintrub, Henry Johansson, Fred Spindel, and Daniel O'Brien, who all provided insightful information and assistance on several issues, are especially noteworthy. Martin Satinsky, Barry Subkow, Donald Clement, Jr., Philip Sider, and Edward Donaghy devoted much time and effort to helping us clarify a number of other technical areas. Special thanks also go to Roger Kopstein, our editor, whose persistent demands for logical narrative flow kept the book on the right track. Finally, we thank Mort Meyerson, Coopers & Lybrand's director of communications, who first conceptualized and helped us develop this work.

SEYMOUR JONES
M. BRUCE COHEN

New York, New York
October 1982

CONTENTS

THE EMERGING BUSINESS

MANAGING FOR GROWTH

CHAPTER
ONE

STRATEGIES FOR
GROWTH

The entrepreneur or owner–manager is the very backbone of our American economy. Even today, in an economic climate dominated by large-scale business enterprise, small business accounts for 87 percent of the nation's new jobs in the private sector and should provide 50 percent of our gross national product by the end of this decade, according to the White House Commission on Small Business.

What are entrepreneurs? What makes them tick? What are their strengths, their weaknesses? Why do they do the things that they do? What must they do to be successful? The typical entrepreneur has a background in sales or marketing and perhaps in the area of production; in other words, he or she knows how to produce or sell a product or service. On the other hand, most owner–managers are not experienced in the areas of finance and administration.

A major functional characteristic of the entrepreneur is that the person and the business are inseparable in terms of financial planning. Accountants and financial advisors who have worked with both professional managers and entrepreneurs recognize that it is fundamentally impossible to serve a closely held business without understanding and relating directly to the needs, hopes, and dreams of owner–managers. In this respect, the entrepreneur differs markedly from the professional manager.

A cross section of the "middle market," representing small to medium-size businesses, reveals the prototype of a closely held company operating in a highly competitive market with limited resources. Typically, such companies are thinly capitalized and highly leveraged so that debt service is a heavy burden. Because of their financial weakness—which can coexist with high profitability in operations—the attitude of the financial market toward these companies is skeptical. Added to their difficulties of obtaining credit and capital are the problems that arise from the lack of a sophisticated staff or middle management. In an economy such as the present one, characterized by alternating recession and inflation, these handicaps tend to make it difficult for the entrepreneur to survive, let alone prosper.

Our collective experience indicates that a major reason for failure among new businesses is inadequate financial management. Together with inadequate capitalization and/or financing, this deficiency can destroy a business even if the basic idea behind that business is viable—that is, if the product or the service has found a favorable reception in the marketplace.

The essence of financial management lies in balancing future growth and profitability with liquidity. In a period of economic downturn or tight money, the proper performance of this "balancing act" will help put the business in a position to take advantage of opportunities when the cycle changes. Thus it may be advisable to stay lean in terms of inventory, even though this may mean forgoing sales that would otherwise be profitable. Simply stated, *survival* may be more important than *profitability.* This is not to say that businesses are not often in the position to increase both profitability *and* liquidity; reduction of overhead and administrative cost cutting are examples. There will, however, be times when one factor can be maximized only at the expense of the other, and when that happens, it is usually liquidity that should be favored. The point is that business strategies and actions must often be dictated by financial considerations.

The foundation of financial management is information. You must have complete and continuous data on backlogs, inventory, accounts receivable and payable, and a host of other key factors. With this input, you can formulate a cash-flow forecast, which must serve as the fiscal basis for nearly every decision you make. Normally, cash flow should be projected a year ahead. In the pages that follow, we will cover the fundamentals of starting your own business and running it from the outset to maturity.

We begin by asking the question, should you be or can you afford to be an entrepreneur? We believe that the immense personal gratification to be derived from owning and managing your business can be as great as the financial benefits and rewards. This must be balanced, however, against the stark failure rate of new businesses—a mortality, incidentally, due primarily to lack of managerial expertise. We strongly recommend that you have a thorough knowledge of the business you are considering before committing yourself to such a significant financial undertaking. We also urge the would-be entrepreneur to consider the strong personal commitment involved—a commitment without which the success of the business would surely be in doubt. Personal commitment goes far beyond financial resources to the very essence of what you are cut out to be. Because you cannot surround yourself within your company with all the necessary financial, legal, accounting, and administrative talent required for a successful business operation, you will have to depend, to some extent, on consultants. We give you some pointers on using them, with emphasis on getting the most from their talents and on controlling the cost of their services.

We then deal with the business plan, without which you should not take any step involving arrangements with or commitments to others. The business plan should be a management tool as well as an instrument to raise the necessary capital and financing. Most businesses in the middle market are highly leveraged. Without a definitive business plan, it is difficult to command the respect of financial institutions. An entrepreneur who has borrowed less than subsequently proves necessary can always appeal for more funds, but the implied admission of poor planning is hardly reassuring to the lender.

We discuss all of the elements of a financial plan including a basic description of the business itself; staffing, with emphasis on qualifications of key personnel; and the development of cash-flow analysis to identify the need for outside financing. Break-even analysis and estimating profit margins are discussed, as is the need for contingency plans, which become so critical in a period of uncertainty.

We then describe some sources of financing, providing tips on how to utilize credit and how to mix it with equity. We discuss venture capitalists, banks, insurance companies, financial institutions, and the government, and we describe various funding devices, suitable for the small and medium-size businessperson, available through these sources. We also take a look at tax planning from the point of view not only of maximizing profits but also, more specifically, of retaining capital in the business. The importance of the loan request or presentation is hard to overestimate. We include a commentary on how these presentations should be made, what documents should be submitted, what attitudes should be assumed, and, of course, what professional services should be employed in preparing these vital compilations.

Once you have a formalized business plan in hand and have determined your source of financing, you must then establish the proper business format. We have a section on selecting various forms of doing business, with a full discussion of their advantages and disadvantages that takes in tax as well as legal aspects. For those interested in acquiring a business, there is the chapter "Buying or Selling a Business," dealing with various methods of acquisition, the decision whether or not to buy, and the criteria for arriving at the appropriate price and means of payment.

Here again, tax planning is critical if the deductions and other advantages available under the Internal Revenue Code and related regulations are to be realized by the owner–manager.

We also discuss in the same chapter selling your business. There is nothing inappropriate about this. If you are successful, you will reach a point where you must consider either what will happen to the business in the event you are no longer able to function or, alternatively, how you can capitalize on your efforts. The method of disposition as well as the terms of payout are governed by personal as well as tax considerations. Frankly, we look upon the entire notion of selling your company as "how to cash in."

Next we describe the mechanics of cash management. Effective cash management is critical to the survival of the business, particularly in periods like the present, in which high interest rates are combined with substantial inflation. Paradoxically, the faster a business is growing, the more important it is to plan for preservation of cash flow. A business that is losing money may be able to contract its operations if there are cash-flow problems, but a business that is growing out of control can easily absorb too much cash before anything can be done about it. It is by no means unheard of for an entrepreneur to go under simply because he or she permitted sales volume to outpace the capacity of the business to handle it. Financial planning for growth has two aspects: first, determining the rate that can be financed internally *without strain* or externally from assured sources; and second, instituting controls to prevent waste of cash and also to ensure that growth limits are not exceeded.

Our treatment of accounts receivable management includes a discussion of appropriate methods and procedures for handling credits and collections. In the area of inventory, we deal with systems and procedures that are critical to any product-oriented company. Inventory is the most difficult asset to manage, because inventory levels directly impact sales volume as well as liquidity. Here again, the entrepreneur is likely to increase the volume base at the expense of liquidity. To be optimal, however, the level of inventory must be consistent with the planned growth level of the company. When inventory gets out of hand, it tends to drain away cash and ultimately produce markdowns and increased operational costs, which in turn can cause serious financial loss. Inventory levels must be constantly regulated in conjunction with sales levels

and liquidity. Inventory management involves understanding both product and carrying costs. It requires establishing perpetual inventory records and cost controls.

Finally, under asset management, we deal with capital budgeting and
the need to provide for fixed asset acquisition, be it real estate, machinery
and equipment, rolling stock, tools, or office furniture and fixtures. All of
these items need to be properly budgeted, planned for, and financed so
that the short-run cash position of a business is not adversely affected.
Asset management—that is, the technique of managing what you have in
the most productive and economic way—will be one of your fundamental concerns.

A reliable flow of at least basic information is virtually essential to running any but the most rudimentary business. Assuming you have no
creditors, investors, or other interested parties to report to (including, in
some cases, customers and suppliers), you might survive without an information system, but it would only be by sheer luck. As an
owner–manager, you have too much at stake to trust to blind instinct.
Our chapters on accounting and reporting systems (including management controls) and small computers cover the kinds of data you will
need to run your business. They also address the problem of how to determine whether computers are applicable under certain sets of circumstances and how to pick the best one for the job. (Today, there are available highly cost-effective minicomputers as well as numerous applications
and software packages.) Postponing computerization when you clearly
need it is unwise and can be dangerous. If your operations break down
because of inadequate accounting and reporting systems and controls—
and this is especially liable to happen if your business is expanding
rapidly—it may be difficult to get things going again. Businesses in this
predicament have been known to fold.

One of the main reasons for going into business for youself is to control your own destiny and determine your compensation. Rewards for
running a successful entrepreneurial business can indeed be quite high.
We believe, however, that there are significant extras that the
owner–manager can develop for both himself or herself as well as key
employees. Publicly held companies offer significant fringe benefits in order to attract and retain key employees. The plans of closely held
companies have a somewhat different structure, but they too can offer

significant benefits both to you and to your employees. These fringe benefits, their related cost, and how to shop for them form the subject of one of our chapters.

The chapter on tax strategies and traps for the closely held business represents a comprehensive overview of tax planning. The benefits are many; travel and entertainment and use of country clubs, cars, and apartments are examples. Yet there is always the question of how far you can go; not only how much you can show to be business related and therefore deductible but also what is good for your business *notwithstanding* the element of deductibility. The nondeductibility of an item can be a critical factor in assessing the related business cost. This is one of the points brought out in our discussion of tax traps. In this chapter, we show how Internal Revenue Service (IRS) rulings and regulations as well as recent tax cases can be significant to your operations. An example is the special problem that arises when the entrepreneur's thinly capitalized company is in debt to him or her.

The owner–manager is inseparable from the business he or she owns and manages. Therefore your estate and personal financial planning should be geared directly to the available benefits of running your own business. In this connection, there are many ways in which to minimize or reduce tax burdens and conserve assets under the applicable rules and regulations. The field is highly technical, however, and many entrepreneurs who have attempted to limit or reduce their tax burdens by improper methods have subjected themselves and their families to serious legal and fiscal complications. In general, you should be prepared to treat your business planning and your estate and personal financial planning as integral parts of a strategy that has as its centerpiece the successful management of your financial life.

The government is an important source of business opportunity. Although the official attitude toward small and medium-size businesses is favorable (as evidenced by legislation specifically targeting certain segments of government business for these categories of enterprise), relations with government agencies are subject to rules and regulations that can be somewhat complex. As a result, inexperienced entrepreneurs tend to shy away from this potentially rewarding market. To help you understand how to do business with the government, we take up such key questions as: What are the various rules and regulations? What are the special provisions applicable to the middle market? and, finally, how does one expedite transactions with the government? We also discuss the various kinds of procurement contracts that are out for bidding.

We have included a chapter on "going public," because of the significance of this strategy to successful emerging businesses. Although the move involves the owner–manager in a whole new set of financial responsibilities, it offers vast possibilities for raising capital, and it also makes possible favorable tax treatment where it might otherwise be unavailable.

For those already involved in managing their own businesses, we conclude with the chapter "Evaluating Business Performance," which summarizes techniques for critical comparisons with other businesses (and with alternative investments) and offers guidelines for subjective— that is, nonquantitative—evaluation. The chapter presents a lengthy, diagnostic checklist that will permit you, as entrepreneur, to rate yourself on how well you are managing your business.

There are abundant indications that in the coming decade the entrepreneur will have to face both inflation and recession. Under these conditions, protecting your business and your personal financial interests will be more difficult than it was in times of rising productivity and mild inflation, such as the period between the Korean and Vietnam Wars. This does not mean that the climate is uncongenial to new small enterprises. We have said earlier that the entrepreneur is the very backbone of the American economy. Notwithstanding the growth of large-scale businesses, the fostering of small and middle-size enterprises has been, and will continue to be, a fixture of public policy in this country. We believe that with sound financial management, any enterprise that is fundamentally viable in a commercial sense should be able to survive and prosper in the decade ahead.

CHAPTER
TWO

WHAT DOES IT TAKE TO BE AN ENTREPRENEUR?

Then are an estimated 12 million small businesses in the United States, employing more than 54 million Americans. They include manufacturers of industrial and consumer goods, distributors, and providers of all types of services. Owner-managed businesses not only are a source of new employment and productivity in this country but also have historically been a great source of innovation and creativity. Products such as cellophane, air conditioning, the jet engine, the helicopter, and the felt-tip pen were developed by individual entrepreneurs and small companies. In medicine, small business has contributed insulin and penicillin as well as sophisticated neurosurgical equipment; in the field of military technology, it can claim credit for the Sidewinder missile and the atomic submarine.

Some entrepreneurial businesses have had a profound effect on our lives and have amassed, for their owners, vast personal fortunes. Some obvious examples are Henry Ford, Henry J. Heinz, and Helena Rubenstein—and some not so obvious, Chester Carlson (Xerox), Herbert Marcus (Neiman-Marcus), Steve Jobs (the Apple Computer).

THE CHALLENGES

Although it is true that no enterprise can succeed without a salable product or service and an effective marketing strategy, managing a business takes a good deal more. The successful entrepreneur must raise the initial capital to start up or acquire a business. He or she must prepare detailed operating plans that cover, among other things, planned production, sales, expenses and capital expenditures. Initially, he or she must assume responsibility for every detail of daily operations. He or she has to meet payrolls, comply with a myriad of governmental regulations, obtain and maintain adequate financing and sources of supply, and, all the while, generate profits. What's more, even if he or she is able to cope with all of these concerns, the entrepreneur still has no assurance of success. Products become obsolete when someone makes a better mousetrap. Tastes change; hula hoops, hot pants, and coonskin caps have all come and gone. Several hundred thousand small businesses—and some large ones—fade away every year.

In fact, the statistics for any given year are disheartening enough to discourage all but the hardiest soul. In the year ended June 30, 1981, there were over 47,000 bankruptcies. If 100 businesses were started at the same time, the odds are that 20 of them would be gone by the end of the first year; 17 more would fade in year two; and by the end of the fifth year, a total of about 67 would have been left by the wayside. Why? Of the 100, 33 survive; 67 do not. By evaluating the reasons for one or the other, can we give ourselves a little more of an edge toward becoming one of the 33 potential success stories? Yes, we can.

Success (and failure) come down to two words: *managerial ability.* Dun & Bradstreet has consistently reported that about 90 percent of all business failures result from lack of managerial aptitude and experience.

Every owner–manager must, at the very least, learn financing techniques and the elements of business planning. He or she must understand asset management and management information systems. But even these qualifications do not ensure success. There are certain personal qualities that are indispensable.

THE ENTREPRENEURIAL PSYCHOLOGY

Contrary to the popular view, most people who forgo employee status for that of employer are not motivated primarily by monetary considerations, although the possibility of reaping substantial financial rewards is certainly recognized. Rather, their primary motive is the desire to be their own masters. Prominent among entrepreneurs is the type of person who cannot be happy working for others and who has a strong need for achievement. Such people want to make decisions, especially the kind of decisions that produce results in short order. They want to try out ideas without consulting a sub-, ad hoc, standing, or executive committee. In short, they want a freedom of action they could never get as employees.

Essential Characteristics

On the basis of our experience and on the findings of several studies, we have identified a few characteristics that we think are essential to the successful entrepreneur. Before we discuss them, however, we advise the reader that most of the studies we used were biased, as they were compiled only from interviews with successful businesspeople. The unsuccessful ones were not around to be interviewed. Hence, one may tend to conclude, erroneously, that if a given characteristic works for a successful individual, an unsuccessful one must have lacked it.

In a study published by the U.S. Small Business Administration (SBA), five characteristics were associated with the successful businessperson: drive, thinking ability, human relations ability, communications ability, and technical knowledge.

Drive

In our experience, drive is the most significant factor associated with the successful businessperson. In the early years of any business, the hours are often long, the problems endless, and the frustrations many. Unplanned production, supply, or inventory problems can result in many missed holiday outings, forgotten anniversaries, and disarray in the family social calendar. "Nine to five" is only a fantasy to the owner–manager.

In regard to long hours, there is the story of a venture capitalist who visited unannounced the business premises of a prospective investee on a Saturday afternoon and found the place empty. He immediately withdrew his plans for investment, explaining to an acquaintance—not the owner–manager—that if the survival of the struggling business was not important enough for the owners to be there on a Saturday, the prospects of the business's ultimate survival were bleak.

In light of these factors, a supportive family is most helpful, if not critical. The owner–manager who faces problems from customers, employees, bankers, and vendors all day must have a home where frustrations can be vented and forgotten.

In another SBA study, the categories rated as most important in a survey of successful businesspersons were perseverance, initiative, confidence, self-reliance, and the need to achieve. All of these characteristics relate to drive.

Thinking Ability

This quality is defined by the SBA as "original, creative, critical and analytical thinking." To test your thinking ability, ask yourself the following questions: Can I make a reasoned decision? Can I plan my business strategy and assume responsibility for it? Do I know when I need help and where to get it?

The entrepreneur must be able to act rather than to react. He or she must think about tomorrow—changing economic conditions, competition, new or improved products or services, new production techniques, and so on. Contingency plans for reasonably predictable events, such as changes in competitor pricing or loss of a source of supply, should be in place. Control systems that promote efficiency, minimize cost, and reduce risk of loss must be designed and implemented. The line-on-the-wall inventory system—that is, when you can see the line, it is time to order or produce more—is ineffective in all but the smallest businesses.

The owner of a successful manufacturing company on the East Coast had a great deal of drive. As the company grew larger, however, it became more and more difficult for him to make the necessary, hard decisions. Eventually, vital matters were left unattended to unless employees took the necessary initiatives. Ultimately, the decision as to the future of the company was made for the owner by a trustee in bankruptcy.

Aptitude for Human Relations

You must be able to deal effectively with people. The entrepreneur has to motivate employees, sell customers, negotiate with vendors, and convince lenders. This is a constant and unremitting challenge.

The owner–manager cannot, however, simultaneously assume the roles of sales manager, production manager, controller, and president for long. No one can be an expert in every business operation. The entrepreneur must learn the delicate technique of delegating without abdicating.

He or she must also be resilient. The entrepreneur must be able to suffer occasional economic defeats—perhaps disasters—and yet maintain his or her balance.

A client of ours reengaged its former president when it became apparent that the company was on the brink of bankruptcy. With over 50 major (and hungry) creditors and no liquid assets, only the most resilient of entrepreneurs would have taken on a course other than a "chapter." This president, however, designed a plan for survival, met with lenders, and motivated them (or, more precisely, sold them) on his concepts for a "work out." He had to encourage dismayed employees, reassure vendors, and, most importantly, convince lenders. Although there were many tense moments, all cooperated and the company not only survived but also has since prospered. That entrepreneur's ability to relate to others, as well as his drive, self-confidence, and thinking ability, saved the company from becoming a statistic.

Ability to Communicate

Can you make yourself understood? Can you persuade? A struggling entrepreneur of our acquaintance talks incessantly, shifts thoughts in mid-sentence, and punctuates his discourse with such phrases as "ya know," "in no way, shape or form," and the ever popular "if you know what I mean." He often shouts, and his memos tend to be unnecessarily long and caustic. The result of all this ineptitude is that much of what he says goes unheard or unread. And no wonder! When communications are muddled or abused in this way, inefficiency and redundancy are inevitable.

You can test your communication skills by instructing someone in how to put on a suit coat that has been draped over a chair. Allow the instructee to perform only the precise movement you describe. Most people find this to be a somewhat challenging task.

In communicating, never lose sight of the listener's or reader's expectations, experience, and abilities. If you are like the manager who told an inexperienced lab assistant to "modify the diameter of the arteriovenous shunt by 10 percent for use in the hemodialysis research project," you are well-advised to carry a fire extinguisher at all times. Succinctness is important, but it must be tempered by the need to be *understood.*

When the wrong product or the wrong quantity of a product is shipped or received, when customers or employees are unnecessarily disturbed, or when sensitive information is mailed to a competitor, 9 times out of 10 the cause is faulty communications. Without doubt, poor communications have contributed to the demise of many businesses.

Technical Knowledge

The owner–manager must know his or her product and market and must have the technical know-how to determine whether to use distributors, a direct sales force, or a combination thereof. The entrepreneur must be able to consider the short- and long-range effects of marketing techniques and must know the strengths and weaknesses of his or her competitors.

An entrepreneur we know formed a leasing company that avoided intense competition by specializing in small-dollar leases that competitors did not want. He learned how to market his service effectively through direct mail solicitation, while he continued to devote most of his own time to developing and marketing products. Meanwhile, he hired lawyers to collect past-due lease contracts, a controller to maintain the financial records, and accountants to prepare financial statements. Thus he was able to develop technical knowledge while effectively utilizing the talents of others.

This example illustrates an important point. You do not have to master every skill that might enter into the conduct of your business. You must know your weaknesses, however, and make sure that you have effective backup in the form of partners, employees, or consultants. It may be a question of taking in a partner as a means of getting investment capital, personal contacts, or a needed talent (a "mister inside and mister outside" arrangement), or of hiring an experienced plant manager to compensate for a lack of production experience.

USING OUTSIDE PROFESSIONALS

Even before you actually begin operations, you will probably have to rely on outside professionals for legal, tax, and accounting advice. Later, when your business gets off the ground, you will need the services of an independent accountant and possibly of management consultants as well. Few small and medium-size companies find it practical to hire lawyers, tax specialists, or management consultants as employees. Even those that do can seldom furnish these people adequate backup in the form of staff, research facilities, record keeping, and so on.

The Certified Public Accountant (CPA)

The independent accountant's basic function is, of course, to report on financial statements. His or her knowledge of your business, however, and of business in general makes the CPA an indispensable adviser on a wide range of matters. Here are just a few of the myriad services your accountant can perform for you: evaluating the financial implications of major business decisions, such as whether to buy or lease, build or purchase facilities, or to acquire or be acquired; identifying weaknesses in internal controls; and rendering vital assistance in tax planning, financial forecasting, and choosing sources and type of financing. Few businesspersons will, or should, take a significant financial step without consulting their CPA.

In selecting the CPA, you will probably do best if you prepare a list of likely candidates and narrow it down by elimination. You should be able to get five or six names from business acquaintances without any trouble. Each firm should be interviewed and asked pointed questions concerning its approach to service, experience in the industry, range of services offered, personnel, and fees. In evaluating the answers, think in terms of future as well as current needs. Outgrowing advisers in a short time can be costly.

You should not ignore your reaction to personalities in evaluating a professional consultant. It is important to be comfortable with the persons with whom you will come into contact. An atmosphere of cordiality and mutual trust makes for the most productive relationship.

The Lawyer

A lawyer should play an integral role in any of your decisions with legal implications. Thus, contracts, leases, notes, and the like should be prepared, or at least reviewed, by competent counsel. Like accountants, lawyers often have a competence in general business matters that goes far beyond their primary professional discipline. For example, a corporate lawyer experienced in acquisitions is likely to be a skilled negotiator.

Range of Services

Corporate reorganizations, real estate, and estates and trusts are generally within the competence of most law firms. You would not, however, presume that a firm is experienced in, say, pension plans, without specific confirmation of that fact. Accounting firms may offer services in many areas of business management besides financial reporting. Examples are acquisitions and reorganizations, international taxation, data processing, accounting systems, production planning, and materials management. Some accounting firms offer specialized consultation in such areas as employee benefits planning, engineering and valuation, and computer services.

The roles of the lawyer and the CPA can overlap, and, in fact, some practitioners are members of both professions. It is inadvisable, however, to use one professional to satisfy both roles. Few individuals can attain, and fewer can maintain, a high level of expertise in two demanding professions. The ideal arrangement where both disciplines are needed is to have the CPA and the attorney work together to consider the financial, tax, and legal effects of business transactions.

Fees and Other Factors

Professional fees are ususally based on time and on the level of the personnel used. For defined tasks, such as reporting on financial statements or preparing tax returns, a fee can usually be estimated in advance. For other services, you can ask for a range of hourly rates. Fees should not be an overriding concern; they are often recovered many times over as a result of professional advice.

Such considerations as firm location, size, and possible conflicts of interest may also influence your choice, not only of attorneys and accountants but also of any professionals.

Summary

A successful business can provide not only the satisfaction of being one's own master but also substantial financial rewards.

Success as an entrepreneur requires:

A great deal of energy

The ability to make decisions

Self-knowledge, including a faculty for knowing what you do *not* know

The ability to deal effectively with a variety of people—employees, customers, suppliers, and lenders

The ability to make yourself understood

A knowledge of the product and the market

A lot of luck

To the above list, we might add the ability to select the right professionals and to use them effectively.

CHAPTER
THREE

BUSINESS PLANNING

Business planning is the systematic forecasting of developments, internal and external, covering a specified period, in order to formulate a course of action for that period. The course of action is spelled out in a document termed the *business plan*. Business planning, strategic planning, and long-range planning generally are the same thing. Budgeting and financial forecasting deal with the financial implications of the business plan. They are necessary, but secondary, parts of the planning process.

THE BUSINESS PLAN

Most companies, large and small, carry out business planning either superficially or not at all. Perhaps large companies with their massive resources can afford poor planning, but the entrepreneur with limited resources of people, money, equipment, and time must utilize them wisely. A good basic business plan should contain:

A statement of objectives

A penetrating appraisal of the organization's opportunities, strengths, and weaknesses

The planning assumptions

An evaluation of alternative courses of action

Selection of a course of action

An implementation plan including organizational changes, schedules, and financial forecasts

An annual update including regular review and refinement

Why Plan?

Effective practical planning enables you to control the direction of your business and stabilize it. In our society, change is a way of life; planning is one way of effectively guiding your company through a rapidly changing environment. By taking as your time horizon a period of several years, you can constantly reassess your current strategy in the light of opportunities and dangers. The ability to do this is the mark of a successful business.

Planning enables the entrepreneur to achieve results on a much broader scale than is possible on a day-to-day or month-to-month basis. Someone once commented that since almost no one devotes any effort to planning, success is assured to those who do. Success is far from assured, but without soundly based objectives and carefully formulated strategy, you are navigating blindly and will eventually commit serious errors that you might have avoided.

Importance in Raising Capital

A business plan is not only a management tool but also a means of raising equity and borrowed capital. The potential equity investor wants a large return on the investment plus the original amount of the investment, both at minimum risk. To appeal to investors, a business plan should answer a number of questions. First, in connection with return *on* investment, the plan should answer:

When will you begin or expand operations?
How rapidly will the business grow?
How will this growth take place?
Where will this growth take place?
Will the growth be profitable?

Second, in connection with return *of* investment, the business plan should answer:

How will the investor be paid? By buyout?
When can the investor expect the investment to be returned?
What form should the investment take?
What is your commitment (as owner–manager) and that of your employees?

Third, in connection with risks, the business plan should answer:

What investment will the planned growth require?
Will the investor have to spend more money to protect the initial equity?

What threats exist in the business environment, and how will the entrepreneur cope with them?

What are the company's strengths and weaknesses?

How will the owner capitalize on opportunities?

To appeal to lenders, the plan should answer:

Will cash flow cover debt service cost (interest and repayment)?

Does the enterprise have assets that creditors can secure?

Who loses in case of business failure?

Is the equity investment sufficient to cover the lender's risk?

Planning Problems

Planning is at best an imperfect art. It requires accurate long-term forecasts of inflation rates, market growth, and costs of materials, labor, and overhead. Since absolute precision in economic forecasting is unattainable, there is, in all plans, an element of wishful thinking—financial hopes filled with "polite numbers." Another factor that cannot be taken fully into account is the pace of change. Financial performance must be tied to time in a plan, yet organizational change, product development, and the like do not occur on a monthly or quarterly basis. Innovation does not follow neat accounting periods. Here are a few rules for avoiding some of the pitfalls of business planning:

Separate the process of planning from the financial aspects of planning, and emphasize the former. Also, separate planning from budgeting.

Develop the plan to correspond to events. Do not try to shape events to correspond to the plan.

Develop a reasonable schedule based on time for each project. Use it as a basis for expenditures and for periodic progress evaluations. At each major infusion of money the project should be reevaluated. You can expect to have some losers. Do not throw good money after bad; dump them quickly.

Develop a plan to minimize balance-sheet (investment) risks. Risks that involve major investments in property, plant, and equipment are much more serious than risks that involve salaries and marketing expenses.

Update the plan each year; adapt it to change; be flexible and alert to new opportunities.

The Planning Process

Before you get down to the actual mechanics of planning, you must ask yourself three questions concerning your company's future:

What are the basic objectives over the planning term?

What are the long-term profit objectives?

What is the appropriate rate of growth?

On the first point, most business plans cover a 5-year period. Companies that require major capital investment may plan in terms of 10 or even 20 years.

Objective Setting

In posing these questions, you begin the first phase of planning: objective setting. To answer the questions, you must define what you want in terms of sales, profits, product development, service level, and personal rewards for you and your people.

Objectives in Employee Relations.   Incidental to its importance in planning, formulation of objectives has utility in employee relations. Many companies have made themes out of one or two objectives that they continually stress to their personnel. Examples are 3M's product innovativeness and IBM's customer service. You do not have to be a giant to do the same. Be careful, however, that your themes are not overly ambitious or complex. What you want to do is to serve notice as to where your company is going in realistic and easily understood terms.

Self-Appraisal

Once you have a set of objectives, it is necessary to develop a working plan or strategy to attain these objectives within your designated time frame. The first step in this process is systematic self-appraisal or assessment. Set down, at some length, a realistic description of your business, including background, products or services, location and facilities, marketing and distribution, competition, labor relations, skill levels, key personnel, and financial resources. Then ask yourself the following questions:

What business am I really in?

What skills in our organization are valuable or unique?

What is my position in the industry?

What is the nature of our markets?

What customers am I serving? Where is my market?

How do major customers view us?

What image do we have in the marketplace?

What image changes would we consider desirable?

What market share do I want? When?

What major changes are likely:

　　In our present services and projects?

　　In the technology of our industry?

　　In the nature of our competition?

What, if any, plans should I have for product improvement?

What are my five greatest strengths?

What are my greatest problems?

What are my objectives for profit improvement?

What business do I want to be in, in three to five years?

How can I finance growth?

Will my objectives require capital expenditures?

What specific steps do I need to take if the organization is to achieve my objectives?

Planning Assumptions

All factors that can influence the development of your business over the planning period must be formally provided for in your plan; that is, they must be the subject of specific assumptions. These factors include but are not limited to:

Rate of inflation

Interest rates

Status of employees vis-à-vis collective bargaining

Demand patterns

Long-range market growth

Tax rates

Labor supply

Make sure your assumptions are reasonable and conservative. Where you already have data, as might well be the case with such factors as existing resources, share of market, and competition, you must assume that those figures will remain constant unless you have hard evidence to the contrary. Businesspeople are all too familiar with planning failures that occurred because the plans were based on unrealistic (usually overoptimistic) expectations. (Often, as a result of this sort of fiasco planning advocates within the organization are deprived of their credibility and the vital planning function is virtually abandoned.) Also, since the factor of uncertainty is greater in proportion to the number of assumptions, try to keep only to essentials. Finally, it is a good idea to document your assumptions for the benefit of interested parties—that is, lenders and investors.

Alternative Assumptions.   In many areas you will not be satisfied with one assumption per factor. You will wish to introduce several alternative assumptions about the same factor into your plan—for example, four different interest rates. You can do this because of the versatility of modern planning techniques.

Development of Strategies.   Alternative analysis can be used to develop business strategies, that is, means of achieving particular objectives. Thus, for a targeted growth for sales and earnings, you might consider the following alternatives:

Growth from existing products through more effective distribution and marketing

Growth from new products in the same marketplace, which usually involves analysis of the marketplace and customer needs

Growth by entering new markets either on a product or territory basis.

Note that business strategies may be implemented by internal means or by acquisition.

In selecting a particular strategy, you should answer questions along the following lines:

What will be the effect on my current organization? Do I have the proper management, or must I recruit?

What is the likely impact—short range and long range—on my financial statements? Can I afford this course of action?

Can I raise the necessary funds for implementation? How much will I need? When?

Does this strategy utilize my strengths and minimize my weaknesses?

What will be the reaction of my bankers, stockholders, customers, and community?

What is the probability of success, and what must I do to improve my chances?

What is the risk of doing nothing?

How long will implementation of my plan require, and what will be the results?

In what ways can I minimize the risks?

When will I break even?

What would be the impact of outside forces in respect to changing customer demand, recession, government regulation, labor unrest, and competition?

When should the plan be reevaluated for possible revision?

Financial Aspects

A plan that takes no account of the financial implications of your business strategies is incomplete. For each strategy, financial projections must be developed to evaluate fully the impact of various alternatives. For an existing enterprise, the current financial statements should be examined to determine present position and trends. For the start-up company or new project with no financial experience, the absence of financial statements must be made good by assumptions. As financial data becomes available, assumptions can be revised.

The plan should include a financial forecast covering the plan's life. The forecast should normally include two projections, one for sales and collections and the other for expenses. The first years of the projections should be broken down into months (budgetary units), with subsequent periods projected in quarters. Care must be taken to show the impact of investments in fixed assets as well as the impact of sales growth on inventory and accounts receivable.

There are computerized projection models that can greatly simplify financial forecasting. At Coopers & Lybrand we have an easy-to-use model that makes it possible to project the financial impact of forecasted changes in sales, expenses, plant investment, working capital, and other factors, in order to produce a balance sheet and income and cash-flow statements for any number of prior assumptions. With this kind of model, you will be able, once you have developed your basic forecast, to change at will the numerical values of key factors that impact cash flow, such as gross margin, inventory turns, accounts payable, and sales growth rates, to determine the effect on cash flow of different quantitative mixes of these factors. Moreover, you can introduce new factors into the projection to determine what would happen if certain events occurred. This process of evaluating the effect of contingencies, commonly desribed as "answering the what-if questions," is a critical part of planning. Thanks to computerized projection models, a complex exercise that would otherwise require an enormous amount of time on the part of someone well-versed in mathematics, statistics, and accounting can be simplified to the point where the nonspecialist can prepare clear and meaningful projections.

Many executives find it helpful to involve professional advisers in the process of planning and the subsequent development of financial forecasts. The consultant, with special knowledge of the planning process and an independent viewpoint, can assist by providing professional help as needed.

FINANCIAL FORECASTING

A financial forecast is an estimate of a company's financial position and results of operations for one or more future periods. Forecasting may be aimed at exterior factors, such as the economy in general or conditions within an industry, or at interior factors, specifically the forecasting operation's performance. Large companies such as IBM cover all three perspectives; small businesses can focus on the third, relying on published forecasts for whatever predictive data they need for their industry or the economy as a whole. The accuracy of a forecast is a function of the knowledge and skill of those who prepare it, the stability of conditions not considered in the forecast during the period covered, and the length of that period. Modern business forecasting depends heavily on formalized analysis with documented assumptions, but the element of judgment is still important.

What Does Forecasting Accomplish?

Forecasting is implicit in virtually every business activity, including financial planning, budgeting, purchasing, production scheduling, and inventory management, to name only a few. Forecasts supply important input in determining the feasibility of an acquisition or merger. Formalized forecasts may be demanded by lending agencies.

It is important to distinguish between forecasting and budgeting. A budget is used to make and coordinate plans, communicate those plans to the persons responsible for carrying them out, motivate managers, and control and measure performance. A forecast, on the other hand, is "passive." It does not represent a plan, nor does it provide motivation or control. Yet forecasting has budgeting implications. For example, assume that an owner–manager calculates that sales for the following year will be approximately the same as for the current year. A host of budgeting possibilities arise from this conclusion. To cite two, a company may budget sales at:

Forecast levels, focusing attention on cost control to sustain or increase current profit margins

At higher than the forecast levels, while trying to raise sales expectations with activities such as additional advertising, augmented sales force, or new product packaging.

In this example, the forecast enabled the owner–manager to determine that changes were necessary for the company to maintain its position.

Forecasting is part of the foundation on which a budget should be based. Except in an unusually stable situation, a company cannot budget effectively without forecasting. On the other hand, a company may forecast without budgeting.

Developing Financial Forecasting Assumptions

A forecast is no more reliable than the assumptions that underlie it. It is important, therefore, to develop assumptions with great care, using the best available information. Forecast assumptions must deal with both external and internal conditions. External conditions are beyond your control—for example, the general state of the economy, income tax rates, and availability of the necessary supply of raw materials during the period being forecasted. Internal conditions are those that you can influence, such as sales and production.

External Conditions

The subject of your assumptions will naturally be conditions critical to your business during the forecasting period. These conditions may vary from period to period because of such factors as changes in the Internal Revenue Code, market conditions, and so on. There are many sources of information needed in formulating external assumptions. For the state of the general economy, for example, you can use economic indicators, a Federal Reserve Bulletin, and published business surveys. For industry trends, there are the publications of trade associations, as well as published surveys.

Internal Conditions

The recommended procedure for developing assumptions about internal conditions is as follows: first, collect relevant historical data; second, determine what factors influence data patterns of key variables; third, formulate your plans and strategies for the forecast period; and finally, evaluate these plans and strategies with respect to marketing, manufacturing, and financial policies.

Historical Data.   The form in which historical data for any item—for example, sales—should be collected varies from company to company and is determined by factors such as the size of the company, the diversity of its products or services, and the stability of its operations. For sales, aggregate data such as units sold or total dollars of sales may be used with single-product companies. For other companies, aggregate data are of little value in forecasting sales. Instead, monthly data by product class or by salesperson and territory are used. Historical data are especially useful in forecasting accounts receivable. The pattern of collections helps determine the timing of cash inflow, the accounts receivable balance at any point in time, and the probable improving or worsening credit picture. The amounts of uncollectibles for several periods allow you to gain perspective of the company's collection history; this, combined with information on the general economy, credit picture, and forecasted receivables, should help forecast uncollectibles much more accurately.

Factors Influencing Key Variables.   To identify these factors, ask yourself why historical data show the patterns they do. In other words, can any useful relationships be discerned between past and future variables? Are there causal relationships that will better predict a particular variable? Can changes in various elements of revenue and expense be associated with specific factors?

The Sales Forecast.   Since sales have a major impact on financing, let us consider the factors that affect sales. Some of these are:

General economic conditions

Advertising policies

Geographical characteristics

Size and composition of the sales force

Composition of the company's product mix

Price changes

Competition

Seasonal demand changes

One way to estimate sales volume is to take a statistical approach, using either extrapolation or correlation. Extrapolation involves analyzing secular trends, seasonal fluctuations, and cyclical variations in detail and then projecting them mathematically over some future period. Correlation involves studying sales volume and independent external variables over a period to determine their relationship. For a somewhat oversimplified illustration: if sales of a certain product tend to increase each year at the same rate as the Gross National Product (GNP), sales volume could be projected in relation to assumed GNP growth. Actually, the statistical method involves developing an estimating equation that specifies the relationship between sales volume and several variables. By plugging currently available data into the equation, a sales forecast can be derived. This method usually involves much detailed work to establish the "best" equation. If you are going to rely on statistical methods, you may have to employ expert assistance.

Management Strategies.   Some of the questions that commonly must be answered in evolving assumptions about the effect of management strategies on internal conditions are:

Will new products be introduced or old ones discontinued?

Are any changes in the structure or composition of the marketing channels planned?

Will there be any material changes in the advertising budget?

Are there any anticipated material changes in the size or composition of the company's labor force?

Will the level of fringe benefits be changed?

How will required external financing be obtained?

How will obligations coming due be liquidated?

Documentation

In order to obtain maximum benefit from the forecasting process, document your key assumptions. Documentation facilitates comparison of forecast and actual results and provides a basis for developing future forecasts or revising existing ones. In addition, if you did not prepare the forecast yourself, documentation of the underlying assumptions will enable you to compare your perceptions of conditions affecting the forecast with those of the forecast preparer. Do not try to be too detailed; most assumptions, by their nature, can be stated only in broad terms.

Regular Comparisons with Performance

You must continually compare forecast results with actual results and analyze the deviations. In effect, you are monitoring the efficiency of the forecasting   exercise   and   learning   about   weaknesses—many correctable—in methods and approaches. Do not limit the comparative analysis to financial results; extend it to the underlying factors and key assumptions, such as sales volumes, prices, and production rates. Especially important are the so-called leading indicators, such as order rates, backlogs, and changes in productive capacity.

Summary

You cannot avoid financial forecasting. Even when you have not prepared a formal forecast, you are still making assumptions about the future and translating these into operating decisions. The preparation of a formal forecast tends to ensure a more careful and systematic analysis of relevant data, a better analysis of possible activities and strategies, and improved communication within the organization. Your forecast will probably never duplicate actual results, but it will enable you to determine why differences occurred and to react accordingly.

OPERATIONS BUDGETING

Budgeting is a planning process involving the coordination of resources and expenditures performed to identify the most profitable course of action open to a company. A budget is simply a road map indicating the direction the company expects to follow over a particular period. Although the principal purpose of budgets is to control and evaluate performance, budgeting, as we shall see later, can also be extremely useful in motivating individual performance as well as in communicating planning strategy.

Basic Procedure in Developing a Budget

The basic source of information for the budget is the company's historical financial data, such as annual, quarterly, or monthly financial statements, prior years' tax returns and budgets, and other available historical data. In addition, you should give careful consideration to any factors that may affect expected results in the upcoming period. Using this data, prepare initial estimates of sales, cost of sales, and other related items. In doing this, be sure to consult everyone in your organization who is responsible for an activity being budgeted. Their views could help you un-

derstand budgetary requirements. Once you have prepared the initial estimates, finalize them by adjusting them, as necessary, in light of circumstances or special considerations of which only you may have knowledge.

Following are some do's and don't's in budget preparation:

Build flexibility into the budget so that you can adapt it to unforeseen
circumstances.

Make the budget period short enough to minimize the element of
guesswork in the estimates, but long enough to involve considerations
of policy, strategy, and procedure.

Make the budget simple, concise, and understandable. Budget reports
will be read by nonaccountants, so avoid technical language. Designing the original form of the report merits great care on your part. Once
you have the design, stick to it throughout. Constant change in the
form and content of the report will multiply the difficulties of understanding it.

Don't clutter the report with unimportant information.

Don't strive for absolute accuracy. There is a happy medium between
promptness and perfection. Accuracy with respect to insignificant
items should be sacrificed to achieve this compromise.

Tailor the report to the needs of your readers. Conceivably, the format
used for internal circulation might differ somewhat from the version
you circulate to lenders or investors. (An example of how a set of assumptions is translated into a budget is provided in Chapter 7.)

Understanding Variances

Part of the control function of budgeting is to enable you to put your fin-
ger on weak spots by noting deviations or variances between actual and
budgeted expenditures. If a production foreman spends $600 on factory
supplies when he is only budgeted for $400, something may be wrong;
similarly, if he spends $150, something is amiss, even though the variance
is termed "favorable." This technique embodies what is sometimes called
the exception principle.

When variations between actual and budgeted expenses are turned
up, it is not enough just to indicate the difference. You must explain and

analyze the underlying factors causing the variances. In the following pages, we show how this is done for five major budget items.

Variances in Sales

Budgeted sales differ from actual sales because of differences between budgeted and actual volume and budgeted and actual sales prices. Assume the following facts:

	Units	Price per Unit	Total
Budgeted sales	180,000	$1.50	$270,000
Actual sales	200,000	1.44	288,000
			$18,000

The total sales variance is broken down by quantity and by price variation as follows:

Actual sales at budgeted sales price[a]		
(200,000 × $1.50)	$300,000	
Budgeted sales at budgeted sales price		
(180,000 × $1.50)	270,000	
Variance in quantities sold		$30,000
Actual sales at actual sales price		
(200,000 × $1.44)	288,000	
Actual sales at budgeted sales price		
(200,000 × $1.50)	300,000	
Variance in sales price		(12,000)
Total variation		$18,000

Variances in Gross Profit

Variations in gross profit may be the result of changes in sales price, quantity sold, or cost of goods sold. Assume the following facts:

	Actual	Budget	Variance[1]
Sales	$288,000	$270,000	$18,000
Cost of sales	180,000	162,400	(17,600)
Gross profit on sales	$108,000	$107,600	$ 400
Gross profit as a percentage of sales	37.500%	39.852%	
Unit sales price	$1.44	$1.50	

The total variance in gross profit is broken down into its three constituents as follows:

Actual sales stated at budget prices		
$\dfrac{(\$1.50)}{(\$1.44)} = 1.04167 \times 288{,}000$	$300,000	
Actual sales at actual prices realized	288,000	($12,000)
Change in volume		
Actual sales stated at budgeted prices	$300,000	
Budgeted sales	270,000	
	30,000	
Times budgeted gross profit as a percentage of sales	39.852%	11,956
Changes in cost of sales		
Actual cost of sales	$180,000	
Actual sales stated at budgeted prices *times* budgeted gross profit as percentage of cost of sales, or $300,000 × (100% − 39.852%)	180,444	444
Total variance		$ 400

1. Here and in the above example, unfavorable variances are shown in parentheses.

The analysis shows that there are three reasons for the $400 change in gross profit:

The realized value of gross sales is $12,000 lower than the budgeted value because the actual unit sales price was $1.44, or $0.06 per unit, less than the budgeted unit sales price of $1.50.

The actual gross profit is $11,956 higher than the budgeted amount because the sales volume of 200,000 units exceeded the budgeted volume of 180,000 units.

The actual cost of sales is $444 higher than the budgeted amount because the actual costs of producing the units sold was less than the budgeted cost of producing the units sold.

Variances in Costs of Materials

The variance between the actual cost of materials and the budgeted cost is made up of changes in volume (efficiency of) usage, and price. Assume the following facts:

	Budgeted	Incurred	Variances
Units produced	180,000	195,000	15,000
Unit of raw material per unit of finished product	3.0000	2.8718[1]	.1282
Units of raw material	540,000	560,000	
Material cost per unit	$ .10	$ .095	$ .005
Total material cost	$ 54,000	$ 53,200	$800

Analysis:

Volume variance	15,000	
Budgeted unit of raw material per unit of finished product	3.000	
	45,000	
Budgeted cost per unit	.10	
		$4,500
Usage variance	.1282	
Incurred units	195,000	
	25,000	
Budgeted cost per unit	.10	
		(2,500)[2]
Price variance	$ .005	
Incurred units of raw material	560,000	
		(2,800)
Total material cost variances		($800)

1. Computed.
2. In this example, parentheses indicate favorable variances.

The analysis shows that the favorable variance resulted from the combination of two favorable changes—one resulting from a more efficient use of raw materials ($2,500) and the other from a decline in the cost of raw materials ($2,800)—and an unfavorable change, an increase in volume used ($4,500).

Direct Labor Variances

The three component factors in direct labor variance are changes in total volume produced, rate of salary, and average worker output. These variances are determined after budgeted direct labor is adjusted to the actual level of operations. Assume the following facts:

	Budgeted	Incurred	Variances
Units produced	180,000	195,000	15,000
Hours per unit	.2000	.1949[1]	.0051
Hours incurred	36,000	38,000	
Hourly rate	$ 2.00	$ 2.10	$ .10
Direct labor costs	$ 72,000	$ 79,800	

Analysis:

Volume variance	15,000	
Budgeted hours per unit	.200	
	3,000	
Budgeted hourly rate	$ 2.00	
		$6,000
Output variance	.0051	
Incurred units	195,000	
	1,000	
Budgeted hourly rate	$ 2.00	
		($2,000)[2]
Rate variance	$ .10	
Incurred hours	38,000	
		$3,800
Total direct labor cost variances		$7,800

1. Computed.
2. Parentheses indicate favorable variances.

The analysis indicates that the volume variance, $6,000, is due to units actually produced exceeding units budgeted by 15,000. The favorable output variance of $2,000 resulted from an increase in output per direct labor hour of 0.0015 per unit. The unfavorable rate variance of $3,800 resulted from the average wage rate of $2.10 exceeding the budgeted rate by $0.10.

Overhead Variances

The three constituent variances are in budget, volume, and efficiency. The analysis of manufacturing overhead variances may differ somewhat depending upon whether fixed or variable budget procedures are being used.

For the *fixed budget approach*, assume the following facts:

	Direct Labor Hours	Budgeted Overhead Rate	Total
Budgeted overhead at budgeted operations	36,000	$1.00	$36,000
Budgeted overhead at actual operations	39,000	$1.00	39,000
Actual direct labor hours	38,000		
Overhead expenses incurred			41,830
Unfavorable overhead expense variance			($2,830)

In the preceding example, the direct labor hours for budgeted overhead are derived as follows: budgeted operations, budgeted finished goods production (180,000) multiplied by standard direct labor per unit (0.2); actual operations, finished goods produced (195,000) multiplied by standard direct labor per unit (0.2).

Analysis:
   Budget variance
       Actual burden incurred $41,830
       Planning budget allowance   36,000
                                         ($5,830)[1]

Volume variance
    Actual direct labor hours   38,000
    Budgeted direct labor hours
        at budgeted operations   36,000
                                                    ─────────
                                                     2,000
                                                    ─────────
    Budgeted overhead rate $ 1.00

                                                                    2,000

Efficiency variance
    Budgeted direct labor hours at
        actual level of operations   39,000
    Actual direct labor hours   38,000
                                                    ─────────
                                                     1,000
                                                    ─────────
    Budgeted overhead rate $ 1.00

                                                                    1,000
                                                                   ─────────
    Total overhead variances   ($2,830)
                                                                   ─────────

1. Parentheses in this and the following example indicate unfavorable
    variances.

The budget variance represents the difference between manufacturing
overhead incurred and overhead that would have been applied had the
work been done exactly as had been planned in the budget. This variance
is not a significant indicator of the efficiency with which work is done. It
does not take into account the effect of the volume of work done on
budgeted costs.

The volume variance measures the cost of idle or excess capacity. The
presentation of the variance has two flaws. First, idle capacity is shown as
the difference between planned and actual hours in production rather
than the difference between planned and standard hours. Second, the
volume variance is related to the overall burden rate rather than to fixed
costs only. Fixed costs alone are related to idle plant capacity. The efficiency variance shows the difference between actual and standard production hours. Variable costs are the measure of efficiency, and the inclusion of fixed costs in the burden rate would be erroneous.

For the *variable budget approach,* assume the same facts as under the
fixed budget except that the manufacturing overhead can be broken
down into fixed expenses of $18,000 and variable expenses of $.50 per di-

rect labor hour. The overhead rates per direct labor hour were computed as follows:

	Budgeted Overhead		Budgeted Volume in Direct Labor Hours		Budgeted Overhead Rate (per hour of direct labor)
Fixed	$18,000	÷	36,000	=	$0.50
Variable (36,000 × $0.50)	18,000	÷	36,000	=	0.50
	$36,000		36,000		$1.00

Analysis:

Budget variance

Variable budget allowance for actual
hours worked, $18,000 + ($0.50 × 38,000) $37,000

Actual manufacturing overhead   41,830   ($4,830)

Volume variance

Applied manufacturing overhead at standard   39,000

Variable budget allowance for standard
hours in production, $18,000 + ($0.50 × 39,000) 37,500   1,500

Efficiency variance

Variable budget allowance for standard
hours in production, $18,000 + ($0.50 × 39,000) 37,500

Variable budget allowance for actual
hours worked, $18,000 + ($0.50 × 38,000)   37,000   500

Total variance   ($2,830)

Since actual costs are compared with budget allowances adjusted to actual work done, the budget variance serves to indicate the effectiveness of manufacturing overhead control. The variance may be analyzed for individual items of overhead in each department by isolating the controllable and uncontrollable causes of the variance, such as prices of items that have varied from budgeted prices, and usage of overhead items that have varied from budgeted usage. Corrective action may be taken where required on the basis of a detailed evaluation of the budget variance.

Excess capacity used is properly measured in this illustration. The planning budget was set at 36,000 hours. The standard hours necessary to complete 195,000 units were 39,000. Since fixed costs properly measure idle capacity, the excess hours multiplied by the fixed overhead rate (3,000 × $0.50) give a favorable variance of $1,500.

Since variable costs increase proportionately with direct labor hours, the overhead efficiency variance is expressed in terms of variable expenses only. The adjusted budget allowance for 195,000 units was 39,000 direct labor hours. The difference between this adjusted budget and actual hours of 38,000 multiplied by the variable overhead rate of $0.50 gives a favorable variance of $500.

Reviewing and Revising the Budget

When the monthly reports show significant change, you have a choice of preparing a new budget using new projections or continuing with the existing budget and making the necessary short-term adjustments needed to deal with the observed variances. Your decision should depend on the types of deviations that emerge as well as on their extent. (For this reason, variance reports should provide a space for explaining the reason for the variance.) Except in extreme cases, preserving the budget with suitable reservations is generally preferable. Remember that the budget is only a road map representing a plan for the company's future. To recast the plan because of roadblocks that necessitate small detours is hardly wise.

Break-Even Analysis

Break-even analysis is a special type of budgeting. Whereas ordinary budgeting is aimed at controlling operations, break-even analysis enables you to determine what level of operation is required to cover all costs. Above this level—the break-even point—the business will show a profit; below it, a loss. To develop a break-even analysis, you use your fixed and variable costs to construct a chart that will give you a clear picture of your company's profit position.

Fixed Costs

Fixed costs are costs that are constant over the entire range of output for a given capacity. The best examples are rent, property taxes, owner's salary, and insurance. These expenditures may vary somewhat, but such variations are caused by factors other than output. For example, property taxes may vary from year to year in accordance with the rate and valuation of the property. Similarly, the owner–manager's salary may vary from year to year in accordance with his or her needs and with the financial position of the company. Fixed costs usually vary on a year-to-year basis but not by rate of output.

Variable Costs

These are costs that vary in direct proportion to output volume. An increase in volume of 20 percent causes an increase in cost of about 20 percent. Such factors as efficiency, technological changes, and diminishing returns may distort the relationship. Generally, though, this pattern holds true. Examples of variable cost items are power, materials, direct labor (excluding overtime pay), and salespersons' commissions on sales.

Semivariable Costs

These costs are fixed over relatively narrow ranges of output but change over the wider range. When the limit of the narrow range is surpassed, the costs jump to a higher level, where they again become fixed for a certain range. Examples of semivariable costs are clerical help, indirect labor, maintenance and lighting, and delivery expense.

Break-Even Chart

The break-even chart, shown in Figure 3.1, is a device widely used in planning. It shows the expected relationship between costs and revenue at certain volumes. The measure of volume may be based on the number of units sold or on sales revenue. The total-cost line on the chart in the figure actually starts from the Y axis at the point of intersection with the fixed-cost line. This cost line includes both variable and semivariable costs. Revenue is plotted on the assumption of a constant selling price per unit.

At the break-even point, costs equal revenue. In the chart this point occurs where volume is 3,000 units and both expected revenue and total costs are approximately $37,000. The amount of profit or loss is expressed as the difference between the total-cost and expected-revenue lines. As volume increases past the break-even point, expected profit rises rapidly.

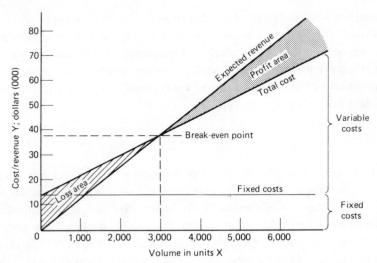

Figure 3.1. Break-even chart for cash management.

The relationships depicted in the chart tell us that if a volume of 4,000 units were budgeted, the company would incur total costs of $45,000 on revenue of about $50,000, for a profit of $5,000. If volume has been projected at 6,000 units, however, we would expect total costs of $58,000, revenue of about $72,000, and a profit of $14,000. By increasing volume 50 percent (from 4,000 to 6,000 units), the company would be able to increase profits by 180 percent. The break-even volume is not usually the same as the "normal" volume used to calculate the overhead rate. In a profitable business, in fact, the normal volume would be considerably higher than the break-even volume.

If you want to gain maximum benefit from break-even analysis, you should use it in contingency planning. This involves preparing a series of charts, each designed to provide answers to a group of hypothetical questions. Several revenue lines can be drawn, for example, each representing what would happen at different levels of operation. Also, different cost lines can be drawn to portray what the company's profit position would be under various cost conditions.

Summary

Budgeting indicates to the owner–manager the effectiveness of control maintained over operations. The best-planned budget serves little purpose unless actual operations are compared periodically with budgeted operations and the differences analyzed to isolate the factors that give rise to the variance. Variation analysis isolates controllable variations and indicates areas of possible cost savings. It gives management the ability to focus attention swiftly on the problem and to cope with the consequences and plan effectively. It provides a risk-free and relatively inexpensive method for conducting a "dry run" of operations, discovering and correcting weaknesses, and otherwise perfecting the plan of action.

CHAPTER
FOUR

SOURCES OF FINANCE

A common characteristic that one sees in a profile of all successful enterprises is adequate capital. In fact, adequate capital may well be the single most critical factor in determining whether an emerging business will survive. By adequate capital we mean *available* capital, that is, not only money or liquid assets but also capital you can raise from outside sources *when you need it.* All other factors—cost, restrictions, reporting requirements, and so on—are secondary to this single consideration.

Just how concerned entrepreneurs are over availability of capital was demonstrated in 1980 when delegates representing over 30,000 businesspeople from all over the country convened in Washington for the White House Conference on Small Business. At that conference, the workshop on capital formation and retention led the other 11 workshops in popularity. Furthermore, all 5 issues resulting from that workshop were included in the top 15 priorities the conference sent to the president.

Volumes have been written about financial presentations, cost of capital, sources of money, types of collateral, negotiating terms, and so on. In this discussion, we will touch on most of these points, but our emphasis will always be on maintaining liquidity and funding growth through access to capital. The discussion is presented in three sections. In the first, we deal with the basic information demanded by lenders or investors, including your personal character, the nature of your business, your financial needs, and the guarantees you intend to offer for payment of interest or dividends and, in the case of loans, redemption of principal. In the second section, we cover the technicalities of business finance, including:

The debt-versus-equity decision, with the relative advantages and disadvantages of each method

Leverage, its upside potential, and downside risk

Cost considerations

Evaluating sources

Acquisition financing

Retaining your present capital through effective tax and financial planning

The third section deals with negotiating loan agreements, the provisions you want, and those you do not want.

THE BASIC THREE QUESTIONS

All vendors and investors, however diverse their needs and objectives, will demand satisfactory answers to the following questions:

Who are you?

How much do you need, over what period, and how will the money be used?

When and how will you pay the money back?

Who are You?

This question is concerned with certain of your basic characteristics and those of your business; notably, your qualifications and aspirations, the management structure of your business, and your strategic position.

Personal Characteristics

Your prospective financing sources will want to know about your background, education, experience, and business goals. Naturally, you will highlight whatever demonstrated capabilities you have for developing and managing a company. In describing your business goals, refer to specific time periods, ideally one year, three years, and five years.

Management Structure

Lenders know that good management can succeed despite bad balance sheets, and bad management can easily destroy the best of financial positions. They will want answers to the following questions:

Do you have a management team, or are you a one-person show?

If you are in it alone, do you intend to keep things that way?

If something happens to you, how will the business continue?

If your goal is growth and physical expansion, is there enough depth of talent to manage those expanding operations?

What provision have you made for assuring the continuity of your business, that is, by grooming an associate or an employee to take over?

Your business may well represent your most significant asset, and its success may depend on the quality and continuity of management. If your ultimate goal is a sale, continuity may be less of an issue, but even here there are financial implications best faced up front. Certainly, when they know that the entrepreneur will eventually sell the business, lenders or investors will look more closely at the collateral or assets of the company than they would otherwise. Assuming the worst case, that is, that something happens to you and management is weak, they may be forced to liquidate their position.

Strategic Position

The next fundamental "identity question" concerns your strategic position, a concept that takes in the nature of your market as well as what stage of the economic cycle you are in. This last point refers to the developmental stages through which all entrepreneurially managed businesses evolve:

Start-up
Initial growth
Physical expansion
Mature growth
Possible going public or sale

You should be prepared not only to identify the stage you are in but also to describe how you hope to develop through later phases. Your position in the economic cycle has a bearing on appropriateness of the kind of financing you have in mind from your point of view, and possibly that of the prospective lender as well. For example, most new businesses start up or receive "seed" capital from the owner, his or her family, or other sources not in the business of making loans. On the other hand, many successful high-technology companies were started by owners who convinced venture capitalists to support them from the beginning. These entrepreneurs understood their particular products and their niche in the marketplace.

Other features you may wish to touch on in conveying your strategic position are seasonal financing needs, acquisition financing, and, in some cases, financing losses or capital squeezes caused by recessionary trends in your industry.

Always try to understand the investor's or lender's viewpoint. If you have a unique technology or marketing idea, be explicit about it. You cannot assume that the new investor or lender will know that fact. For example, even though the chemical industry is a basic industry, many specialized chemical companies are recognized as high-technology operations. Their access to capital is greater, in terms of sources and amounts, than many comparable companies in other industries. You, the entrepreneur, know your product and market best and can best identify its technological potential.

How Much, For How Long, and For What Purpose?

The basic tool for answering these questions is a set of financial projections. With your accountant and financial advisers work out the most *realistic* forecast of your profit, cash flow, and balance sheet position for the coming year on a monthly basis, and for four years thereafter, on an overview basis.

Let us look at some basic principles for developing these plans:

1. Spell out your assumptions carefully. This will go a long way toward answering many questions that might ultimately be raised.

2. Be realistic. An overly optimistic forecast will understate your real cash needs. Take into account the probability of reverses. If you do not, you will lose credibility with lenders when you approach them for emergency funds. Loss of credibility with lenders is to be avoided at all costs.

3. Present only an overview, but have plenty of supporting data available. Most lenders or investors do not have the time or inclination to spend hours poring over a detailed forecast. When they do dip into detail, they do it selectively, so that you must have a great deal of

information readily available that ultimately may not be asked for. Very likely, however, the prospective lender will compare your data to industry averages, evaluate your own historical patterns, and ask questions about margins, trade credit, customer terms, and so on. Your answers should not be more than a telephone call away.

4. Know the sensitive factors in your forecast and plan adequately for any downside risks in those factors. This is sometimes called cushion financing. It involves analyzing such critical factors as sales, costs, and margins to determine what would be the capital impact if performance in these areas were at the worst levels foreseeable and arranging backup financing with a line of credit or alternative source for that contingency. Investors and lenders tend to consider "worst-case" planning as evidence of creditable realism on the part of management.

5. Work closely with your financial advisers in developing your plans. We all have a tendency to fix upon our goals and develop a kind of tunnel vision, centered on those goals. By working with advisers and reviewing our plans carefully as we progress, we can subject our logic to the constant critique of those whose opinions we respect. Business is too complex today for any one individual to spot all of the problems, let alone resolve them.

6. Arrange your financing when you do not need it! From a tactical point of view, this is probably the single most important piece of advice we can give. Commonly, companies seek to arrange financing or borrow money when faced with a crisis such as the inability to meet a payroll or the sudden need for the acquisition of expensive new facilities. These are precisely the situations in which lenders tend to be toughest. They see your position as weak, and they are reluctant to lend. Remember, most financiers are basically merchants whose stock and trade is money. They want to put their commodity to work with people who they feel confident can earn them a good return. To them, a successful entrepreneur, planning well ahead for long-term needs, will typically offer the most favorable prospects.

7. Be sure to consider trade credit adequately in your plans. Are you stretching the trade as far as you safely can (without jeopardizing deliveries)?

8. Identify the collateral you can offer. Forecasted balance sheets will reflect potential assets that would support greater capital levels. As your business grows, receivable and inventory levels will also expand with two vital implications: capital will be needed to finance their expansion, and the higher asset levels themselves will provide collateral to support greater amounts of financing.

When and How Will You Repay?

All financial sources, equity or debt, need some reasonable assurance that their original investment will be returned to them. Any plan that you present must indicate the how and the when of the payback.

Debt Financing

When you are seeking debt financing, make sure your presentation contains the following items:

1. A cash forecast that shows how you plan to repay. If the forecast indicates the need for further debt to refinance what you are presently borrowing (which should not in itself be prejudicial to most lenders), you and the lender should evaluate whether you are structuring the loan appropriately. If your forecast indicates a continuous need for funds over the forecast period, your loan should probably take the form of a revolver (accounts receivable or inventory financing). It might also be structured as a medium- or long-term loan over a five-to-seven-year period.

2. A balance sheet forecast that provides the lender some indication of what values will be available to him or her for collateralizing the loan. If the projected values are in the form of receivables and inventories, you should probably be dealing with a commercial bank or commercial finance company, using a revolver or some form of secured-asset-based financing designed to vary with the level of assets. Such financing has provided an excellent source of capital to many growing companies because their access to capital increases in proportion to their volume and their working capital needs. Furthermore, the amount of indebtedness accepted by lenders under these types of financing can be greater than the capital in the business.

In addition, note the following basic guidelines for preparing a presentation for debt financing.

1. Base your loans for facilities and equipment on the life cycle of those facilities. Many small and growing companies have made the mistake of trying to finance major expansions over too short a period, with the result that they strapped themselves with insufficient cash flow. Remember that when the new facilities come on-stream, your demands for current types of financing will probably also increase with expansion of sales volume, receivables, and inventory levels. If one looks back over the past few years, the value of establishing long-term loans for expansion of facilities at fixed interest rates is readily apparent. Later, when we talk about some overlooked sources of financing, we will discuss some possible low-cost methods of securing such capital.

2. Identify the term over which you actually need the financing. If, in fact, you have a permanent capital need to support working capital growth, admit the need and approach lenders on that basis. Too often entrepreneurs try to start with short-term or other loans requiring a fixed payback, failing to recognize that increased volume as they grow creates greater financing demands. As a result, the entrepreneur spends too much time worrying about financing matters, specifically in trying to arrange new financing instead of concentrating on the basic problems of the business. It is good to follow the principle, "Do not finance long-term needs with short-term money."

Equity Financing

If you are financing out of your own invested funds, your major consideration is the value of subordinated debt versus equity. From a tax point of view, money invested as equity cannot be returned except on liquidation or sale of the company, and then only at a tax cost. As subordinated debt, however, funds can be returned with no tax consequences. From the financial community's point of view, subordinated debt is treated in most quarters as effective equity, resulting in the same leverage capabilities for the entrepreneur.

In securing funds from any outside equity investor, it is useful to have, at the time of investment, a buy-out formula to establish clearly the cost to you of regaining the entire value of your company. If you and the investor can agree on an equitable formula based upon anticipated growth and establish an appropriate put (where the investor can force the company to buy his or her stock back) *and* a call (where the company or entrepreneur can call back the investor's stock), you will greatly reduce the potential for future stress.

Here again, consider the investor's position. If your goal is ultimately to create a public company, the investor will probably resist any formula that would allow you to buy him or her out at a price substantially lower than a future public offering might entail. Therefore, in any financing agreement, some clauses will give the investor rights to share in any public offering with you, to prevent dilution of his or her equity interest, on a percentage basis and to seek "piggyback" rights on any stock registration you file. Such rights allow the investor to sell his or her stock at the same time as yours, with the company bearing the cost. All of these terms and conditions are common and should be expected as a normal part of negotiations by the entrepreneur. However, the terms should be negotiated carefully. The key point is to agree clearly and definitively on a buy-back formula or approach up front, in order to reduce the possibility of friction with lenders and financial strain.

OUTLINE OF OPERATIONS

For best effect, your presentation should be organized around a business or operating plan. An outline of this plan should be a part of your presentation.

Preparing the Outline

The outline should be brief—8–10 pages at most. If prospective lenders want more detail, they will ask for it. One mistake of many entrepreneurs is to present voluminous plans, which may discourage potential sources that have neither the time nor the inclination to wade through them.

First, break down the plan by major topics:

Objectives.

Specific Goals.   These are benchmarks for achievement of objectives.

Strategic Position. Strategic position includes:

History of business

Products

Marketing and competitive posture

Sources of materials and labor supply

Facilities and capital expenditure forecast

Current and prospective capitalization

Management. This includes:

Organization

Résumés of key people

Plans for growth

Pro Forma Financial Statements. These include critical assumptions.

Then identify the key factors that determine whether the investor or lender will become involved. Each case is different. In light of the issues discussed earlier, focus on the five or six areas that, for your particular business, make the ultimate difference for your successful operation. Explain your plans to your advisers; tell them what you are doing and why. They will probably have input that can help you and greatly increase your chances of success.

Prepare a one-page loan request indicating what funds you want, in what form you want them, and how you plan to pay them back. Close the outline by indicating the three best reasons for the financier to invest. Attach your brief plan to the request. Expect to be challenged. When meeting with lenders or investors, do not be defensive. Be prepared for a critical attitude, and for questions in reply to your answers. Some of the questions may seem almost provocative, reflecting an unsparing scrutiny of your motives and capabilities. You should remain cool and calm, replying in a manner that reflects confidence in your product and company. This composure will greatly increase your chances of success. Too many entrepreneurs become agitated, unable to understand why others question their obvious talent. Many financing opportunities have been lost, even as late as at the closing, because of the entrepreneur's hypersensitivity.

An example of a corporate plan outline is shown in the Appendix to this chapter.

TECHNICAL POINTS

Having dealt with the basic questions of the financier, let us look at a few more technical aspects the entrepreneur should be familiar with.

The Debt-versus-Equity Decision

Two major considerations in financing are the type of arrangements to be used—that is, debt or equity—and the amount of indebtedness to be incurred. In the choice of financial arrangements, the entrepreneur may be able to use one of a variety of hybrid instruments, reflecting both debt and equity, such as debt issued with equity kickers—warrants, options, or other stock rights—designed to provide investors with additional incentives. In determining the amount of indebtedness to be incurred, the owner–manager's objectives as well as what the market will accept are of prime importance.

Advantages and Disadvantages of Each

Essentially, all types of debt have a commonality in respect to advantages and disadvantages, as do the various sources of equity. There are some meaningful differences, however, such as preferred versus common stock, and these differences must of course be considered.

Debt   The advantages of debt are:

> Interest is typically a known cost. (However, current trends toward rates that are variable and without a ceiling may eliminate much of this advantage.)
>
> Normally debt confers no claim on the future earnings of the company. Indebtedness may be used as a tool for increasing returns on equity, such as through leverage (discussed later).
>
> Interest is tax deductible; therefore, in a profitable and growing company, debt typically has a lower effective cost to the borrower.
>
> Debt involves no dilution of the owner's interest.

The disadvantages of debt are:

Interest is a fixed cost and increases the break-even point for the company. If the business experiences difficult times, debt will augment financial problems.

Repayment schedules increase the cash outflow of a company and must be considered in future plans. Even in a revolving situation, where debt increases or decreases with asset levels, provision must be made for refinancing at the end of the agreement.

Debt is not permanent capital with an unlimited life; provision must be made to refinance or repay.

Debt instruments typically include substantive covenants or restrictions affecting control of the business by the entrepreneur and management. These will be discussed in greater depth later.

Equity.   The advantages of equity are:

Equity financing has no fixed cost; typically, its cost depends on the future value of the company. (Where the equity is in the form of preferred stock with required dividends, this advantage may disappear.)

A higher equity base provides leveraging capacity to gain more capital through debt financing. If, for example, for every dollar invested in equity capital, your financiers provide two dollars of debt, you can effectively increase availability of capital by three dollars.

Stock and other forms of equity can provide permanent capital with no required payback. (In fact, however, most equity financings for small and medium-sized enterprises do contain some provision for payback. One device commonly stipulated is a put.)

If the new equity is preferred stock, dilution of the current owner's equity and value does not occur. (Admittedly, it can be difficult for a growing entrepreneurial-type business to finance on this basis without providing for convertibility to common or equity.)

The disadvantages of equity are:

Dilution can be significant. Each case is different, but whatever percentage of equity you give up, you are sacrificing that percentage of all future growth. This sacrifice represents the true cost of the amount of capital received.

Because of dilution, equity—not being tax deductible when repaid in the form of either dividends or liquidation—typically has a higher cost than does debt. When you consider the potential dilution of future value against money received up front, the cost can be staggering.

Equity provides the investor with an element of control over your business. How much control depends on the terms you obtain but, in many cases, even a less than 50 percent interest can convey substantial powers, such as the right to elect board members or veto major transactions. Significantly, there is a definite trend toward recognizing the rights of minority interests. The holder of a majority interest may have a fiduciary responsibility to minority shareholders. Finally, the investor may request similar restrictions to those found in loan agreements, if certain unfavorable events occur.

Note on Hybrid Instruments. Hybrid instruments present a special problem. Here it is necessary to determine if a reduced fixed-cost disadvantage of debt is offset by an unknown future cost of the equity kicker.

The Decision-Making Procedure

Once you understand thoroughly the implications of the various financing arrangements, you can make your choice. From a purely financial point of view, the key factors in your decision will be:

Cost.   This is calculated and based upon projections of the company.

Cash Flow.   This is reviewed against projections of the company over the short run.

Risk.   This is determined by amount involved and method of repayment.

There is also a nonfinancial consideration: how much loss of control you will be able to live with. Give this factor careful consideration. Businesspersons who overlook it often realize later that they cannot continue in business under conditions they accepted at the outset.

Leverage

The concept of leverage is critical to most financing decisions and strategies for growing companies. Simply stated, leverage is the ability of the company to use a lender's money (debt) to increase the return on a company's equity base. Figure 4.1 illustrates in a simplified way how financial leverage works. Company A and Company B are identical, with one important distinction: Company B has borrowed an additional $100,000 of long-term debt on the same terms as an earlier $100,000. Company B earns the same rate of return (15 percent) on the additional funds as it would have on only $100,000 and pays the same tax deductible fixed interest on the debt (10 percent). By borrowing the extra $100,000, Com-

Company A

Long-term debt, 10%	$100,000
Stockholders' equity	200,000
Total capitalization	$300,000
Earnings before interest and taxes (15%)	45,000
Interest expense (10% × $100,000)	10,000
Earnings before taxes	35,000
Taxes (50%)	17,500
Net earnings	$ 17,500
Rate of return on equity ($17,500 ÷ $200,000) =	8.75%

Company B

Long-term debt, 10%	$200,000
Stockholders' equity	200,000
Total capitalization	$400,000
Earnings before interest and taxes (15%)	60,000
Interest expense (10% × $200,000)	20,000
Earnings before taxes	40,000
Taxes (50%)	20,000
Net earnings	$ 20,000
Rate of return on equity ($20,000 ÷ $200,000) =	10%

Figure 4.1. Example of financial leverage.

pany B has increased its net earnings from $17,500 to $20,000 and its rate
of return on equity from 8.75 percent to 10 percent.

We can summarize the advantages of leverage as follows:

If an investment opportunity exists to provide a rate of return higher
than the fixed rate of the indebtedness, leverage will operate as indicated in Figure 4.1.

Higher amounts of debt or equity capital at work open up more opportunities. Acquisitions of companies or expansion of facilities become
more realistic with more money at work.

Debt used for leverage does not provide any direct control over the
business to the lender.

All this looks great, but it is not the whole story. Leverage has its negative as well as its positive side. For example:

If invested funds do not earn as high a rate as the debt, or if you have a
loss, the interest on the debt must still be paid. Interest is a fixed cost
that increases your break-even point and exaggerates the effect of
downturns in your operation. This is the exact reverse of what leverage
was intended to do.

Debt has a maturity and repayment schedule, affecting your future
cash flow.

Restrictions in loan agreements affect operations of your business.

You must consider all these pros and cons and analyze investment opportunities as well before putting funds to use. Empires have been built
upon leverage, not only in real estate (a good example) but also in all
types of business. Conversely, some of our greatest bankruptcies resulted
when bad situations were made worse and the process of decay accelerated because of substantial debt.

Cost Considerations

The entrepreneur should be able to assess the full cost of the capital he
or she is seeking. In the case of borrowed capital, the ultimate cost is determined on the basis of various factors, many difficult to anticipate, of

which the current interest rate is only one. The ultimate cost of equity capital is reckoned in terms of dilution of equity and value.

Interest Cost

Commonly, the true or effective interest cost is much higher than the nominal interest rate. This is due to certain factors that can be grouped into three categories: those that reduce the amount of capital available, those that raise overall cost, and those of a hybrid nature.

Factors that Reduce Available Capital.   Available capital is reduced by:

Compensating Balance Requirements.   These are funds that must be left on deposit with the lender. The following example illustrates the cost impact that compensating balance requirements may have:

Loan amount	$100,000
Less compensating balance requirement (10%)	10,000
Available capital	$ 90,000
Interest at 14%	$ 14,000
Effective interest rate ($14,000 ÷ 90,000) =	15.56%

If you have a "float"—that is, a difference between book and bank balances reflecting uncleared checks—and that float maintains a consistent level, you can apply it to fulfilling your compensating balance requirement, thereby reducing, to the extent of the float, the amount of available capital you must segregate in these balances.

Up-Front Loan Discounts. The lender takes his or her finance charges or interest in advance.

Lags in Clearance of Checks Received from Customers by Lenders on Accounts Receivable.   In essence, the bank or finance company is delaying your collection of the receivables, effectively increasing your cost of capital.

Factors that Increase Overall Cost.   These factors, which may operate up front or over the loan term, are:

  Points or other fees charged at the closing of the financing, which up-front costs represent current dollars to be amortized over the life of the loan to determine the effective interest rate
  Commitment fees for committed lines not used
  Prepayment penalties if a loan is paid off before maturity

Hybrid Factors.   Other factors that create costs are:

  Equity kickers such as warrants, options, or convertible features
  Puts, which allow the financier to force the company to buy back an equity kicker, which in most cases establishes a minimum additional cost

Calculating the Cost.   The preceding factors must be quantified to determine the average amount of capital available during the loan term together with the total costs on a year-by-year basis. Then, by discounting the annual costs back to present-day dollars at an appropriate interest rate, you can determine the current effective cost of capital. The interest rate must be adjusted for inflation, since a dollar today is worth more than it will be 5, 7, or 10 years from now. Present value tables are available to help you compute these amounts.

Equity Cost

Determining the true cost of equity capital—whether in the form of common stock, convertibles, warrants, or options—is a somewhat more difficult exercise than determining the cost of borrowed capital. The key factors are:

  The percentage of common stock ownership that the investor ultimately receives
  The company's projections of future growth in earnings and value (Typically investors are skeptical of forecasts and will discount them by as much as 50 percent)
  An appropriate multiplier for earnings in the industry

When you compute the cost of an equity financing, you will typically find the rate of return or effective cost very high. Whether you should consummate the transaction will depend on two main considerations: first, your evaluation of investment opportunities exceeding the computed cost rate; and second, your ability to use the funds as a leverage base for further financing.

Choosing Financing Sources

An important factor, perhaps the principal factor, in your choice of the type and source of financing should be your business objective. For example, if your ultimate goal is to build a professionally managed technology company, you should probably talk, in the very early stages, to groups specializing in venture capital and in other forms of equity finance. Why? Because these groups understand, and are comfortable with, the financing of technology and growth and can provide a wide access to capital for technological ventures. They can also help you secure a professional management team.

Alternatively, if you are building a growing and profitable family enterprise with a basic product or service, your concern may well be to maintain a certain market niche in the foreseeable future. In this case, your focus should be on building contacts with banks, finance companies, and other traditional debt sources. The entrepreneur's ultimate goal here is to ensure access to capital without creating any future calls on the equity position of the business.

For emerging businesses, the chief sources of funds are banks, institutional investors (which may, of course, include banks), and all levels of government. These institutions generally follow clear-cut criteria in selecting their borrowers and investments, and they generally provide printed information on the types of loans and investments they make. You should not assume, however, that these institutions, even those in the same class, will respond identically to your proposals. At any one time, a bank or investing body may be more or less conservative than other organizations of its kind, may be interested in a specific industry, or may offer unique financing arrangements—unique not so much in respect to rates as to term and other conditions of repayment and amounts offered.

Commercial Lending Institutions

Commercial banks and commercial finance companies are the chief sources of commercial credit. The finance companies, however, are willing to deal with higher risk operations, often providing credit to new or expanding smaller companies that cannot secure adequate lines from banks. The finance companies rely to a greater degree on collateral values than the banks do, but their rates generally reflect the greater degree of risk they assume.

Some Tips on Approaching Lenders.   It is best to approach your source when your need for funds is not acute. At other times, your negotiating strength may not be as great. Ask a number of banks or investing groups—three or four will normally be ample—to evaluate your business and propose a financial package to meet your needs. They should respond readily; this type of project is very much in their line.

Tell all parties what you are doing at the outset. Give the fullest and most objective consideration to the proposals, and then make your selection. The process of selection and the implementation of the proposal must be reasonably expeditious. If you fail to act on the proposal, you may give the impression that your intentions were not serious, that is, that you were just dabbling. The financial community is close-knit, and a reputation for insincerity could close doors to your company.

Government Sources

Government agencies often provide financing on more favorable terms in respect to amount, interest rates, and conditions of payment than do private sources. If you are in an area of high unemployment, for example, the Economic Development Authority may give priority to your loan request. If you are building a plant in a rural area, the Farmers Home Administration may guarantee a term loan to your business to support physical expansion or increased working capital needs. To entice you to a particular community, a local development company (quasi-governmental or private) may, in combination with the Small Business Administration and local banks, provide capital for expansion at average rates lower than those of normal banks. In many urban or depressed areas, grants such as Urban Development Area Grants (UDAG) may be available to reduce the financial impact of your expansion. Many federal and state agencies even make outright grants in certain cases.

Your bank or financial adviser should be able to supply you with information on this kind of financial assistance. In addition, you can consult your local chamber of commerce, the appropriate office of your state or local government or of the federal government, and your trade association. Once you have a lead on a particular opportunity, do not hesitate to ask the agency involved for further information and assistance in applying for financing. That is what they are there for.

Some Financing Vehicles

Financial analysts distinguish a number of stages in the development of business. The first two stages are initial growth and physical expansion. In the first stage, the financing picture is dominated by three borrowing vehicles; in the second stage, more specialized types of financing are also feasible.

The Initial Growth Stage

A new business usually has a tremendous need for funds. Typically, its accounts receivable and inventories are growing rapidly, and even though profits may be good, the maintenance of cash flow, through credit lines, is critical to support higher levels of working assets.

Three types of financing vehicles commonly available to support this growth are:

1. *Revolving Lines of Credit.* Revolving credit is a continuous arrangement whereby the funds available to the borrower at any time represent the difference between a maximum established at the outset and the amount of loans outstanding. Typically, commercial revolving credit is collateralized by accounts receivable.

2. *Accounts Receivable Financing.* Funds are advanced as goods are shipped, on the basis of a defined proportion—typically 80 percent—of eligible accounts receivable. Normally, the lender has some say in the matter of which customer accounts it must accept as collateral. Usually invoices are financed only for a specific period, normally 90 days from shipment. A variant of accounts receivable financing is factoring. Here the receivables are sold rather than

used as collateral. This technique costs more than borrowing on receivables, but it eliminates some of the costs inherent in maintaining the accounts on the books and also the burden of assuming the credit risk.

3. *Inventory Financing.* Normally this kind of financing is provided in tandem with accounts receivable financing. Because of the comparative illiquidity of inventory (which is seldom valued at more than 50 percent of the value for finished goods, lower for raw materials, and even less for work in progress), the advance rate on this form of asset is characteristically below that for receivables.

In negotiating any of these three financing vehicles, there are a number of features that you can stipulate to maximize the amount you receive. In the case of credit line, for example, the maximum granted might be tied to some growth factor in your business.

Other features that could be advantageous to you in connection with these vehicles are:

Maximized advance rate on receivables and inventories based on *quality of your assets*

Maximized time period for eligible invoices

Provision for periodic temporary overadvances as an emergency capital source

An inventory value defined for advance purposes as sales value or current costs [*never* last-in, first-out (LIFO) costs]

Physical Expansion Stage

Typically, physical expansion involves creation of new employment, an advantage in securing certain specialized financing vehicles, among which are:

Industrial Revenue Bonds (IRB). Many states have established programs to facilitate construction of new or expanded facilities, essentially plant and equipment. You isssue bonds, but the state underwrites them. The interest paid on IRB's is tax exempt and therefore bears a lower interest cost (typically about 70 percent of normal long-term rates). Often it can be used to provide 100 percent of new capital needs.

Leasing.   Assets, or more properly, the use of assets, may be acquired by leasing. This method may, in certain circumstances, be less costly than direct purchase.

The advantages of leasing are:

100 percent financing of asset cost, often including installation, is available.

The investment tax credit may go to either party; that is, it is negotiable.

Current loan agreement covenants may not be affected.

Payments are level over the term.

The terms may be longer than those available under other types of financing and are inherently more flexible.

The disadvantages of leasing are:

Costs are usually higher than they are for debt; that is, the implicit interest rate is higher.

When the operation is profitable, property ownership provides an acceleration of tax benefits due to the offset of accelerated depreciation versus level rental payments.

Residual value may not revert to lessee unless stipulated in purchase option or renewal clauses.

Acquisition Financing

The acquisition of another business is a major event. Before embarking on this venture, you should carefully analyze the business and tax implications of the move (see Chapter 6). Do not try to go it alone; consult with your financial and legal advisers and with your key managers.

Some Guidelines

It would be difficult to furnish a complete syllabus of acquisition procedure because no two acquisitions are exactly alike. The following recommendations, however, are widely applicable.

Assets of the Acquired Operation.   Look closely at financing potential in
the assets of the proposed acquisition. Often you will be able to generate
considerable cash from these assets, through either borrowing or outright sale of excess capacity. Acquisitions funded in this way are referred
to as leveraged buy-outs.

The following example illustrates this kind of acquisition; in this case,
the acquired company is a consumer goods manufacturer.

	Capital Provided	Source
Real estate loan	$750,000	Savings banks
Equipment loan	800,000	Commercial banks
Working capital		Commercial finance
(receivables and inventory)	500,000	company
Subordinated acquisition debt	350,000	Seller
Equity	25,000	Entrepreneur
Total	$2,425,000	

The company in this example was able to consummate this highly leveraged deal because the business was basically sound, the assets had significant financing value, and the seller was willing to take a portion of the
sales price over a five-year period.

Intangibles.   Where the seller seeks a significant amount for goodwill or
intangible assets, negotiate for a deferred payout over several years, sub-
ordination to the other creditors, and either lower-than-market interest
rates on the payment or a balloon payment or both. The amounts finally
agreed on should be discounted to current dollars at an appropriate interest rate. These recommendations are designed to protect you from
overpaying for intangibles.

Allocation of Price.   The more of the purchase price that is allocated to
tax-deductible items, the more is the advantage to you. If you can pay less
for goodwill, which is not tax deductible, and more for a convenant-not-
to-compete or consulting agreement, the tax benefits can reduce your
net cost substantially. If these items are paid out over several years, the
current cost (or present value) is reduced even further. Frequently, sellers
are willing to trade tax benefits, deferred payouts, or low interest rates in
return for receiving a price at or close to the asked price.

Tax Implications. With combined federal and state tax rates typically around 50 percent, tax savings or deferrals can be significant sources of future cash flow (thereby reducing financing needs). In the case of marginally attractive acquisitions, the net tax result may be the determining factor in whether to go ahead.

Minority Shareholders.   If there are minority shareholders or key management people who want to stay in or invest, consider offering them equity at a fair price. They provide equity financing and reduce the cash you need to acquire the company.

Contingent Payouts.   Where possible, avoid payouts hinged on future earnings without a dollar limit. These arrangements may well involve you in legal complications. There is, furthermore, a real possibility that the seller will gain legal rights at your expense or even substantial control of your business. If necessary, concede the seller a higher fixed price in return for a long-term payout. The present value may be within both your and the seller's acceptable range. Generally speaking, you should travel the contingent payout route only where all other options fail.

Ownership of Real Estate.   Evaluate with care ownership of any real estate to be acquired. Usually it is best to own real estate separate from the operating company. This ensures maximum flexibility in the selling of either the company or the real estate and provides an avenue (rent) to secure funds from the operating company.

Retaining Capital in the Business

No matter how much capital you obtain from outside sources, you will not get far in your business if you let that capital leak away without being put to effective use. The most common cause of capital leakage is poor cost control, especially the failure to give priority to more urgent expenses over less urgent ones. A probable second in rank is poor asset management, as evidenced by insufficient turnover of accounts and the presence of idle facilities and equipment that could be either put to use or sold. Other deficiencies that waste capital are:

Unprofitable Product Lines.   This defect is usually a direct result of unrealistic sale policies.

Failure to Utilize Internal Capital Sources.   Examples are failure to secure appropriate trade credit terms so that deliveries balance cash flow, overly liberal sales terms and collection policies; and neglect of cash sources such as life insurance policies.

Excessive Tax Payments.

Tax Planning

Tax rates are high; for every dollar your company earns before taxes, federal and state governments probably take 50 cents. They are, in effect, equal partners in your business without sharing the risks. Remember that every tax dollar saved goes directly to increasing profitability. The benefits of deferring taxes are also important; in certain cases the fiscal consequences of deferring a tax can be practically the same as those of not paying the tax at all. If the deferral lasts long enough, the amount of the tax will be defrayed in reduced interest expense.

In an inflationary period, the dollar return from tax planning tends to increase significantly for several reasons. First, both current-year taxes and estimated tax payments for the coming year are reduced. In a growth company, estimated taxes are typically based on the prior year's taxes. Thus a *double cash-flow benefit* can be achieved. Consider the value of this at today's interest rates. Second, at the high interest rates prevailing today, the present value of taxes (and other obligations) deferred for long periods is minimal. Finally, certain specific tax concepts that can operate to the taxpayer's advantage become relevant to more taxpayers than they do in normal times.

Consider the following tax-saving techniques

LIFO Inventory.   Under inflationary conditions, the use of the LIFO method for inventory increases cost of sales to reflect current and latest costs, resulting in significant deferrals of tax. There are ways of maximizing the benefits of LIFO with a minimum of disruption to your business. In fact, with recent relaxation of IRS restrictions, it is now possible to report results of operations simultaneously on both a non-LIFO and a LIFO basis to meet banking, credit, and investor needs.

Depreciation.   Try to deduct the cost of fixed assets, including property, plant, and equipment, over as short a period as possible. (Shorter recovery periods are now permitted, thanks to the Economic Recovery Tax Act of 1981.)

Installment Sales. You may be able to defer the tax on the gross profit on sales reflected in your year-end accounts receivable. You can do this if you are on the installment method of accounting for tax purposes. You can elect this method if your sales terms require or contemplate more than one payment—for example, 10 percent, either at point of shipment or point of order, with the remaining 90 percent payable in one or two installments due on normal terms. This requirement is flexible, not absolute. If credit or marketing considerations dictate that the installment terms should not be extended to all customers, you can still implement the installment method on sales to specific customers. You can also limit installment sales to late in the year (say, the last quarter) when collection by year end is unlikely. If you elect the installment method for tax purposes, you are not bound to use it for financial statements. Therefore, there will be no adverse effect on reporting results of operations; all profits are reported on a normal accrual basis.

Export Sales. If you have significant amounts of export sales, consider the benefits of establishing a Domestic International Sales Corporation (DISC). Essentially, a DISC will allow you to defer tax on a portion of the income produced by export sales. The period of deferral is maximixed if you establish a DISC corporation having a fiscal year ending one month later than that of the existing operating corporation.

Utilization of Losses. Be sure that any loss operations are either in a branch or a subsidiary corporation that may be included in a consolidated return. This ensures that loss will be converted into current tax savings through offsetting taxes on profitable operations.

Separate Tax Treatments for Component Operations. Examine all areas of your business to determine if any particular components can be treated as a separate entity and accounted for on a cash basis. In that way you will pay taxes on the income from that operation only when cash is received. This articulation is usually feasible if inventories are not a major component of your business. For example, any service operations involving extensive repair on maintenance work, especially under warranty, might qualify.

Do not wait until the end of the year to formulate strategies with your tax advisers. If you do, you will almost always find that the opportunity for effective action has been lost. In fact, the later in the year you act, the harder it will be to implement most of these opportunities.

NEGOTIATING LOAN AGREEMENTS

Most entrepreneurs approach negotiations involving money with intense anxiety. Too often they are either defensive to the point of belligerence, or they are too meek and get less than they should have gotten in respect both to amounts and to terms. If you adhere to a few basic principles, you should be able to keep to the path of moderation between the two extremes.

Some Guidelines

First, make full use of your advisers, particularly your lawyer and your accountant. They may help you understand the significance of some of the points raised and determine which points are worth fighting for. Second, never suppress any of your objections to or misgivings about any point. Remember that all terms are negotiable—until the agreement is signed. Third, remember that you are dealing essentially with an institution and not an individual. A loan officer or financier may use reassuring formulas such as, "Don't worry; if anything goes wrong, I'll be here to help you, and give you a waiver," but in the long run it is the written word that will bind. You have no way of knowing whom you will be dealing with in the future or what will be your negotiating position. Finally, look at everything from a long-range point of view. Restrictive clauses and covenants may not seem burdensome now, but four or five years from now they may be serious impediments. If you are apprehensive about the effect of any restrictive provision over the long term, try to build in a cushion. One way to do this is to link the restriction—by percentages, formulas, and ratios—to factors that can be expected to grow with the growth of the company.

The preceding guidelines deal with general principles. The following suggestions focus on more specific points:

Try to establish a ceiling on the interest rate demanded. If necessary, offer a floor to fix your financing cost within a certain range. The more severe inflationary conditions are, the harder it will be to obtain this concession.

Try to maximize the average use of capital. Among the possibilities you might propose are moratoriums on principal and/or interest for 1–2 years, balloon payments (for example, a 10-year loan with a 20-year payoff schedule), or any other expedient that would increase average capital and reduce payments in the early years.

Seek a right of prepayment without penalty to allow you to refinance if rates go down.

If financial statements are required from independent accountants, it may be possible to arrange for limited reviews, as opposed to full audits. Limited reviews cost less but still provide the financier with a certain level of comfort.

Evaluate personal liability provisions very carefully. Try to set a limit on personal liability and also exempt specific assets, such as your home.

Covenants and other tests should not be too restrictive; otherwise, growth may be hampered. Severe limitations on capital expenditures are particularly burdensome. Restrictions on other borrowings should not preclude future financing.

Consider eliminating debt-to-net-worth ratios from the debt test, if possible, or alternatively exempting such items as deferred taxes and accrued salaries and wages, to allow more room for tax planning alternatives.

Ask for 30 days to cure a default, if default provisions trigger. Further, suggest the provision not trigger until notification is received from the financier.

Do not make too much of limits on dividends. The IRS, under certain provisions of the Internal Revenue Code, can assess a stiff tax on the company for unreasonably accumulating retained earnings. A limit or barrier on dividends in a loan agreement is one argument for not paying dividends and thereby avoiding the tax.

Define clearly and in writing all unusual or subjective terms utilized in the agreement. Both parties should be able to look to the agreement for a clear definition of terms used.

Minimize collateral to maintain flexibility for possible future financings.

Consider carefully the nature of the collateral you are pledging in the light of future dealings with vendors and other third parties. In your industry it may be unusual for companies to collateralize debt with inventory or receivables. If so, point this out to the lender or investor. If this policy could put you at a competitive disadvantage, you have a strong argument against it.

If you pledge your stock, take a close look at provisions triggering default. They may allow the financier effectively to take control of your company.

APPENDIX: ANALYSIS OF A CORPORATE PLAN OUTLINE

The following report was prepared by a client of Coopers & Lybrand (name, product data, and dates have been changed). It outlines the company's present status—in terms of strategic position, sources of materials and labor, capital expenditures, capitalization, and management. A series of forecasts in the form of pro forma financial statements cover income, manufacturing, overhead, marketing and administrative expenses, cash flows and balance sheet for a five-year period.

Outlines of this sort have proven to be useful tools in:

Formulating long-range goals
Determining financial needs
Securing equity and debt financing

The company in this example is a manufacturer of heavy equipment. The basic concepts underlying the plan and the approach, however, would be the same if we were dealing with a supplier of audiovisual aids or a foodstore chain. The development of this outline follows the standard format for any type of organization (as described in this chapter), although this plan outline, like any other, has its own special emphases.

Allied Engineering Corporation

Allied Engineering Corporation (hereinafter referred to as the "company") is a Massachusetts corporation organized on June 30, 1982. Its offices are located at 100 Industry Avenue, Springfield, Massachusetts. The company was founded in 1970 by John Anderson, a graduate mechanical engineer with a BSME from the University of Massachusetts. Prior to 1979, Anderson worked for manufacturers in the machine tool field for a 10-year period, holding various positions involving the design, manufacture, sales, and service of machine tools.

The company began as a manufacturer's representative in the field of machine tool accessories, handling product lines such as power chucks, power work rests, feed drives, and various grinding wheel dressing devices.

This activity became profitable after nine months, at which time the company acquired a distributorship for the power chuck and power work rest lines. Territorial coverage, at first restricted to New England, was expanded into upper New York State, New Jersey, and Eastern Pennsylvania by the appointment of subagents. At approximately the same time, the company began to design and manufacture, through subcontractors, complete hardware packages, including electrical controls for use with the power work rest. This activity proved profitable and helped stimulate further territorial expansion, this time into Ohio. In Ohio, the company established business relations with a whole new group of important machine tool builders.

In mid 1980, the company became an importer and U.S. agent for the machine tool products of an English company. This line has been very successful, and the company has acquired a similar position vis-à-vis two other English firms.

In late 1981, the company became aware of certain problems associated with the manufacture of lathes, specifically with the feeding of bar and tube stock into various turning machines.

Foreseeing a substantial market for lathes of advanced design (in light of the rapid expansion in the use of numerically controlled turning equipment), the company began to investigate several design concepts. After a three-month effort, a simple, realistic solution to bar feed problems was found. The concept and design criteria of what came to be known as "the Guide" were then turned over to a professional designer, Mr. Paul Johnson, for development. Mr. Johnson, who had been self-employed in the design and building of special machinery since 1968, had formerly been with the Acme Machine Corporation, where, as vice-president of engineering for 10 years, he was in charge of product development and design. Mr. Johnson ironed out the engineering problems and, in addition, designed the entire production process.

To date, the company has received two firm written orders for the Guide and has built, shipped, and received payment for the first of these orders. Six additional machines have been manufactured and are available for shipment.

On September 1, 1982, a patent application for the Guide was made at the U.S. Patent Office in Washington, D.C.

The Product

Thousands of products in many industries begin their existence when a long bar of steel is fed into the spindle of a screw machine of automatic lathe. One end of the bar is held in a chucking device and rotated at high speed. At this point, many and various cutting, drilling, and threading tools perform a sequence of machining operations. When the multiple machining is complete, the newly machined piece is cut off the end of the bar, which must then be moved further through the spindle, exposing another length of bar stock, and the machining cycle is repeated. The process just described is accomplished by automation, the byword of modern industry. One can understand from this description that the feeding of bar stock is itself nonproductive and that, therefore, manufacturers want to accomplish it with a maximum of efficiency in a minimum of time. The concept of efficiency takes into account such factors as safe operation, low noise levels, efficient loading of multiple bars, smooth control of bars as they are fed, minimum floor space consumption, rapid changeover from one stock diameter to another, simplicity of electrical interconnection between the bar feeder and the machine tool to which it is coupled, and the ability to handle a wide range of stock diameters.

The Guide resolves these problems and provides solutions that are presently not available to machine tool builders and users. Today's manufacturing machines are becoming more efficient and are operating at higher rotational speeds. To handle this requirement, the Guide utilizes supports that retain the bar stock every 36 inches between three rollers. In addition to promoting safety, these rollers operate at a lower noise level than other feeders that allow the stock to whip inside a steel tube in a V-trough. The Guide handles multiple bar stock with a simple loader mechanism. The bars are fed into the front of the machine instead of into the rear, as is done in much of the equipment that is presently in use.

The Guide translates the bar stock by rotating the bar and simultaneously skewing rollers in the triroll supports.

This approach provides smooth, easily adjusted feed control, eliminating the stock bounce that is unavoidable with the pneumatic rams and chain drives utilized in other designs. The absence of rams makes the Guide a very compact machine. Other feeders must be longer than the bar stock to provide room for the ram to push on the end of the bar; some feeders are as much as eight feet longer than the Guide's. The Guide provides extremely simple adjustments from one stock size to another via a hand wheel at each station. From this one adjustment, the support and loader mechanism are set to any bar size in the range of the Guide. Changeover of the four-station Guide is accomplished in a comfortable five minutes, a time unmatched by other feeders. The control package supplied with the Guide provides manual control as well as operation by today's most sophisticated numerical control systems. Interconnection to a turning machine is accomplished with as few as four wires.

The Guide utilizes modular construction, which costs less to manufacture and makes possible the simple conversion of the basic machine to several models. The first model handles various lengths of stock from one-half inch to two-and-three-quarter inches in diameter. At present, the company is developing a feeder utilizing the same principles that will be designed for use with multispindle turning equipment.

The Guide is the most universal and versatile stock feeder available today and provides effective engineering solutions to various problems associated with all other similar equipment.

Marketing

The Guide in its present form has a market price of approximately $10,000 per unit. The company intends to market it in the United States through machinery distributors and manufacturer's representatives, which will handle sales to the user. The company has concluded agreements with several such organizations, which have been established for many years in their field. Sales to original equipment manufacturers (O.E.M.) will be handled by the company. In previous years, O.E.M. lathe manufacturers have designed and built most of the stock feeding equipment supplied with their machinery. Newer turning equipment designs have substantially changed the stock feeder capability requirements, particularly in terms of very high rotational speeds. In addition, stringent regulations imposed by the Occupational Safety and Health Administration concerning safety and noise pollution have further served to make existing stock feeder equipment obsolete. Today's lathe manufacturers are extremely busy and in this position have little or no surplus engineering hours to devote to the development of new accessories such as stock feeders, a fact that may account for the high interest manufacturers are currently showing in the Guide. The company feels that the O.E.M. potential constitutes a significant new market and will contribute as much as 85 percent of the company's early business and average approximately 50 percent over extended periods of time. A considerable number of contacts have been established with some of the more prominent lathe manufacturers. These contacts have generated requests for quotations in the amount of $400,000. A substantial portion of this equipment, if ordered, will eventually be shipped to a division of an automobile manufacturer. The company envisions an annual U.S. sale in excess of 400 machines by 1987.

The company is presently involved in negotiations with a large British corporation with annual sales of approximately 2 billion dollars. The company, which specializes in automotive components and stock feeding equipment, presently produces a stock feeder oriented primarily to the automatic screw machine market. In late 1982, Mr. Anderson visited the British company at its invitation and inspected its machinery division. Subsequent to this meeting, the British expressed in writing their interest in becoming the company's agent for distributing the Guide in Common Market countries and also raised the possibility of eventually becoming a licensee for manufacturing the Guide. The company replied by sending them a sales agent's agreement for execution and a quotation covering a fully automatic Guide which, on acceptance of agreement terms, is to be regarded as an initial order.

Competition

There are few manufacturers of stock feeding equipment in the United States, and investigation turned up only one manufacturer whose sole product is stock feeding equipment. The company feels that this manufacturer is its most significant competitor. Other manufacturers of stock feeding equipment are typically very small entities operating within larger companies, and their sales represent an extremely small percentage of the parent company's overall sales. Investigation of all known stock feeding equipment, both inside and outside the United States, has not uncovered any model that utilizes the principles of the Guide or that is comparable to it, particularly in regard to rotational speeds, safety, and noise levels.

Sources of Material and Labor Supply

The company subcontracts the manufacturing of the product's components and subassemblies, performing only the assembly function in house. In the building of the first seven machines, approximately five subcontractors were used, and the company feels that there are a substantial number of other subcontractors within easy access that are capable of fulfilling the same requirements. The company plans to absorb most of the operations presently subcontracted during the next three years.

At present the company has 10 employees. It is not anticipated that the acquisition of additional personnel as required will present any problems.

Manufacturing Facilities and Capital Expenditures

The company occupies premises at 100 Industry Avenue, Springfield, Massachusetts, pursuant to an oral agreement; rental is $1,500. These facilities encompass approximately 15,000 square feet, of which 5,000 square feet are taken up by the company's office and manufacturing activities, and 10,000 square feet are left unoccupied. Management believes that its facilities are presently adequate for the company's requirements but will not be so for long. On the basis of business projections, management has planned a tentative 5,000-square-foot expansion in the third year of operation and believes that this expansion will provide adequate facilities for the ensuing five years. The premises are leased from Mr. Anderson, their sole owner.

The following is a schedule of estimated capital expenditures for the next five years:

First Year, Early

Item	Condition	Quantity	Price
Bridgeport miller	Used	1	$ 1,700.00
Surface grinder	Used	1	3,000.00
Engine lathe	Used	1	4,000.00
Band saw	New	1	1,200.00
Cutoff saw	New	1	1,200.00
Drill press	New	1	500.00
Sunnen hone	New	1	4,000.00
Belt sander	New	1	500.00
Bench grinder	New	1	200.00
Arbor press	New	1	300.00
Flame cutting equipment	New	1	3,000.00
Black oxide equipment	New	1	3,000.00
Fork lift truck	New or used	1	4,000.00
			26,600.00
Tooling and inspection equipment			7,400.00
Shop storage and warehouse equipment			25,000.00
Office equipment and furniture			2,000.00
Truck	New	1	4,000.00
Research and development: electrical and pneumatic test equipment and experimental hardware			10,000.00
Total			$75,000.00

Equipment prices include cost of freight and installation in all years.

First Year, Late

Item	Condition	Quantity	Price
Numerical control drill	New	1	$35,000.00
Plain miller	Used	1	7,000.00
Multispindle drill (4)	New	1	2,000.00
O.D. grinder	Used	1	3,000.00
Bridgeport with optics	New	2	8,000.00
Bridgeport	Used	2	4,000.00
Hardinge lathe	Used	1	5,000.00
Compressor	New	1	2,000.00
			66,000.00
Jigs, fixtures, and perishable tools			9,000.00
Total			$75,000.00

Second Year

Item	Condition	Quantity	Price
Bridgeport	New	2	$7,000.00
Machining center	New or used	1	125,000.00
Surface grinder	New	1	7,000.00
Engine lathe	New	1	9,000.00
			148,000.00
Jigs, fixtures, and perishable tools			12,000.00
Shop storage and warehouse equipment		25,000.00	
Office equipment and furniture		2,000.00	
Total			$187,000.00

Third Year

Item	Price
Capital equipment	$100,000.00
Office equipment and furniture	3,000.00
Trade truck	3,000.00
Total	$106,000.00

Fourth Year

Item	Price
Capital equipment	$100,000.00
Office equipment and furniture	3,000.00
Research and development equipment and hardware	20,000.00
Total	$123,000.00

Fifth Year

Item	Price
Additional capital equipment and replacement of earlier used equipment	$100,000.00
Office equipment and furniture	5,000.00
Trade truck	4,000.00
Total	$109,000.00

Management and Directors

The names and addresses of the officers and directors of the company are as follows:

Name and Address	Position
John Anderson Springfield, Mass.[1]	President, treasurer, and director
Phyllis Anderson Springfield, Mass.	Director
Robert W. Clark Springfield, Mass.[1]	Clerk
David Anderson Boston, Mass.	Director
Ralph Davis Longmeadow, Mass.[1]	Director
Paul Johnson Suffield, Conn.[1]	Director

1. Denotes members of the Executive Committee scheduled to meet weekly. Meetings of the full Board of Directors are scheduled quarterly.

The company is actively involved with outside counseling. The Massachusetts chapter of SCORE (Service Corps of Retired Executives), sponsored by S.B.A., is providing substantial guidance in the areas of planning, marketing, and manufacturing. Financial advice is being obtained through a coordinated effort with SCORE and the international accounting firm of Coopers & Lybrand. Corporate counsel is being provided by the law firm of Lyons and Kennedy.

Capitalization

The authorized capital stock of the company consists of 80,000 shares of common stock, without par value. The company is presently involved in a private intrastate offering of its common stock. Prior to the offering, stockholders owned 45,000 shares. The offering to the public is 20,000 shares at an offering price of $10 per share. This price was arbitrarily set by the company; it was not based on earnings, and the company does not represent that the stock has a market value of $10 or could be sold at that price. No dealer, salesperson, or other person has been authorized to give any information or make any representation of the offering. All proceeds will go to the company. To date, 3,400 shares have been purchased by the public, leaving 16,600 shares available. If the offering is completed, the purchasers will own 20,000 shares, or approximately 30.7 percent of the shares that will be outstanding.

Long-Range Plans

The long-range plans of the company encompass expansion of the existing equipment designs, extension of marketing effort into foreign countries, development of additional feeder equipment, and introduction of new machine tool products.

The present Guide designs have been created particularly for applications with single-spindle lathes. This covers adaptations from simple engine lathes to sophisticated, numerically controlled turning centers. With additional engineering, the present design will be adaptable for use with other types of equipment requiring stock feeders, such as single-spindle automatic screw machines, cut-off saws, and presses.

As discussed in the "Marketing" section, considerable efforts have been made toward expanding business into the European Common Market countries through association with a British company. There are other markets of comparable importance, such as the Japanese; to date, however, no contacts have been made in any to them. The company feels that it is in its best interest to begin making such contacts as soon as possible.

The company has given considerable thought to applying the Guide principles to other feeder designs. Currently, interest is focused on developing units capable of adapting to multiple-spindle turning equipment. At least three additional feeder models are envisioned, compatible with four, six, and eight-spindle equipment, respectively. In the five-year forecast, funds have been allocated for use in the development of this new feeder equipment. New product development is also basic to the company's long-range plan. Concepts have been formulated toward the development of a turning machine, and some preliminary engineering work has been done. Management believes there is a tremendous need for such a machine of proper design and price. There is no question that the company's personnel are capable of designing such a machine and producing a prototype. As presently conceived, the turning machine could sell at the rate of several thousand per year, at a unit sales price in the vicinity of $15,000. Should the turning machine concepts prove sound, the company expects that additional capitalization will be required to pursue this effort. (Potential revenues from the sale of these turning machines have not been included in the five-year forecast.)

The following financial statements represent management's best forecasts of financial position and the results of operations during the five-year period ending June 30, 1987.

Allied Engineering Corporation—Forecasts for Years Ending June 30, 1983 through June 30, 1987

a. Income

	1983	1984	1985	1986	1987
Gross sales	$500,000	$1,575,000	$2,640,000	$3,720,000	$5,460,000
Less discounts	34,000	105,000	132,000	186,000	273,000
Net sales	466,000	1,470,000	2,508,000	3,534,000	5,187,000
Cost of sales					
Materials and subcontracting	280,000	585,000	930,000	1,271,000	1,869,000
Manufacturing labor, including fringe benefits	—	105,000	270,000	434,000	651,000
Assembly labor, including fringe benefits	35,000	65,000	95,000	130,000	172,000
Manufacturing overhead, annexed	80,000	126,000	203,000	278,000	352,000
Total cost of sales	395,000	881,000	1,498,000	2,113,000	3,044,000
Gross profit	71,000	589,000	1,010,000	1,421,000	2,143,000

Marketing and administrative expenses					
Marketing	91,000	173,000	274,000	444,000	562,000
Administrative	68,000	99,000	164,000	211,000	261,000
Total marketing and administrative expenses	159,000	272,000	438,000	655,000	823,000
Subtotal	(88,000)	317,000	572,000	766,000	1,320,000
Add gross profit from distribution of other manufacturers' products	26,000	29,000	32,000	35,000	39,000
Operating income (loss)	(62,000)	346,000	604,000	801,000	1,359,000
Less interest expense	(9,000)	(23,000)	(19,000)	(15,000)	(10,000)
Income (loss) before income taxes	(71,000)	323,000	585,000	786,000	1,349,000
Federal and state income taxes	—	(156,000)	304,000	408,000	708,000
Income (loss) before extraordinary item	(71,000)	167,000	281,000	378,000	641,000
Tax benefit from utilizing 1983 net operating loss and investment credit	—	44,000	—	—	—
Net income (loss)	$(71,000)	$ 211,000	$ 281,000	$ 378,000	$ 641,000

b. Manufacturing Overhead

	1983	1984	1985	1986	1987
Rent	$12,000	$ 12,000	$ 24,000	$ 24,000	$ 30,000
Supplies	4,000	7,000	16,000	20,000	25,000
Power	2,500	3,000	6,000	8,000	10,000
Heat	3,500	4,000	8,000	10,000	12,000
Maintenance and repairs	1,500	2,500	6,000	9,000	12,000
Insurance	2,500	4,500	6,000	8,000	10,000
Engineering salaries	22,000	25,000	50,000	77,000	107,000
Engineering services, fees, and consultation	12,000	12,000	12,000	12,000	12,000
Research and development	5,000	10,000	10,000	35,000	50,000
Depreciation	15,000	46,000	65,000	75,000	84,000
	$80,000	$126,000	$203,000	$278,000	$352,000

c. Marketing and Administrative Expenses

	1983	1984	1985	1986	1987
Marketing					
Sales commissions	$16,000	$ 53,000	$132,000	$186,000	$273,000
Sales salaries and fringe benefits	38,000	57,000	68,000	150,000	165,000
Travel and entertainment	15,000	25,000	30,000	50,000	60,000
Autos	5,000	8,000	9,000	18,000	19,000
Advertising, promotion, and trade shows	17,000	30,000	35,000	40,000	45,000
Total	$91,000	$173,000	$274,000	$444,000	$562,000
Administrative					
Administrative salaries and fringe benefits	25,000	35,000	70,000	80,000	100,000
Office salaries and fringe benefits	7,000	19,000	40,000	50,000	60,000
Telephone	1,500	2,000	2,500	3,000	4,000
Supplies	1,000	3,000	4,000	5,000	6,000
Machine rentals and maintenance	1,500	2,000	2,500	4,000	4,000
Legal and accounting					
Normal	3,000	3,000	7,000	10,000	10,000
Patent	10,000	5,000	5,000	15,000	15,000
Dues and subscriptions	1,000	1,000	1,000	2,000	2,000
Consulting and directors' fees	5,000	5,000	6,000	6,000	6,000
Key-man insurance	8,000	8,000	—	—	—
Depreciation	—	1,000	1,000	1,000	2,000
Bad debts	5,000	15,000	25,000	35,000	52,000
Total	$68,000	$ 99,000	$164,000	$211,000	$261,000

d. Cash Flows

	1983	1984	1985	1986	1987
Receipts					
Operating profit (loss) before interest expense and income taxes	$(62,000)	$346,000	$604,000	$801,000	$1,359,000
Add					
Depreciation	15,000	47,000	66,000	76,000	86,000
Increase in accounts payable and accrued expenses	40,000	60,000	62,000	89,000	67,000
	(7,000)	453,000	732,000	966,000	1,512,000
Less increase in accounts receivable and inventories	(142,000)	(179,000)	(211,000)	(258,000)	(292,000)
Cash provided by (used in) operations, before interest expense and income taxes	(149,000)	274,000	521,000	708,000	1,220,000

Less					
Interest expense	(9,000)	(23,000)	(19,000)	(15,000)	(10,000)
Federal and state income taxes					
Final for prior year	—	—	(112,000)	(192,000)	(104,000)
Estimated payments	—	—	(112,000)	(304,000)	(408,000)
Cash provided by (use in) operations	(158,000)	251,000	278,000	197,000	698,000
Sale of capital stock	100,000	—	—	—	—
Term debt	225,000	25,000	—	—	—
Total receipts	167,000	276,000	278,000	197,000	698,000
Disbursements					
Purchase of equipment	150,000	187,000	106,000	123,000	109,000
Payment of bank loan, short-term	18,000	—	—	—	—
Payment of term debt	—	—	50,000	50,000	50,000
Increase in cash value life insurance	—	—	3,000	3,000	4,000
Total disbursements	168,000	187,000	159,000	176,000	163,000
Excess of receipts over disbursements (disbursements over receipts)	(1,000)	89,000	119,000	21,000	535,000
Cash balance, beginning of year	8,000	7,000	96,000	215,000	236,000
Cash balance, end of year	$ 7,000	$ 96,000	$215,000	$236,000	$ 771,000

e. Balance Sheet

	1982	1983	1984	1985	1986	1987
Assets						
Cash	$ 8,000	$ 7,000	$ 96,000	$ 215,000	$ 236,000	$ 771,000
Accounts receivable	22,000	75,000	164,000	279,000	393,000	576,000
Inventories						
Raw materials and purchased parts	—	33,000	63,000	94,000	138,000	172,000
In process and finished	34,000	90,000	150,000	215,000	315,000	390,000
Total current assets	64,000	205,000	473,000	803,000	1,082,000	1,909,000
Cash value, life insurance	—	—	—	3,000	6,000	10,000
Equipment, net of accumulated depreciation	3,000	138,000	278,000	318,000	365,000	388,000
Total assets	$67,000	$343,000	$751,000	$1,124,000	$1,453,000	$2,307,000

Liabilities and stockholders' equity

Bank loan, short-term	18,000	—	—	—	—	—
Accounts payable and accrued expenses	26,000	66,000	126,000	188,000	277,000	344,000
Federal and state income taxes	—	—	112,000	192,000	104,000	300,000
Term debt, current portion	—	—	50,000	50,000	50,000	50,000
Total current liabilities	44,000	66,000	288,000	430,000	431,000	694,000
Term debt, noncurrent portion	—	225,000	200,000	150,000	100,000	50,000
Total liabilities	44,000	291,000	488,000	580,000	531,000	744,000
Stockholders' equity						
Common stock	37,000	137,000	137,000	137,000	137,000	137,000
Retained earnings	(14,000)	(85,000)	126,000	407,000	785,000	1,426,000
Total stockholders' equity	23,000	52,000	263,000	544,000	922,000	1,563,000
Total liabilities and stockholders' equity	$67,000	$343,000	$751,000	$1,124,000	$1,453,000	$2,307,000

The following statements show forecasts of income and cash flows for four quarters of the fiscal year beginning June 30, 1982.

Allied Engineering Corporation—Quarterly Forecasts for Fiscal Year Ending June 30, 1983

a. Income

	1st Quarter Ended September 30, 1982	2nd Quarter Ended December 31, 1982	3rd Quarter Ended March 31, 1983	4th Quarter Ended June 30, 1983	Total for Year Ended June 30, 1983
Net sales	$ 37,000	$ 93,000	$168,000	$168,000	$466,000
Cost of Sales					
Materials and subcontracting	22,000	56,000	101,000	101,000	280,000
Assembly labor, including fringe benefits	7,000	8,000	10,000	10,000	35,000
Manufacturing overhead	11,400	18,600	25,000	25,000	80,000

Total cost of sales	40,400	82,600	136,000	136,000	395,000
Gross margin (loss)	(3,400)	10,400	32,000	32,000	71,000
Less marketing and administrative expenses					
Marketing	15,500	20,500	27,000	28,000	91,000
Administrative	12,800	14,400	18,400	22,400	68,000
Subtotal	28,300	34,900	45,400	50,400	159,000
	(31,700)	(24,500)	(13,400)	(18,400)	(88,000)
Gross margin from distribution of other manufacturers' products	5,000	7,000	7,000	7,000	26,000
Operating profit (loss)	(26,700)	(17,500)	(6,400)	(11,400)	(62,000)
Interest expense	(500)	(1,500)	(3,000)	(4,000)	(9,000)
Net loss	$(27,200)	$(19,000)	$(9,400)	$(15,400)	$(71,000)

b. Cash Flows

	1st Quarter Ended September 30, 1982	2nd Quarter Ended December 31, 1982	3rd Quarter Ended March 31, 1983	4th Quarter Ended June 30, 1983	Total for Year Ended June 30, 1983
Receipts					
Sale of capital stock	$100,000	$ —	$ —	$ —	$100,000
Term debt	50,000	75,000	$ —	100,000	225,000
Total receipts	150,000	75,000	$ —	100,000	325,000
Disbursements					
Net loss	27,200	19,000	9,400	15,400	71,000
Less					
Depreciation	(3,000)	(3,000)	(4,000)	(5,000)	(15,000)

Increase in accounts payable and accrued expenses	$ —	(10,000)	(10,000)	(20,000)	(40,000)
	24,200	6,000	(4,600)	(9,600)	16,000
Add increase in accounts receivable and inventories	$ —	46,000	34,000	62,000	142,000
Cash used in operations	24,200	52,000	29,400	52,400	158,000
Purchase of equipment	65,000	10,000	$ —	75,000	150,000
Payment of bank loan, short-term	18,000	$ —	$ —	$ —	18,000
Total disbursements	107,200	62,000	29,400	127,400	326,000
Excess of receipts over disbursements (disbursements over receipts)	42,800	13,000	(29,400)	(27,400)	(1,000)
Cash balance, beginning of period	8,000	50,800	63,800	34,400	8,000
Cash balance, end of period	$ 50,800	$63,800	$ 34,400	$ 7,000	$ 7,000

Basic Assumptions

Operating

Sales. Sales terms will be net 30 days. Two-thirds of the sales volume during 1983 and 1984 will be handled through distribution to the user market. In 1985 and thereafter, one-half of the sales volume will be to the O.E.M. market and one-half to the user market. Sales to the O.E.M. market will be the net of a 10 percent discount to the O.E.M., while sales through distributors will be at full list price but will result in a 10 percent commission to the distributor.

Management estimates that average selling prices and volume during the forecast period will be as follows:

	1983	1984	1985	1986	1987
Volume in units	50	150	240	310	420
Average gross selling price	$10,000	$10,500	$11,000	$12,000	$13,000

The higher selling prices after 1983 are primarily the result of more advanced phases with more capabilities than the initial model. Management intends to pursue a vigorous program of cost reduction in order to maintain the sales price of the Guide at competitive levels. Thus it is expected that, while the sales prices of the present models may decrease in later years, more advanced models will account for a greater percentage of sales volume, with a resulting higher average selling price in future years.

Cost of Sales. Materials and subcontracting costs are based on actual costs to date of constructing bar feeders, adjusted after 1983 to reflect:

A gradual transition over the period from purchase of all parts to full manufacture by the company of its own parts

Increased costs resulting from the manufacture of a more advanced model

The expected results of management's cost reduction program and economies resulting from higher volume levels

Manufacturing labor will increase over the period as more manufacturing activity is performed to replace subcontracting. At the same time, labor rates are expected to increase at approximately 10 percent per year. Fringe benefits have been included for all types of labor at 25 percent gross payroll.

Anticipated increases in assembly labor are based on management's estimate of the manpower required to handle expected volume levels and expected increases in labor rates. Management expects to employ the following number of people in assembly:

1983	2
1984	4
1985	6
1986	8
1987	10

Manufacturing overhead, as shown in the detailed schedule, is based on management's estimate of the amount and type of costs required for the volume levels projected. Rent is raised in 1985 to reflect additional space used. Engineering salaries are based on the salary and fringe benefit costs of the following number of people:

1983	1
1984	1
1985	2
1986	3
1987	4

Anticipated research and development costs for new and improved products and new product lines have also been included.

Depreciation is based on the accelerated cost recovery system under the Economic Recovery Tax Act of 1981.

Marketing Expenses. Marketing expenses as shown in the editorial schedule are based on management's estimate of the effort required to achieve the forecast volume levels. Commissions reflect 10 percent of the sales volume forecast to be handled by distributors. Sales salaries are based on the following staff, including, in the later years, a full-time sales executive:

1983   2
1984   3
1985   3
1986   5
1987   5

Advertising consists primarily of trade advertising, and provision has been made for one trade show in 1983 and two shows in all other years.

Administrative Expenses.   Administrative salaries increase significantly after 1984 to reflect the addition of an officer to assist the president on a full-time basis and to provide for continuity of management. Office salaries are based on the following number of people, including an office manager or controller in the later years:

1983   2 (part-time)
1984   3
1985   4
1986   5
1987   5

Provision has been made for legal costs expected in connection with the company's patent activities. Key man insurance will be carried on the president and, for the first two years, on the company's consulting engineer. From 1985 on, the policies will build cash value approximately equal to their yearly cost. Bad debts have been provided for at 1 percent of sales as the company expects to pursue an aggressive sales policy.

Federal and State Income Taxes.   Income taxes have been provided for at an overall 53 percent (the approximate rate presently in effect) during the period to allow for both federal and Massachusetts taxes. It is assured that the investment tax credit will remain at 10 percent, and tax credits for research and development are expected to remain unchanged. The timing of cash payments for income taxes and related estimates is based on current provisions of the laws.

Accounts Receivable.   Projections are based on an average of 40 days sales in receivables at all times. This average provides for possible payment delays by customers. Customer deposits and prepayments have not been considered for projection purposes.

Inventories. Management estimates that one month's supply of raw material and purchased parts will be required to be on hand at all times. The projections reflect this estimate. The projections reflect an inventory of three months' sales as in process and finished at an average of 50 percent complete. This is consistent with the 12-week manufacturing cycle estimated by management.

Accounts Payable and Accrued Expenses. Projections are based on an average of one month's raw materials and purchased parts carried in inventory plus a comparable amount for the material and parts content of the in-process and finished inventory.

Financing Assumptions

Management is presently seeking sources of equity and debt capital. The ratios of equity and debt financing cannot be determined at this time. For purposes of the projections, however, the following has been assumed:

1. The company will raise $100,000 of equity capital during 1983.
2. The company will secure debt capital of $250,000 during 1983 and 1984. The assumed terms of such debt include interest at 9 percent and principal payback at an equal rate on each August 1 from 1984 through 1988.

Capital Expenditures

The projections include capital expenditures in the amounts estimated by management and during the periods management believes necessary. Such amounts and periods are as follows:

1983	$150,000
1984	$187,000
1985	$106,000
1986	$123,000
1987	$109,000

CHAPTER
FIVE

FORMS OF DOING BUSINESS

One of the first and most important decisions you will have to face when you go into business for yourself is the choice of the appropriate form of business ownership. This is a decision that will have far-reaching tax, financial, legal, and business implications. With few exceptions, there is no one recommended form for carrying on a particular business activity. That decision must be based on the specific facts and circumstances of each individual situation. And as changes occur or different needs arise, the form of doing business may need to be reexamined and the alternatives reevaluated. In this chapter we will explore the principal forms of doing business with emphasis on the advantages and disadvantages of each. (For a tabular comparison of various forms of doing business, see the Appendix to this chapter.)

PROPRIETORSHIP

A proprietorship is an unincorporated business owned by one individual. You can undertake a proprietorship without any of the formalities associated with other forms of business, such as registering to do business. As with a partnership, one of the disadvantages of doing business as a proprietorship is that you are personally liable for the obligations of the business. On the other hand, you have exclusive control.

Taxation

A proprietorship is not a separate entity for tax purposes; therefore, it does not pay a separate income tax. The proprietorship's taxable transactions are attributed to the proprietor, who combines them with his or her income, if any, and pays a tax based upon the total taxable income. You cannot shelter income in a proprietorship. The net profits of the business are taxed to you whether you actually have them distributed to you. The individual income tax rates vary from 12 percent (11 percent after 1982) to 50 percent (The effective tax rate for long-term capital gains ranges from 4.8 percent in 1982—4.4 percent thereafter—to 20 percent.)

The Self-Employment Tax

In lieu of Social Security taxes paid equally by an employer and employee with respect to the employee's compensation, the net earnings of a proprietorship are subject to a special self-employment tax. Beginning in 1983 the maximum income subject to the self-employment tax is indexed (has a built-in factor of change) for expected increase. The factor itself is subject to change; the following table assumes an annual increase of approximately 8 percent.

Year	Rate of Tax	Maximum Taxable Income	Maximum Tax
1982	9.35%	$32,400	$3,029
1983	9.35%	35,000	3,273
1984	9.35%	37,800	3,534
1985	9.90%	40,800	4,039
1986	10.00%	44,000	4,400

In addition to the federal income and self-employment taxes, an individual doing business as a proprietor may also be liable for various state and local taxes.

Nondeductible Expenses

As a sole proprietor, you cannot deduct as a business expense any payments for group hospitalization, life insurance, and medical plan expenses that relate to your personal coverage. (Payments for employee coverage are, of course, deductible). You can, however, establish a self-employed retirement plan and deduct from income the contributions made to the plan. For defined contribution plans (see Chapter 10), the maximum allowable deduction is currently the lesser of $15,000 or 15 percent of self-employment income. For years beginning after 1983, the dollar limitation increases to $30,000, and the percentage limitation will be 15 percent for profit-sharing plans and 25 percent for pension plans (see Chapter 10). For defined benefit plans, the contribution limitations must be actuarially determined. Unlike a corporation or partnership, a proprietorship is not permitted to deduct the amortization of organization costs as a business expense.

Tax Year

The tax year of a proprietorship coincides with the tax year of the individual and is, therefore, normally a calendar year. The IRS will normally permit a fiscal year only if you can justify the change on the ground that the fiscal year conforms more closely to the cycle of your business's activities. Even then, the IRS will generally require that the tax year end shortly after the peak business season.

Liquidation of Business

You can liquidate your proprietorship entirely by selling it, by ceasing to do business and assuming personal control, or by incorporating. You can carry out a partial liquidation by selling part of the business and either operating as a proprietorship with the remaining interest or continuing the business in partnership with the buyer or buyers.

In most forms of disposition, partial or total, the proprietorship is viewed as selling the individual assets of the proprietorship. Thus whether your gains or losses are recognized and whether they are either capital or ordinary will depend upon the basis and nature of the assets sold (see Chapter 6). If, for example, you sold a business that consisted only of accounts receivable, inventory, and plant and equipment, you would be required to allocate the sales price to the assets sold before determining the nature of the resulting gain or loss. Any gain or loss recognized on receivables and inventory would be ordinary since they are not capital assets. Any gain recognized on the sale of plant and equipment would be subject to the applicable depreciation recapture laws— that is, ordinary income must be recognized to the extent that depreciation or cost recovery was claimed in the past since depreciation is used to offset ordinary income—and accordingly would be ordinary or a combination of ordinary and capital. If your proprietorship is several years old, capital gain will be recognized to the extent that you can allocate the sales proceeds to intangible assets, such as goodwill. Be sure to spell out in the sales agreement your allocation of the sales proceeds; otherwise, the IRS might try to impose a different allocation.

Closing out a business does not automatically trigger recognition of gain or loss on the assets of that business. Recognition will not occur until you actually dispose of the assets and may therefore be deferred indefinitely. The death of the proprietor has no income tax significance for the proprietorship, even though the value of the business is included in the proprietor's estate. (You should, of course, provide for the disposition or continuance of your business after your death.)

PARTNERSHIP

For tax purposes a partnership is defined as "a syndicate, group, pool, joint venture, or other unincorporated organization, through or by means of which any business, financial operation, or venture is carried on, and which is not, within the meaning of the Internal Revenue Code, a trust or estate or a corporation." If an organization meets this definition, it will be classified as a partnership regardless of the wishes of its participants. To be classified as a corporation under tax law, an organization must have more corporate than noncorporate characteristics: any organization that meets this requirement cannot escape corporate status.

Two Classes

Generally speaking, there are two types of partnerships: general partnerships and limited partnerships.

The General Partnership

The legal definition of a general partnership is "an association of two or more persons to carry on as co-owners a business for profit." General partnerships are typically found in associations that are service oriented and not capital intensive. This takes in most of the professions, including law, accounting, and medicine. This kind of partnership should not be ruled out for a capital-intensive business if the prospective partners are able to provide the required capital and are willing to accept all of the risks.

Probably the most often cited disadvantage of doing business as a general partnership is that the partners' legal liability is not limited to the assets of the partnership. Creditors may look to personal assets to satisfy the debts of the partnership once the partnership's assets have been exhausted. Mitigating the impact of this drawback, at least where new ventures are concerned, is that owners of corporations sometimes have to accept personal liability. It is common practice for creditors of new corporations, or corporations involved in operations deemed speculative, to exact personal commitments from each founder shareholder to guarantee the corporation's debts.

The Limited Partnership

The limited partnership differs from the general partnership in respect to the nature of its members. In the limited partnership there are in addition to the general partner or partners one or more partners not bound by the partnership obligations. These limited partners are only liable for the partnership debts to the extent of their capital contributions.

Limited partnerships are usually formed where there is a need for more capital than can be provided by the general partners or where the general partners want to spread the risk of a venture (at least to the extent of the limited partners' capital contributions) without utilizing the corporate form. This form of partnership is common in real estate development, oil and gas exploration, and motion picture ventures.

Limited partnerships are treated for tax purposes the same as general partnerships. The danger of acquiring too many corporate characteristics and thus being classified as a corporation under tax law is somewhat greater with limited than with general partnerships.

Taxation of Partnerships

The method by which the income of a partnership is taxed has both its advantages and disadvantages. The partnership itself does not pay any federal income taxes, although it is required to file an income tax return. The partnership functions as a conduit through which the various tax attributes flow to the partners, who report the amounts on their federal income tax returns and, in most instances, on their state income tax returns.

The tax paid on the income of the partnership (or the tax benefit derived from a partnership loss) is a function of the partner's effective tax rate. Your share of the profits or losses of the partnership is combined with your other income (or capital gains) and losses for the year— ordinary to ordinary, capital to capital—and the tax is computed on the total. Your share of the partnership income will be taxed whether or not it is actually distributed.

The federal income tax rate imposed on partnership income could vary from 12 percent (11 percent after 1982) to 50 percent, depending upon the amount of each partner's taxable income from all sources. All or part of the income may also be subject to the self-employment tax. Income of a limited partner, other than guaranteed payments, is not self-employment income. If the partner is a corporation, the corporate tax rates apply. Other examples of items flowing through to the partners are dividends qualifying for exclusion, tax credits such as investment tax credit and targeted jobs tax credit, tax preference items, and nontaxable income.

Your share of the partnership's income or losses may differ from your interest in the capital of the partnership, as long as there is an economic justification for the difference. The same is true for any other tax attributes of the partnership such as capital gains and losses, credits, and so on. Gains, losses, and credits, however, cannot be allocated among partners solely for tax avoidance purposes.

If the loss from operations exceeds your basis in the partnership, the loss recognized in the current year will be limited to your basis in your partnership interest. Your basis is the total of your contributions increased or decreased by your allocated share of profits or losses, respectively, from operations in prior years, increased by your share of certain partnership liabilities and reduced by withdrawals. If you have a loss in excess of the allowable limit for any one year, you can carry the loss forward to be used in a year in which your basis exceeds your loss.

Deductibility of Personal Items

Personal items, such as the cost of membership in qualified retirement (for example, pension and profit sharing) plans, life insurance, or coverage for hospitalization or medical reimbursement, paid by the partnership on behalf of any or all partners are not deductible in computing partnership taxable income. (The payments are treated as nontaxable distributions that reduce the recipient's basis in the partnership exactly as would a distribution of cash.) An exception to the nondeductibility of personal items at the partnership level are so-called guaranteed payments, which are special compensation to a partner or partners for contributions of services not matched by other partners. These payments are taxable income to the recipients. Costs of participation in qualified retirement, medical, and hospital plans are, however, deductible by the *individual* partners on their personal return (subject to limitations). The partnership may, of course, deduct as an expense the cost of any of these benefits on behalf of employees. (Partners cannot be employees.)

Contributions by Partners

When you contribute property to a partnership, the partnership will normally credit you with the property's fair market value. To the extent you receive a partnership interest or an increased partnership interest in return for the property, neither you nor the partnership will recognize gain or loss on the exchange (in most instances). For tax purposes, however, your basis (or increase in basis) in the partnership will be your adjusted basis in the property contributed (generally your cost less depreciation allowed) as of the date of transfer. Similarly, the partnership takes the property at your basis for tax purposes.

To the extent that you receive cash or its equivalent in exchange for property rather than partnership interest, the transaction will be treated as a sale rather than as a contribution. If you contribute services in exchange for partnership interest, the transaction will be treated as compensation in an amount equal to the value of the interest you received.

Treatment of Liabilities. Your basis in the partnership is increased by your share of any liabilities the partnership assumes. Conversely, if you contribute property subject to a liability and the partnership assumes that liability, you are deemed to have received a cash distribution equal to the aggregate liability assumed by the other partners. For example, if you contribute property with a value and basis to you of $100,000, on which there is a $40,000 mortgage, to a partnership with three other equal members, you will be deemed to have received a cash distribution of $30,000, and your basis in the partnership will be reduced by this amount. Accordingly, your basis in the partnership would be $70,000, that is, $100,000 (basis in the property contributed) less the $30,000 liability assumed by the other partners—i.e., the "deemed distribution."

If there is no stated agreement as to which partner will be personally responsible for any liability of the partnership, the liability will be allocated among the partners in the same way as partnership losses are allocated to each partner in determining the partner's basis in his or her partnership interest.

Distribution to the Partners

Distributions by the partnership to the partners during the life of the partnership are generally not taxable. If, however, the partnership distributes money to you in excess of your basis in your partnership interest, that excess will be recognized as a gain to you. The sale or distribution of unrealized receivables and substantially appreciated inventory by the partnership are subject to special rules.

Partners as Outsiders

When you deal with your partnership in a capacity other than as a partner, you must be treated as an outsider. Thus, for example, if you sell an asset to the partnership, for an amount in excess of your basis, you will recognize gain on the sale. If the sale results in a loss, you can also recognize it for tax purposes, unless you have a direct or indirect interest in the partnership's capital or profits of more than 50 percent.

Termination of Partner's Interest

You can terminate your entire interest or a part of your interest in a partnership by selling such interest to other partners or a new partner. (Most partnership agreements provide for the approval of a new partner by the remaining partners and spell out the procedure for liquidating a partner's interest.) It is standard practice to determine a selling partner's share of income or loss from operations by means of a ratable allocation proportioned to the number of days the partner held an interest during the taxable year. This means that the seller must wait until the end of the partnership's taxable year to learn his or her income or loss. Few partnerships would find it feasible, however, to close their books at an interim date.

Tax Aspects of Terminating a Partnership Interest

Under the general rule you will realize a capital gain or loss on the sale of your interest except to the extent that the sales price is attributable to unrealized receivables of the partnership or inventory items that have substantially appreciated in value, in which case you will have ordinary income. The capital gain or loss will be either long or short term, depending on the length of time you held your interest. You can, however, exchange your partnership interest tax free for shares of a corporation as long as the transaction meets certain control requirements. You can also dispose of your partnership interest by gift, without, in most cases, incurring recognition of gain or loss. (There are numerous arrangements for the handling of a partner's interest upon the death of the partner. A sound partnership agreement should address these matters, and a prospective partner should review them with a competent tax planner.)

The sale of a partner's interest will not terminate the partnership unless: (1) no part of the business is continued by any of the partners; or (2) the sale brings to 50 percent or more the proportion of the total interest in the partnership that has been sold or exchanged within a 12-month period.

Taxable Year

A newly formed partnership may use a calendar year as its taxable year, or it may adopt the same taxable year as that of all of its principal partners. Any other taxable year requires the approval of the IRS. Normally, the IRS will approve any tax year that does not end earlier than three months before the principal partners' year end. Therefore, a partnership with calendar-year partners would normally be able to elect any year ending between September 30 and December 31.

Registering to Do Business

Partnerships are generally required to register with the state in which they are organized. They do not normally have to be registered with the federal government. A partnership does need an employer identification

number, however, when filing its income tax return and, if the partnership has employees, when remitting income and Social Security taxes
withheld from salaries. It is best to apply for this number as soon as the
partnership is formed.

THE CORPORATION

The distinguishing characteristics of the corporate form are:

Continuity of Life. The death, bankruptcy, or retirement of, or the di-
vestiture of interest by, any shareholder or group of shareholders will
not of itself cause a dissolution of the corporation.

Limited Liability. A shareholder is not personally liable for the indebtedness of or claims against the corporation (except in very special circumstances).

Free Transferability of Interest. A shareholder generally may sell all
or part of his or her interest to any buyer without the consent of the
other shareholders.

Organizing the Corporation

Organizing a corporation can be considered under two headings: administrative and capitalization. The administrative considerations can be
summarized as follows: obtaining the charter, drafting the bylaws, and
electing a board of directors. Legal consultation is a must in establishing
a corporation.

Capitalizing a corporation involves an exchange whereby cash or
other assets are contributed to the corporation and equity—that is,
shares or interest-bearing obligations, such as securities—is received by
the contributors. The tax implications of debt versus equity financing are
discussed below, under "Pitfalls."

Federal Income Taxation of Corporations

The corporate income tax rates for tax years beginning in 1982 and thereafter are as follows:

Taxable Income	1982	1983 and Thereafter
Up to $25,000	16%	15%
$25,000 to $50,000	19	18
$50,001 to $75,000	30	30
$75,001 to $100,000	40	40
Over $100,000	46	46

The alternative capital gains rate for a corporation is 28 percent, unless income does not exceed $50,000, in which case, the regular rates of 16 percent and 19 percent apply (15 percent and 18 percent in 1983 and thereafter).

Double Taxation

Because corporations do not receive a deduction for dividends paid, both the corporation and the shareholders pay taxes on the same income. (Recipients of dividends have an annual exclusion of $100, or on a joint return, $200.) Where shareholders with a controlling interest in a corporation are also its employees, they could have the corporation declare little or no dividends and instead designate their share of the corporate earnings as compensation. The IRS, however, will accept the compensation claim only for amounts it deems reasonable in relation to services performed. To the extent that payments exceed this limit, the payments will be treated as dividends (see Chapter 11).

Nonrecognition of Gain or Loss in Certain Cases

Corporations may be acquired or formed, as subsidiaries or totally independent entities, without recognition of gain or loss at the shareholder level. Of particular significance in the formation of a corporation is that transfer of assets (including cash) to a corporation is tax free to the transferors if they own 80 percent or more of the value of the corporation's outstanding stock and if certain other conditions are met (except to the extent that the contributor receives property other than stock, such as cash or securities, in which case he or she may have recognized gain on the fair market value of the property received). In addition, the acquisition of one corporation by another can be accomplished by having the shareholders of the acquiring corporation exchange their shares for the shares of the acquiror. The exchange is tax free because the shareholders are considered to be in the same economic position after the exchange as before (see Chapter 6).

Consolidated Tax Returns

Where a corporation owns a minimum of 80 percent of one or more other corporations, it may elect to file a consolidated federal tax return, which, for example, allows the loss of one company to be offset against the income of another.

Favorable Treatment of Recognized Gains and Losses (Shareholder)

When a corporation is liquidated, the shareholder, subject to certain requirements, may receive capital gains treatment on the transaction. Owners of stock in companies that qualified as "small business corporations" at the time the stock was issued (and that issued the stock in accordance with specific requirements) may, if they sell the stock at a loss, be entitled to ordinary-loss treatment.

Fringe Benefits

Under current law, a corporation may deduct larger amounts for contributions to certain benefit plans, notably, employee pension or profit-sharing plans, then can a partnership or proprietorship. However, as a result of the Tax Equity and Fiscal Responsibility Act of 1982, generally effective for years beginning after 1983, partnership and proprietorship contributions to retirement plans will be on a parity with contributions to corporate plans (see Chapter 10).

Corporations have another advantage over partnerships in connection with benefits. Certain benefits are not taxable to employee–recipients whether the employee is of a partnership or a corporation. A shareholder who is also an employee of the corporation (and this status must be evidenced by facts) may be in a position to receive these nontaxable benefits even though the costs are deductible to the corporation. In a partnership this combination of deductibility at one level and nontaxability at the other is not possible if the recipient is a partner, because a partner (even though active in the business) may not be an employee. Note, however, that many benefits, such as qualified retirement plans and noninsured medical reimbursement plans in particular, must be provided on a nondiscriminatory basis to all eligible employees in order to receive the favorable treatment allowed under the law. (A detailed discussion of fringe benefit plans may be found in Chapter 10.)

Pitfalls

The following subjects have been treated elsewhere in this book (see chapter cross-references). This discussion is therefore summary in form.

Collapsible Corporations.   Simply stated, a collapsible corporation is one used to substitute capital gain for ordinary income. The corporation—typically, one engaged in construction—disposes of its shares at the point where its principal activities are about to produce income, and the shareholders claim capital gain. Under the Internal Revenue Code, the proceeds of the sale are treated as ordinary income (see Chapter 11). The IRS has published guidelines to determining whether the amount of ordinary income derived by the corporation is sufficient to avoid collapsible status.

Accumulated Earnings Tax.   This tax is imposed on accumulations of income considered to exceed the reasonable needs of the company. It is a penalty tax and does not reduce the regular corporate levy. The rate is 27.5 percent of the first $100,000 of "accumulated taxable income" plus 38.5 percent of the amount in excess of $100,000.

Currently, the law permits corporations to accumulate at least $250,000 of earnings before there can be any penalty. (For techniques of minimizing exposure to this tax, see Chapter 11.)

Equity versus Debt.   In evaluating the desirability of stock (common or preferred) versus indebtedness as vehicles for capitalizing a corporation, the latter may seem more advantageous. There are two reasons for this:

Interest paid on debt securities is deductible, whereas dividends paid on stock are not deductible by the corporation.

The repayment of debt principal is tax free to the debt holder, whereas redemption of a shareholder's stock may be exposed to dividend treatment unless special redemption provisions are met.

Under the tax laws, however, a small equity capitalization in relation to indebtedness can mean that all or part of the indebtedness will be considered equity, with the interest payments thereby becoming dividends not deductible as a corporate expense (see Chapter 11). Also receipt of securities by shareholders may trigger recognition of gain or loss where it would not otherwise occur (see above, "Nonrecognition of Gain or Loss in Certain Cases").

Personal Holding Company.   A corporation that falls within the definition of a personal holding company is assessed an additional tax of 50 percent of its undistributed personal holding company income. (It is not subject to the accumulated earnings tax.) Since the tax is on undistributed earnings, a corporation can escape this tax by paying sufficient dividends. The purpose of this provision is to discourage the practice of transferring individually owned investment properties to a corporation, or incorporating individual talents or services to get the benefit of the lower corporate tax rate—that is, a maximum of 46 percent versus a maximum individual rate of 50 percent. Typically, a corporation will fall under the personal holding company rules if 60 percent or more of gross income (with certain adjustments) consists of passive-type income such as dividends, interest, royalties, gains from securities transactions, and, under certain circumstances, personal service income (see Chapters 6 and 11).

The reduction in the maximum individual income tax rate from 70 percent to 50 percent has significantly reduced the impact of the personal holding company tax.

Subchapter S Corporations

The Subchapter S corporation, as provided for in the Internal Revenue Code, has some tax attributes of corporations and some of partnerships, as well as certain unique features of its own (see Appendix). The Subchapter S corporation is designed to function as a conduit, that is, to provide for taxation of corporate earned income only at the individual-shareholder level. The shareholder treats the income and the deductions as though he or she personally realized or incurred them.

Requirements for Qualification.   A Subchapter S corporation must:

Be a domestic corporation

Not be a member of an affiliated group of corporations, eligible to file a consolidated return

Have only one class of stock

Not have more than 25 shareholders

Derive no more than 80 percent of its annual revenues from sources outside of the United States

Derive no more than 20 percent of its annual gross receipts from passive investments, such as interest, dividends, royalties, and proceeds from dealing in securities

Have only individuals, estates, or certain types of trusts as shareholders

Not have a nonresident alien as a shareholder

A corporation that meets these requirements may elect Subchapter S status. The election requires the consent of all the shareholders. If it is made after the first 75 days of the taxable year, it will go into effect with the following taxable year.

Termination of Status.   Subchapter S status may be forfeited in any of the following events: any of the conditions for qualification are no longer met; new shareholder affirmatively refuses consent to the election; or all shareholders in the corporation consent to revoke the election.

Taxation of Shareholders.   The shareholders report on their individual returns the Subchapter S corporation's taxable income or loss (with adjustments and limitations) for the current tax year. They must report undistributed taxable income as well as actual distributions because they are liable, as of the corporation's last year end, for all income earned by the corporation during that year and not distributed.

The tax treatment of distributions depends on the source of that distribution, and, accordingly, an order of priority has been established for determining the source or sources from which a distribution is deemed to be made. Distributions made no more than two and one-half months after the end of the corporations's previous taxable year will be deemed to come first out of any undistributed taxable income earned by the corporation during that year and retained by the corporation. Such distributions will be tax free. Distributions made after the two-and-a-half-month period (or during such period, but in excess of the prior year's undistributed taxable income) are considered made, sequentially, from the following sources:

Current year's earnings and profits (taxable as of receipt)

Undistributed previously taxed income retained at corporate year end but earned in previous years (not taxable)

Accumulated earnings and profits (taxable as of receipt)

Original basis of stock (return of capital)

Distributions beyond return of capital (treated as capital gain distributions)

Advantages and Disadvantages. The principal advantages of the Subchapter S corporation over the regular corporate form of doing business can be summarized as follows:

There is no regular corporate tax.

Corporate long-term capital gain, with limited exceptions, is taxed directly to shareholders, thus retaining its character as capital gain.

Corporate net operating losses are deductible directly by shareholders, subject to limitations, and therefore shelter—that is, offset—other income from taxes.

Income tax payments may be deferred by as much as a year if the company uses a fiscal year ending shortly after the tax year of its stockholders.

The tax on unreasonable accumulations of earnings will generally not apply.

Previously taxed earnings may be removed in cash from the corporation without incurring individual tax.

Of the major disadvantages, three have already been mentioned: stringent requirements for qualification; vulnerability to termination or revocation; and the elaborate nature of the rules of governing the amount, form, and timing of income distributions. A fourth disadvantage is the difficulty of retaining in the corporation earnings for operations, especially when the shareholders are in a high bracket and need a sizable distribution to pay their individual income taxes. It is not uncommon for shareholders to have to lend back the balance of their distributions, after paying their tax, to keep the corporation going.

When Should a Subchapter S Corporation Be Considered? The following conditions are favorable to establishing or converting to a Subchapter S corporation. Naturally, no one of them should be regarded as determinative in and of itself.

In the initial year of a business, there is a substantial amount of tangible personal property that will generate an investment tax credit.

The corporation can reasonably anticipate for the ensuing tax year a loss for which there will be no immediate benefit available from a net-operating-loss carryback claim. (This situation is typical of the early years of a company's operations.)

There is more than one corporate entity, and the taxable income bracket amounts must be allocated.

The corporation has a problem with excessive accumulated earnings.

The shareholder or prospective shareholder has children who are in a lower tax bracket so that there would be a tax advantage in transferring the shares to them. If the shareholder is (or anticipates becoming) an employee of the corporation as well, he or she might consider reducing his or her salary, consequently increasing the undistributed income to which (or part of which) the donees would be entitled. If the shareholder does this, however, he or she must be able to demonstrate that this reduced salary is adequate compensation for his or her services. Otherwise, the IRS may claim that some or all of the transferred amount should be treated as compensation (and taxed accordingly) followed by a gift to the children.

A circumstance in which participation in a Subchapter S corporation may be inadvisable arises when the shareholder would be taxed at a higher rate than would be a regular corporation. The following highly simplified example illustrates this situation. Assume a shareholder in the 50 percent bracket and a corporation with a taxable income (after payment of salaries to employee–shareholders) of $100,000. If the corporation were a Subchapter S corporation, the $100,000 would flow through to the shareholder, who would pay a tax of $50,000. If, on the other hand, the corporation were not a Subchapter S corporation and were liquidated shortly after the $100,000 was earned, the shareholder would end up paying a tax of only $40,600, arrived at as follows: tax on the corporation (1983 rate), $25,750; capital gain tax to the individual shareholder on liquidation, $14,850 (that is $74,250 earnings distributed, less $44,550—the latter figure representing the 60 percent long-term capital gain deduction—with the result being taxed at the 50 percent maximum rate on individuals); total tax, $40,600 ($25,750 plus $14,850).

APPENDIX

COMPARISON OF VARIOUS FORMS OF DOING BUSINESS

	Proprietorship	Partnership	Regular Corporation	Subchapter S Corporation
Taxable year	Usually calendar year	Usually calendar year; however, September, October, or November can be elected.	Any year end is permissible.	Optional original choice; changes of fiscal year end generally limited to September, October, November, or December
Expensing of depreciable business assets	Limited to $5,000 in 1982, increasing to $10,000 in 1986	Limited to $5,000 in 1982, increasing to $10,000 in 1986		Limited to $5,000 in 1982, increasing to $10,000 in 1986
Ordinary distributions to owners	Drawings from the business are not taxable; the net profits are taxable; and the proprietor is subject to the tax on self-employment income.	Generally not taxable	Payments of salaries are deductible by corporation and taxable to recipient; payments of dividends are not deductible by corporation and generally are taxable to recipient shareholders.	Same as regular corp.
Limitations on losses deductible by owners	Amount "at risk," except with respect to real estate activities	Partner's investment plus his or her share of the partnership recourse liabilities except for real estate partnerships	No losses allowed to individual except upon sale of stock or liquidation of corporation	The shareholder's investment plus his or her loans to the corporation; basis of loans reduced by losses and distributions

COMPARISON OF VARIOUS FORMS OF DOING BUSINESS

	Proprietorship	Partnership	Regular Corporation	Subchapter S Corporation
Dividends received	$100 dividend exclusion ($200 on joint tax return)	Conduit	85% to 100% dividend-received deduction	Treated as ordinary income; no exclusion or deduction
Formal election required	No	No	Must incorporate under state law	Yes
Capital gain	Taxed at individual level; 60% deduction for long-term	Conduit	Taxed at corporate level; alternative tax rate, 28%	Amounts flow through to extent of shareholder's portion of corporation's taxable income, but (unlike partnership) ordinary losses and capital gains are netted at corporate level.
Capital losses	Carried forward indefinitely	Conduit	Carry back three years and carry over five years as short-term capital loss offsetting only capital gains	Carry over five years as short-term capital loss, offsetting only capital gains
Section 1231 gains and losses	Taxed at individual level, combined with other Section 1231 gains or losses of individual; net gains are capital gains for individual; net losses are ordinary losses for individual.	Conduit	Taxable, or deductible at the corporate level	Net gain is a capital gain to the shareholder; net loss is an ordinary loss to the shareholder; however, corporation's 1231 loses are not netted with shareholder's 1231 gains.

	Individual (Proprietorship)	Partnership	Regular Corporation	Subchapter S Corporation
Basis of allocating income to owners	All income picked up on owner's return.	Profit and loss agreement (may have "special allocations" of income and deductions if they reflect economic reality)	No income allocated to stockholders.	Number of shares owned on the last day of the corporation's tax year
Basis for allocating a net operating loss	All losses flow through to owner's return.	Profit and loss agreement (may have "special allocations" of income and deductions if they reflect economic reality)	No losses allocated to stockholders.	Prorated among shareholders on a daily basis
Group hospitalization and life insurance premiums and medical reimbursement plans	Itemized deductions: for medical expenses, half of insurance premiums up to $150, medicine and drugs in excess of 1% of adjusted gross income, other bills over 3% of AGI; no deduction for life insurance premiums	Cost of partner's benefits are not deductible as a business expense; may be treated as distribution to individual partners, eligible for some possible deduction as if paid by individual.	Cost of shareholder–employee's coverage is generally deductible as a business expense if plan is "for the benefit of employees."	Same as regular corp.
Retirement benefits	Limited to H.R.–10 plan benefits, normally 15% of income up to $15,000; however, some defined-benefit H.R.–10 plans may provide more. For years beginning after 1983, limitation increases to essentially same as regular corporation.	Same as individual	Normal corporate employee benefits subject to maximum pension to retired employees of $10,000 plus inflation.	Corporation can deduct normal corporate employee contribution; however, owner–employee must add income contribution in excess of $15,000 to taxable income. For years beginning after 1983, limitation increases to essentially same as regular corporation.

COMPARISON OF VARIOUS FORMS OF DOING BUSINESS

	Proprietorship	Partnership	Regular Corporation	Subchapter S Corporation
Organization costs	Not amortizable	Amortizable over 60 months	Amortizable over 60-months	Same as regular corporation.
Partner's or shareholder's "reasonable" salary	Not applicable	Treated as an allocation of partnership profits and a conduit		Expense to the corporation, taxable to the shareholder-employee subject to FICA
Charitable contribution	Subject to limits for individual: gifts for the use of private foundation, 20% of AGI; gifts to public charity, cash 50% of AGI; appreciated property, 30% of AGI. Other limitations for specific items contributed	Conduit		Limited to 10% of taxable income before special deductions
Liability	Individually liable on all liabilities of business	General partners individually liable on partnership's liabilities; limited partner liable only up to amount of his or her capital contribution.	Capital contribution is limit of liability of shareholder.	Same as regular corporation
Qualified owners	Individual ownership	No limitation	No limitation	Only individuals, estates, and certain trusts may be shareholders.

Type of ownership interests	Individual ownership	More than one class of partner permitted.	More than one class of stock permitted.	Only one class of stock permitted.
Transfer of ownership	Assets of business transferable rather than business itself	New partnership usually created; consent of other partners normally required if partnership interest is to be transferred.	Ready transfer of ownership through the use of stock certificates; restrictions may be imposed by shareholders' agreement.	Shares can be transferred only to individuals, certain types of trusts, or estates; no consent by new shareholders to Subchapter S election is needed.
Capital requirements	Capital raised only by loan or increased contribution by proprietor.	Loans or contributions from partners (original, or newly created by remaking partnership)	Met by sale of stock or bonds or other corporate debt	Met by sale of stock or bonds, but corporation has only one class of stock and is limited to 25 shareholders.
Business action	Sole proprietor makes decisions and can act immediately.	Action usually dependent upon the unanimous agreement of partners or general partners.	Unity of action based on authority of board of directors.	Same as regular corporation except unanimous consent is required to elect or revoke Subchapter S status
Management	Proprietor responsible and receives all profits or losses.	Except for limited or silent partners, investment in partnership involves responsibility for management decisions.	Shareholder can receive income without sharing in responsibility for management.	Same as regular corporation

COMPARISON OF VARIOUS FORMS OF DOING BUSINESS

	Proprietorship	Partnership	Regular Corporation	Subchapter S Corporation
Flexibility	No restrictions	Partnership is contractual arrangement, within which members can do in business what individuals can, subject to the partnership agreement and applicable state laws.	Corporation is a creature of the state functioning within powers granted explicitly or necessarily implied and subject to judicial construction and decision.	Same as regular corporation
Investment credit	Limited by tax liability up to $25,000 plus 90% of liability in excess of $25,000 (85% for tax years beginning after 1982)	Conduit	Offset to taxes at corporate level; subject to $25,000 plus 90% of liability in excess of $25,000 (85% for tax years beginning after 1982)	Conduit
Tax preferences (minimum tax)	Through 1982, 15% of tax on preferences in excess of either $10,000 or one-half of taxes paid, whichever is	Conduit	Taxed at corporate level; 15% on preferences in excess of either $10,000 or tax liability, whichever is	Conduit

	greater (but capital gains preference and adjusted itemized deductions preference subject to alternative minimum tax). After 1982, add-on minimum tax is eliminated, and all preference items are subject to an expanded alternative minimum tax.		greater. In addition, for years beginning after 1982, benefits of certain preferences are "cut back" by 15% in computing taxable income. Amount of "cut back" preference is reduced for purposes of computing add-on minimum tax.
Character of income and deductions	Taxed at individual level; long-term capital gains deduction; limitation on investment interest deductions	Conduit	Taxed at corporate level
			Except as to long-term capital gains, income and profits are computed at corporate level, so that characteristics are determined at corporate level and do not flow to shareholder.

CHAPTER
SIX

BUYING OR SELLING A BUSINESS

T his chapter is in two sections dealing with nontax and tax aspects, respectively.

NONTAX ASPECTS

Certain points in the following discussion are essentially relevant only to buyers; others are equally relevant whether you are buying or selling.

General Hints for Buyers

To evaluate a business properly, you should know everything, current and historical, that bears on the viability of that business. Unfortunately, the necessary input for this kind of comprehensive understanding is rarely forthcoming from company management. As a practical matter, you will probably have to settle for something less. Few companies will refuse you a balance sheet and profit and loss statement. (You should demand a sequence of these reports going back as much as 10 years, or the life of the company if less.) Some may balk, however, at a request for operating reports covering even 3 years, and your request to inspect plant or facilities in the company of your own experts may meet with an evasive or highly qualified response.

The less cooperative a candidate for acquisition is in providing you with information, the more suspicious you should be. Other negative signs are the failure of the candidate to retain an independent certified public accountant or a record of heavy turnover in independent accountants. (If the company has a CPA, you should insist on his or her cooperation with your accountant as prerequisite to any offer you might make.)

If you are not satisfied with what you have learned yet are still interested in acquiring the company, you can always investigate the company principals. Usually this does not call for an exorbitant outlay of time or money.

Initial Survey

Before beginning your financial analysis of the target company, you should make a general survey of its operations, focusing on strengths and weaknesses that cannot be determined from the kind of data given in the financial statements. Your survey should include inquiries into the target company's products, facilities and manufacturing operations, employees, management, and legal issues.

Products.   Some questions that require detailed answers are:

What is the price, quality, availability, and sales terms of the product?

Are any of the company's products likely to be obsoleted in the near future?

Are there warranties, or other significant product liability exposure?

Who are the customers?

Can domestic or foreign markets be expanded?

Is there a seasonal sales pattern?

Who are the competitors, and how do they impact pricing, customers, or market penetration?

Are there any contractual relationships?

Is there a pattern to selling and distribution costs?

Have the following been reviewed:

Sales forecast as compared to actual?

Reasons for sales cancellation?

Budgeted to actual costs?

Profitability by product line?

The nature of customer complaints?

Patterns of discounts or markdowns?

Facilities and Manufacturing Operations.   Some questions that require a detailed answer are:

Where are facilities located, and what are the advantages or disadvantages of the location?

Is insurance adequate?

Are there any zoning restrictions, liens, or building code restrictions?

What is the quality, value, and remaining life of equipment?

Are there any technical problems in complying with the requirements of the Environmental Protection Administration (EPA), Occupational

Safety and Health Administration (OSHA), or any other regulatory body?

Has current capacity been compared to sales forecasts?

Has a review and evaluation been done of:

  Production planning?

  Production efficiency and layout?

  Availability of raw materials and lead times?

  Inventory storage and warehousing?

  Quality control?

What costs are fixed or variable, and what is the break-even level of sales?

Does the schedule of overhead costs reflect any significant trends?

Have the following been considered:

  Defective production?

  Downtime?

  Scrap?

  Labor turnover?

How long does it take for an order to be processed?

Are inventories stratified by fast- and slow-moving items?

Are there controls on inventory quantities?

What is inventory turnover?

What inventory valuation method is used?

Is there any significant inventory obsolescence?

Is a cost accounting system in effect?

Are there any long-term sales contracts, and if so, do prices escalate to meet projected costs?

What is the cause of any significant adjustments to inventory accounts resulting from physical counts?

Employees. Some questions that require detailed answers are:

  Is there a union, and if so, what are the contract terms and expiration dates?

  How are labor–management relations?

  Is there an incentive compensation system?

  Is there an acceptable safety record?

What skills are available in the area?

Is the surrounding community growing?

Is there a formal management organization chart?

Can managerial positions be filled by promotion from the ranks?

Is there a pension plan, and if so, what are the company's future obligations in connection therewith?

Have the details of all fringe benefits, such as profit sharing, life insurance, travel and disability insurance, deferred compensation, or severance plans, been considered.

What are the company's vacation and sick pay policies?

Management.   Some questions that require detailed answers are:

Is authority centralized?

Is marketing production or administration dependent on only one person?

Is the management style of the seller comparable with that of the buyer?

Are there any apparent management weaknesses?

Is there a long-range operating plan?

Is there a detailed budget, by department, plant, or subsidiary, in effect?

Is there segregation of duties and responsibilities within the companies?

If segregation of duties is not the practice, are there adequate compensating controls?

Does management periodically evaluate its performance?

Legal Issues.   Some questions that require detailed answers are:

What is the status of any current litigation?

Did the company's counsel prepare a representation letter for its auditors, and if so, has the company made it available?

Is the company in compliance with regulatory authority requirements, such as those of OSHA, the EPA, and the Equal Opportunity Employment Commission?

Are there legal issues that are common to the company's industry?

Financial Analysis

After obtaining the answers to the foregoing questions (and any additional appropriate question), you can begin to approach the financial analysis. A comprehensive financial analysis is necessary since it may form the basis upon which the transaction is valued and structured. That is, it can assist in determining how much the target company is worth and may indicate how it can be paid for, such as with equity investment, short-term debt, long-term debt, payments contingent on achieving certain goals, or a combination of all of these.

Before beginning such an analysis, however, you should gather certain data. Thus in the purely financial area you need:

Annual financial statements, preferably audited for up to 10 years

Financial results on a comparative basis by division

The most recent interim unaudited financial statements

Federal and state income tax returns for 5 years

IRS reports resulting from examinations

Schedules of unused loss and investment tax credit carry-overs

Projected financial statements

Current and past sales backlog information

Industry data relating to market trends, economic forecasts, or issues unique to the industry

Bonus or profit-sharing plans

Union contracts

Long-term leases or debt agreements

Royalty agreements

Important data outside the purely financial area include:

The amount of officers' compensation

The extent of transactions with related parties, such as rent paid for a building owned by the company officers and services provided by companies with common ownership

The amount of travel and entertainment expenses incurred by owner–managers.

The company's cash-management techniques

Comparative "aged" trial balance of accounts receivable

Credit policies and amount of uncollectible accounts

Extent of credit memo and the reasons therefor

The name, cost, and carrying value of marketable securities

The details of any investments accounted for by the equity method

The details of any patents, trademarks, or other such intangibles

The details of accounts payable by type and age

A listing of purchase commitments

The details on the company's vacation and sick pay policies

The amount of debt maturing in each future year and the interest rates, assets pledged, and personal guarantees

An overall evaluation of financial management including the electronic data processing (EDP) function

Timeliness of internal financial data

Armed with this data, you can now begin the formal part of the financial analysis. A formal financial analysis of a company can be carried out in two phases (not necessarily in sequence). The first phase is an exploration of the key relationships between accounting items. The second phase is a valuation of the company as an investment on the basis of its projected earnings.

Exploring Key Relationships

Relationships between various items drawn from balance sheet, profit and loss statement, and operational reports can be useful parameters of business performance and financial soundness. When the relationship between two items—expressed as a ratio—deviates from a normal figure, usually a range established for that ratio, there is a possibility that something needs correcting. The "norms" for each ratio are determined from industry statistics (available from several published reports) adjusted in accordance with the target company's performance over a period (see Chapter 15).

Key Ratios.   In keeping with accepted business usage, the following relationships are termed ratios. Strictly speaking, however, they are not ratios until they have numerical values. In this selection we focus on ratios recognized to be of general diagnostic significance. There are many others, relevant to specialized aspects of operations.

1. *Financial Position Ratios.*   These ratios include:

   a. *Current assets to current liabilities.* Widely used as a criterion of solvency, this ratio is a guide to the magnitude of financial margin of safety.

   b. *Trade debt to net worth.* This ratio indicates what portion of financing is provided by suppliers. Overtrading on suppliers' capital may be dangerous and may also involve loss of valuable discounts.

   c. *Total debt to net worth.* This ratio supplements the preceding ratio and compares the longer term indebtedness with the equity capital base on which it was incurred, thereby providing a measure of leverage.

   d. *Inventory to working capital.* This ratio indicates how the least liquid portion of current assets relates to total current assets. When inventories exceed net working capital, the current liabilities (debts that generally must be paid within the year) exceed the funds available to pay them, such as cash, marketable securities, and accounts receivable. Thus, liquidation of inventory may become necessary in periods of stress.

   e. *Fixed assets to net worth.* This ratio indicates the proportion of fixed assets financed out of equity capital rather than by debt. Financing fixed assets by debt rather than equity capital increases a company's vulnerability during periods in which the debt must be serviced out of shrinking margins.

2. *Capital Utilization Ratios.*   These ratios include:

   a. Cash to sales volume.

   b. *Cost of sales to average inventory (in dollars).* This ratio shows the number of times the total inventory in dollars turns over. It is, of course, an aggregate ratio, with products and components of inventory varying widely as to individual turnover rates and cost basis.

c. *Daily sales to average inventory (in dollars).* This is also an inventory turnover measure.

d. *Sales to net worth.* This ratio measures the adequacy of the investment in relation to volume of business as well as the efficiency of capital utilization.

e. *Sales to inventory.*

f. *Fixed assets to sales volume.* This ratio may disclose excessive or inadequate capacity.

g. *Working capital to sales.* One of the standard measures of the adequacy of working capital is its relation to sales volume. (Where working capital is excessive, there is waste; where it is insufficient, the company may not be able to meet its obligations.)

h. *Trade notes and receivables to daily credit sales.* This ratio shows the average collection period, which is a good measure of a company's success in enforcing its credit policies. Daily average credit sales are annual net credit sales divided by 360.

3. *Profitability Ratios.* These ratios include:

a. *Net profit to net worth.* This ratio measures management's ability to earn a return on shareholders' capital. You can compare it with other companies in the industry and evaluate it in relation to risks taken. In the case of closely held companies, adjustments may have to be made for such factors as owner salaries, and so on.

b. *Net profit to total assets.* This ratio measures profit earned on all assets used in the business. Price-level changes and varying depreciation methods may make it necessary to adjust fixed asset values to a common basis for comparative purposes. Methods of computation vary among companies.

c. *Net income to unit of capacity or service offered.* An example of a unit of service would be a ton mile; units of capacity include hotel rooms, hospital beds, and alleys in a bowling alley. This ratio provides significant clues to profitability (or the lack of it).

4. *Operating Cost Relationships.*   These include:

   a. *Costs as a percentage of sales.* This measures the proportion of sales devoted to covering an element of cost.

   b. *A cost to its cost group.* This ratio, of which labor to cost of manufacturing is an example, is primarily useful as a means of describing a trend that can be correlated with other observed trends. For example, an increase in a particular category of costs could be related to an increase in one of the category's constituent items. Thus the ratio must be recorded over successive intervals.

5. *Operating Expense Relationships.*   These ratios include:

   a. *Commissions to sales.* This measures one cost of distribution.

   b. *Bad debt to sales or accounts receivable.* This measures the efficiency of the credit-granting function. This ratio is only meaningful when related to sales volume.

   c. *Sales expenses to sales.* This measures the cost of the selling effort.

   d. *Various expenses to total expenses in the same group.* Like the cost-to-cost group ratio, this type of ratio—for example, machine oiling as a percentage of total maintenance—is most meaningful when applied over time to describe a trend.

Analysis over Time.   As already pointed out, individual performance, as opposed to industry statistics, is an important source for establishing the norms by which to assess the implications of specific ratio values. The best procedure is to present this experience or "historical" data of the target company graphically for each ratio, plotting successive readings to define broad patterns over time. With certain ratios this approach is more or less mandatory, because their value at any one time is not significant. What counts is how the successive values change and how the changes correlate with similarly derived patterns of certain closely related ratios. If you know what you are doing, you can also analyze the resultant graphs predictively to deduce trends that might shed light on the future of the company under present management.

The Discounted Cash-Flow Method

If your preliminary analysis proves positive, you can then undertake the more technical evaluation of the prospective company as an investment. The standard technique for this involves ascertaining the present value of the company's projected cash flow for the life of its productive assets (reckoned as a composite of individual lives). The discount used is based primarily on alternative money market yields, but other factors, such as the estimated risks of the particular enterprise, are usually considered in arriving at a figure. With today's interest rates, discount rates are naturally high, and accordingly the falloff in present value in relation to time is steep. Therefore, if the composite asset life is longer than 10–15 years, you would probably be well-advised to limit your computations to a period in this time span.

To the extent that the target company's discounted future cash flows exceed the asking price, the purchase of the business would, in terms of current cost of capital, be justified.

Cash Flow versus Book Income. Notice that cash flow, not book profitability, is the basis for the present-value computation. A business may show a large book income and still produce an unsatisfactory economic return if net cash flow is not realized from the operation, say, because of indebtedness. (That resumption of cash flows could be anticipated at some future time—in the case of indebtedness, after the retirement of the debt—would not necessarily alter the picture appreciably. Again, the explanation lies in the negligibility, in current terms, of distant prospective inflows.)

On the other hand, a company may show nominal earnings, or even losses, and still have substantial value. This can happen if, for example, substantial amounts that will benefit earnings in the future are being expensed currently. It can also happen when excessive compensation is being paid to the stockholder–employees or if there are unfavorable contracts about to terminate.

If you are selling a business, you will find the cash-flow analysis an excellent basis for setting your price. If, however, you are offered consideration other than cash, especially debt and stock, you will be faced with another type of valuation exercise. Stock, for example, even though listed, may be subject to various restrictions that adversely affect its value. (Instead of selling the company to one buyer, you might consider splin-

various components and selling each separately.
to go public; see Chapter 14.)

e computation in Figure 6.1 is a somewhat
of the discounted present-value method of
is assumed that the company or the operation
ly intact after acquisition and that future capital
e a yield that is at least equal to that currently

...stimated Valuation Based on
Discounted Cash Flow, December 31, 1982
(in thousands of dollars)

Net income for 1982		$10,100
Add:		
Depreciation and depletion[1]	$6,500	
Interest expenses[2]	2,000	8,500
		18,600
Less, interest on excess cash		
investments net of income taxes[3]		500
"Adjusted" operating cash flow		$18,100
Present value of adjusted cash flow discounted at 10% per annum for 13 years[4]		
Factor 7.103		$128,600
Present value of net working capital (at the end of the estimated useful life of the productive assets considering a required return on investment of 10% per annum);		
Current assets	$37,000	
Less marketable securities at cost[5]	16,000	21,000
Current liabilities		8,000
Net working capital		$13,000

FIGURE 6.1

Factor 0.2896[6]	+ 4,000
	132,600
Less long-term debt[7]	38,000
	94,600
Add temporary cash investments at net realizable value[8]	16,000
Total estimated valuation	$110,600
Per share (4,000,000 shares)	$ 27.65

1. This is added back because it was deducted from book income yet represents no actual cash outlay.
2. For purposes of valuation, interest expenses may be treated as dividends on equity, which, unlike interest, do not reduce operating earnings. Since this amount was deducted from net income as interest, it is here added back.
3. This is deducted because it represents interest income from nonoperating assets—in this case, marketable securities.
4. The estimated life of the productive assets is determined on an overall basis by dividing the annual depreciation, depletion, and amortization expense into net fixed assets (undepreciated book cost).
5. This is deducted because it is not a part of operating assets. Deduction is in full amount because securities, being highly liquid, are theoretically usable at any time.
6. This factor refers to the value of an amount available in a future year, not (as in above factor) to the cumulative value of successive amounts over successive years.
7. Because the debt is treated as outstanding equity (Note 2), it cannot be part of operating assets.
8. This is added back because it is still a part of overall valuation.

FIGURE 6.1 (concluded)

TAX ASPECTS

How the transfer of a corporate entity will be taxed can generally be influenced by the way in which the parties structure the transaction. Transactions may be taxable or nontaxable to the seller; normally, the parties can determine which by agreement. If the seller will realize a loss on the transaction, nontaxability is generally not advantageous.

Nontaxable Transactions

If the transaction is to be nontaxable, the seller must receive only stock. To the extent he or she receives money or nonmonetary assets, any gain realized would be recognized for tax purposes. Moreover, if the property is deemed equivalent to a dividend, the tax may be at the ordinary-income rather than at the gentler capital-gain rate.

If the selling corporation exchanges assets for stock, it can distribute the stock received to its shareholders and liquidate tax free. (It may be more advantageous, however, for the seller to continue in existence as a personal holding company to be utilized as an estate and financial planning tool. For a discussion of the personal holding company concept, see "Personal Holding Companies" in this chapter.)

If the acquiring corporation is not publicly held, a nontaxable transaction is generally undesirable to the seller unless its shareholders can arrange beforehand (possibly with the acquiring company) to dispose of the latter's shares at a reasonable price. This might be done with a buy–sell or redemption agreement.

Basis to Seller

Assuming the buyer gives only stock, the seller's tax basis in that stock will be the same as his or her basis in the property surrendered. (Holding periods will also be the same.) The seller will be taxable only on subsequent sale of the stock (in a taxable transaction) and only if the amount received exceeds that basis. If the seller is an individual and holds the stock for life, his or her estate will not be taxed on the gain realized during his or her lifetime.

Basis and Attributes to Buyer

The acquiring corporation will take over the acquired corporation's basis in the property received. In addition, the new owner will acquire certain important tax attributes of the selling corporation (unless the principal purpose of the transaction was avoidance of federal income taxes); net operating loss carryforwards is an example. For acquisitions after 1983, however, these attributes will be proportionately reduced whenever ownership changes by more than 60 percentage points in a period of three years or less. On the other hand, losses generated by the acquired corporation in any year in which the buyer–parent owned 40 percent or more of the issued and outstanding stock for the last half of the year are not reduced. The ownership test is based on the percentage of ownership the selling corporation's shareholders acquire from the buying corporation as a result of the acquisition. (The 60-percentage-point test, with certain exceptions, goes into effect in 1984—that is, for tax years beginning 1983—superseding the current test of 80 points.)

Taxable Transactions

Generally, a transaction will be wholly taxable where the consideration received by the seller is not primarily stock. Furthermore, as pointed out later, the buyer must also consider the tax aspects of the purchase, since he or she may trigger an income tax that will raise the purchase cost.

The interests of the buyer and the seller may conflict when it comes to deciding on whether the buyer will receive stock, or assets. From the seller's standpoint, sale of stock is the simplest procedure for selling ownership of a corporate business in a taxable transaction. Once taxable gain is realized, the seller is relieved of all contingencies attaching to the corporation (other than those stipulated in the sales agreement with the buyer), and he or she does not bear the additional costs and expenses if the selling corporation is liquidated. Also, in this transaction, the seller generally avoids the problems generated by the recapture rules (see below).

Buyer Purchases Assets

Usually it is to the buyer's advantage to acquire assets rather than stock. For one thing, with assets, he or she avoids the problems of contingent liabilities, paying for unwanted items, and incurring additional costs if the acquired company is liquidated. If, moreover, the purchase price of the assets is higher than the seller's basis in them, the buyer will receive a stepped-up basis. Finally, outright ownership of assets may make it possible to allocate basis advantageously—that is, more to such items as inventory and depreciable property—and less to nondeductibles such as goodwill. (Both the stepped-up basis and the opportunity to allocate are obtainable if the buyer receives stock instead of assets, but, from the buyer's point of view, there may be drawbacks to this mode of acquisition, as will be pointed out.)

Buyer Purchases Stock

The buyer in a stock purchase may liquidate the acquired corporation or continue it. If, however, he or she wants to get a step-up in basis, an election will be necessary.

Two Alternatives. When contemplating a stock purchase, the buyer must consider whether he or she wants his or her basis in the underlying assets to be equivalent to the purchase price or whether he or she prefers to take over the seller's basis in those assets—that is, their underlying tax basis. If the buyer's preference is for the former—which would be logical if the purchase price were higher than the seller's basis—stock constituting control (80 percent or more) must be purchased within 12 months. A further requirement for stepped-up basis in this circumstance is that the corporate purchaser must make an election within 75 days of the date of the acquisition, under which the acquisition will be treated as though the assets had been purchased and the acquired company had been liquidated. Under this election, no gain or loss will be recognized except as required under the recapture rules (see below).

If, on the other hand, the buyer wants a basis in the acquired assets equal to the transferor's former basis (a so-called carry-over of basis)—for example, because this basis exceeds the purchase price—he or she need not be concerned with the time it takes to achieve 80 percent control, and no affirmative election need be made.

Under the first alternative—asset basis determined by purchase price—the buyer–parent will lose any favorable tax attributes of the acquired corporation. In addition, the acquired company will recognize gain taxed as ordinary income to the extent that certain recapture rules are applicable. The recapture rules cover:

Depreciation taken on depreciable personal property

Depreciation on nonresidential real estate acquired after 1980 if depreciated pursuant to an accelerated method

Accelerated depreciation in excess of straight-line depreciation on depreciable real property acquired prior to 1980 and residential property acquired after 1981

The LIFO layer—that is, the difference in pricing inventory under the LIFO (last-in, first-out) method compared with that under the FIFO (first-in, first-out) method (This recapture rule applies only to transactions entered into after December 31, 1982.)

Previously expensed items that generated a tax benefit in the year expensed but that still have value—for example, supplies and tools

Provisions for bad debts to the extent no longer needed

Accumulated earnings of certain foreign corporations

Investment credit, to the extent that holding period requirements have not been satisfied

Where the election is made to increase the basis of the acquired corporation's assets, the corporation will be treated as if it sold its assets tax free, except for income realized pursuant to the recapture rules, on the last day the seller owned the stock. This prevents the buyer from utilizing its tax attributes to offset any income tax arising from making the election. Note that if the acquired corporation had previously filed a consolidated income tax return with its corporate seller, that seller may be liable for the recapture tax.

Under the second alternative—asset basis carried over—there will be the same carry-over of favorable tax alternatives mentioned in connection with nontaxable transactions, including the post-1983 provisions. Until 1984, if there is a change of ownership (based on a 50-percentage-point change) by purchase, within a two-year period, and if the nature of the trade or business has changed, none of the acquired attributes can be carried forward.

Deferred Taxation.   If in a taxable transaction the buyer pays in installments, the seller can use the installment method of accounting and thereby defer taxation on a portion of the gain. Moreover, even if the seller does not use the installment method, the Treasury requires that the seller impute 10 percent interest with respect to a portion of each deferred payment unless the contract calls for actual interest of at least 9 percent. The portion of the deferred payment treated as imputed interest is deductible by the buyer as interest expense and is ordinary income to the seller, even if the principal of the payment is capital gain. Of course, the portion of the purchase price treated as imputed interest is not included in the basis of assets acquired by the buyer.

Liquidation by Shareholders

Instead of selling stock, the stockholders can liquidate their corporation and incur a taxable gain, generally at the capital rate, to the extent the fair market value of the assets exceeds the stockholders' basis in them. The fair market value will be the basis of the property received—so that the new basis represents a step-up—and no gain or loss will ordinarily be realized when the property is sold. Thus there is no taxation at the corporate level (except what might result from the operation of the recapture rules); the shareholders will be taxed only when they receive the proceeds of liquidation. This type of liquidation is not available to corporations that are owned 80 percent or more by another corporation, because no gain or loss can be recognized to the parent on the liquidation of an 80-percent-owned subsidiary.

When a liquidation is accomplished by having the stockholders instead of the corporation sell the corporate trade or business, it is important that the corporate officers not be parties to the transaction. Otherwise, the gain may be taxed to the corporation despite the liquidation. As an additional safeguard, it is strongly recommended that the sale not be negotiated until after the liquidation. Gain on assets "deemed" sold before the liquidation could be subject to double taxation—that is, be taxed at the corporate level, with the balance taxed to the shareholders.

The Twelve-Month Liquidation.   Usually compliance with these requirements will be enough to secure nonrecognition of gain at the corporate level. If, however, the stockholders want greater assurance, they should consider utilizing the special 12-month liquidation, whereby the corporation adopts a plan of complete liquidation and thereafter liquidates entirely within 12 months. Under this procedure, the corporation generally has no recognized gain or loss, with two exceptions: first, income generated under the recapture rules, and second, gain or loss resulting from disposition of installment obligations and inventory. (Gain or loss will not be recognized on inventory that is substantially sold in one transaction to one purchaser during the 12-month period.) The nonrecognition of losses can, of course, be disadvantageous, but the courts have sometimes allowed the recognition of loss on a sale of property where the sale took place prior to the adoption of the plan of complete liquidation.

A liquidation that meets the requirements for a 12-month liquidation will come within the nonrecognition provisions whether or not the taxpayers desire it. Accordingly, taxpayers who have adopted a plan of liquidation yet want recognition should make sure that the liquidation is deferred. This can be done by retaining in the corporation a significant portion of the assets to be distributed until after 12 months have elapsed.

The liquidation of a corporation by its shareholders (whether or not under the 12-month plan) can be deemed a reorganization, where the assets of the liquidated entity are sold to another corporation. The shareholders need only own more than a "nominal" amount of stock in the second corporation to trigger the reorganization. If there is a reorganization, the cash and property received by the stockholders in liquidation of the selling company may represent dividend distributions subject to ordinary-income and not capital-gains tax. This possibility must be reckoned with whenever a degree of common ownership exists with respect to the selling and buying corporation. The courts, however, have generally refused to find a reorganization in such circumstances where the shareholders of the liquidating corporation own, in the aggregate, less than 50 percent of the outstanding stock of the acquiring corporation.

The One-Month Liquidation. The Internal Revenue Code also provides for a special one-calendar-month liquidation. Under this plan, stockholders are generally permitted to liquidate their corporation without recognition of gain and to substitute their stock basis for the corporate tax basis of the property, provided the corporation has no accumulated earnings and profits and no cash or stock or securities. If the liquidating corporation has any of these two items, gain is recognized to the extent of the greater of the two amounts. For corporate shareholders, the gain is treated as capital. In the case of noncorporate stockholders, a portion of the recognized gain equal to a pro rata share of accumulated earnings and profits is taxed as ordinary divided income, and the balance of the gain, if any, is taxed as capital gain. The one-month liquidation is generally not available to ˸ corporate stockholder owning 50 percent or more of the liquidated corporation.

The one-month liquidation is a useful technique in planning a taxable disposition in special circumstances. For example, it may be used to great advantage if only a portion of the corporation's assets are to be sold. In addition, the one-month liquidation may make it possible to defer gain by converting the corporation's cash, stock, and security investments into real estate.

The one-month liquidation is elective, and the election is irrevocable. Noncorporate shareholders will not be covered by the election—and thus will not be entitled to its benefits—unless those who make the election own at least 80 percent of the voting stock held by the noncorporate shareholders. With corporate shareholders, the equivalent proportion is 50 percent of noncorporate-owned voting stock. Stock owned by an ineligible shareholder—for example, one who owns 50 percent or more of the shares—cannot count toward this minimum. There is no requirement that both groups must elect, and, therefore, one group may qualify without regard to the others. Elections must be filed by stockholders on Treasury Form 964 not later than 30 days after the adoption of a plan of complete liquidation by the corporation.

With the one-month liquidation, as with liquidations by stockholders carried out on other terms, care must be taken to avoid having the sale of the trade or business by the shareholders attributed to the corporation. If this happens, the gain will be subject to tax on the corporate level and the balance—gain less tax on the gain—will be treated as ordinary dividend to the shareholders. Furthermore, the adverse tax consequences that may result where stockholders have interests in both the buying and selling corporation are a factor with this type of liquidation as well as with previously described variants.

Sale Instead of Liquidation.   Thus far, the discussion of liquidations and sales by shareholders has focused on maximizing aftertax proceeds. If, however, a corporation has property on which a loss is anticipated, it may be advisable to take the loss on that property by selling it before liquidation or, in the case of a 12-month liquidation, before the adoption of the plan. The loss may then be applied to offset the tax realized under the recapture and other rules, with the balance of the loss carried back against prior years' income to produce a tax refund.

There are circumstances in which it is desirable to sell the assets without liquidating the corporation. Continuation of the corporation's existence may be advantageous where the corporation has substantial net operating loss carry-overs. These carry-overs may be used to offset gain, if any, realized on the sale of the business assets and also to offset future income from the reinvested proceeds from the asset sale. Where the corporation is continued, the personal holding company provisions of the code (discussed below) may be applicable.

Whenever the stockholder's taxable gain on liquidation will be substantially greater than the corporation's gain from the sale of its assets, there will be a tax saving in keeping the corporation alive. Apart from this consideration, an elderly stockholder may find it desirable to keep the corporation alive so that the stock may pass through his or her estate, thereby acquiring an increased basis without giving rise to a liquidation tax. The personal holding company can be an effective tool, for this purpose.

Personal Holding Companies

A personal holding company (PHC) is a closely held corporation that derives its income primarily from investments. The technical requirements that a corporation must meet if it is to qualify as a personal holding company can be summarized as follows:

1. At any time during the second half of the taxable year, more than 50 percent of the value of the outstanding stock must be owned by (or on behalf of) five or fewer individuals.
2. At least 60 percent of the adjusted ordinary gross income must fall into one or more of several defined classes of income.

Adjusted ordinary gross income is gross income less:

1. Gain from the sale of capital assets and from sale of property used in trade or business
2. Certain exclusions and deductions

The items of income considered in determining whether the 60 percent requirement is met, include:

Most forms of passive income, including—with certain limitations— dividends, interest, royalties, and rent

Income earned under a personal service contract

A personal holding company is subject to taxation on its undistributed income. The PHC is also subject to double taxation on the appreciation of its assets: once when the corporation sells them, and again when the shareholder receives the proceeds or other property as dividend or on liquidation. Notwithstanding these tax drawbacks, the personal holding company is a valuable financial planning tool.

Valuation of Shares

Most PHCs are unlisted and have comparatively few shareholders. The stock of these companies is not readily marketable and is therefore generally valued, in the hands of the shareholder, at below the level of the underlying assets. Thus a gift of shares representing a 10 percent interest in a typical PHC whose only asset is 1,000 shares of General Motors would be worth considerably less than a gift of the GM shares. The IRS has allowed discounts of as high as 20 percent below the assets of the company; the courts have been more generous, granting allowances as high as 55 percent. If the shares convey the right to force a voluntary liquidation (as opposed to dissolution in bankruptcy) under state law, the value of the shares of the personal holding company may then be equal to its net asset value.

Tax Advantages

The personal holding company offers important tax advantages that can minimize, in some cases to the extent of virtually eliminating, the impact of double taxation.

Deductions. The combination of the standard 85 percent dividend-received deduction and deductions for the compensation of the owner–manager and for operating expenses can easily exceed ordinary income, thereby generating a net operating loss. Furthermore, this net operating loss can be applied against long-term capital gain, reducing it to the point where the effective corporate tax rate is less than the individual rate. Thus the tax cost to a PHC when it disposes of assets at a gain may, in some cases, be substantially lower than the tax would have been to the former outright owner of these assets had he or she sold the assets and realized the same gain. Finally, a PHC's capital loss can be carried back three years, whereas there is no such provision for individuals.

Deferral. It may be possible to defer the payment of any tax on the appreciation of an asset held by a PHC. The key to this deferral is to have the PHC distribute the assets, say, securities, as a dividend to the shareholders instead of selling them. The individual shareholder will have a basis in the securities received equal to their fair market value (and thus, on subsequent sale of the securities, can be taxed only on appreciation over that value). The shareholder's basis in the stock of the PHC will, however, be decreased by the fair market value of the securities received.

In addition to getting a fair-market-value basis, the shareholder will not be taxed on the distribution except to the extent that: (1) the PHC has accumulated current earnings and profits, in which case the distribution will be ordinary income to the extent of the accumulation; or (2) the fair market value of the securities received exceeds the shareholder's basis in the PHC stock, in which case the difference will be a capital gain.

In this transaction, the shareholder in effect allocates his or her basis in one security—stock in the PHC—to his or her basis in another—the distributed securities. If the shareholder increases his or her basis in the stock of the PHC—that is, by contributing more assets—he or she may be able to further defer recognizing and paying tax on appreciation realized when the securities are sold. Thus, the PHC may be used as a vehicle to acquire, tax free, a diversified portfolio. This deferral technique must be used with moderation, however. If it is used too often, the IRS may treat the sale of the stock by the shareholders as a sale by the PHC rather than as a dividend of the sale proceeds.

Fringe Benefits. The PHC may maintain fringe benefits such as a qualified pension or profit-sharing plan, a medical reimbursement plan, or life insurance on behalf of one or more shareholders. The cost of these plans is an operating expense. If the taxpayer should die before receiving all the benefits from the qualified plan, up to $100,000 of the amount paid to his or her beneficiary may be excluded from the estate.

Gift Giving. Because of the difficulty in marketing PHC shares, these shares have been used to make direct gifts where otherwise a trust would have been deemed obligatory. Considering the formalities and petty expenses associated with setting up a trust, you should at least look into this alternative if you are contemplating a restricted donation of any kind.

Summary

In buying or selling a business, tax considerations should be a prime determinant of the form of the transaction. Taxation may influence even the buy–sell price; often the party picking up the tab for the additional taxes generated will take that amount into consideration in making the offer. There are, however, many expedients for minimizing taxes: installment sales and personal holding companies are two of those most often used.

CHAPTER SEVEN

ASSET MANAGEMENT

Monitoring
    Tracking and Postaudits
A Final Note

Effective management of assets is critical to the successful operation of a business. Under ideal conditions, you might be able to get away with a certain amount of laxity, but in periods of inflation or recession or both, protecting your balance sheet is just as important as maximizing the bottom-line figure on your next year's income statement. In fact, under high interest rate conditions, next year's profit might depend on how well you "turn" your assets.

In this chapter, we deal with three basic kinds of assets: cash, inventory, and capital items. Cash management is essentially a question of maintaining liquidity. Inventory management involves a balancing of delivery versus carrying cost to find and maintain optimal levels for thousands of separate items. Capital budgeting is an approach to controlling investment in capital assets by evaluating the profitability of each asset, both prospectively and on the basis of demonstrated performance.

The rules of asset management make sense for enterprises of any size. For emerging businesses, however, especially in times of economic adversity, they are the lifelines of survival.

CASH MANAGEMENT

A company's cash flow is the barometer of its economic health. Having cash to meet obligations as they fall due is the primary requirement for continued business existence. Handsome profits are not as meaningful if all your cash is tied up in inventory, machinery, or other noncash assets. A certain degree of liquidity is essential in any business.

Next to human error, lack of effective control over cash resources is the most common cause of business failure. The casualty rate from this defect is particularly high for smaller businesses in their formative early years. Paradoxically, prosperity itself is often the problem. Flourishing sales entail heavy expenditures for raw materials and payrolls in order to meet increases in volume, and the company finds itself with an unbridgeable gap between accounts payable and accounts receivable.

No business can be completely insured against adverse circumstances, but with a well-designed financial management system, you are at least in a position to minimize the financial consequences of these circumstances. Essentially, cash management involves:

Knowing how much cash you will need, when you will need it, and where you can get it

Adjusting spending plans realistically to meet changes in financial expectations

Maintaining an appropriate balance of cash—neither so little as to constrict operations nor so much as to forfeit significant earnings from putting the cash to productive use

Cash-Conserving Techniques

Cash management employs a wide variety of techniques, ranging from the obvious to the most sophisticated.

Accelerating Collections

From the time you deliver to the customer to the time his or her money is credited irrevocably to your account, there is a chain of procedures, many of which you can expedite. For example, you can:

Streamline banking arrangements by shortening the time lag between payments of funds by customers and the deposit of those funds to the company's bank account. If your company has more than one logical collection point for remittances, consider having all remittances sent to a single address, such as a postal box number. You can give a bank with a branch near that post office the authority to collect the remittances from the postal lockbox and send you daily a list of receipts. Many banks will grant you a zero-balance account, whereby you can borrow up to a limit based on the average balances of remittances in the lockbox account with them.

Factor accounts receivable or, alternatively, honor bank credit cards. Your choice would hinge on which expedient offers the lower cost.

Allow discounts or modification of other terms on accounts receivable to promote quicker payment by a customer. Here, the validity of a particular rate offered would depend largely on how the effective annual rate of the discount compared with the highest available bank interest.

Expedite the transmittal of invoices and statements to customers; a delay of even one day is costly. Invoices should be issued at the time of shipment.

Review accounts receivable continuously for delinquencies and step up collection procedures. If an amount is due 30 days after shipment, call for payment on the thirty-first day if the cash is not received. Do not wait another 30 days.

Credit Policies

One way to avoid a collection problem is to ship only cash on delivery (C.O.D.). In most businesses, however, this kind of stringency would seriously reduce volume. The chances are, therefore, that you will have to grant credit to most, of your customers. This means that you will have to evaluate all your customers on the basis of their financial strength and their reputation. There is no shortcut to this evolution process in the granting of credit; poor credit management is a major factor in many small business failures.

Centralization is essential to an effective credit program. Credit policies should be explicit, written down, and circulated to all concerned, including of course, salespeople. All orders should be subject to confirmation by a credit officer.

It is possible to obtain credit insurance as a blanket protection against bad debts. This kind of insurance is costly, but it can be worthwhile if your customers are all or for the most part in a line of business that is vulnerable to economic or technological developments.

Delaying Disbursements

With disbursements, you are at the opposite end of the chain of procedure between delivery and final transfer of funds. Nevertheless, the same principle applies, only for "expedite" read "delay." Thus, you can:

Make sure bills are not paid before their due dates.

Take advantage of any latitude in payment terms. For example, with various forms of insurance—notably, workmen's compensation insurance—it is often possible to pay premiums in installments without finance charges.

Make it a policy to release checks at the latest acceptable time, and impose the policy throughout your organization. Mail checks at the end of the day and, where possible, at the end of the week.

Give full consideration in your choice of bank to the factors of mailing and clearing time.

Taking Advantage of Discounts

The standard 2 percent discount for payment within the first 10 days is equivalent to interest at an annual rate of about 36 percent, probably far exceeding anything you can earn from a bank or elsewhere. If your cash position is so weak that you are unable to take advantage of discounts—say, because of difficulty in paying bills in an orderly way—you may be able to borrow the necessary funds from a bank for the purchase. The cost of borrowing may be well below the annualized savings from the discount. On the other hand, if you can delay paying a bill for 60 days without alienating the vendor, the effective rate for the discount drops to less than 15 percent.

Temporary Cash Investments

The essential function of cash management is maximizing the productive use of cash. This means ensuring that cash not needed for operations is invested in some manner. The following discussion covers some more common short-term cash investment possibilities (also summarized in Table 7-1). Note that many instruments can mature in as little as one day.

Money Market Funds.   These are pooled investments in the short-term money market. They operate on the same principle as mutual funds and offer much the same advantages of diversified risk and professional management. Unlike some mutual funds, money market funds can be redeemed anytime; many permit withdrawals by check. Before investing in this kind of fund, ascertain the priorities of the management in regard to safety, yield, and growth.

Certificates of Deposit.   These are time loans to banks collateralized by savings accounts in the lender's name. The term is anywhere from 30 days to one year and interest is at a set rate. Certificates of deposit are backed by the full faith and credit of the issuing bank. Liquidation of the account before term is subject to heavy penalty.

Table 7.1

SOME SHORT-TERM INVESTMENT VEHICLES

Type of Investment	Usual Maturity	Minimum Investment	Liquidity	Interest Paid	Description
Money Market Funds	7 days average	$1,000	Marketable	Daily	Mutual funds concept of diversified investments with portfolio management
Certificates of Deposit	30 days–1 year	100,000	Marketable	At maturity	Bank time instrument issued for a specified period earning interest at a stated rate
Bankers' Acceptances	30–270 days	10,000	Marketable	At maturity	Time draft drawn on and guaranteed by a bank
Repurchase Agreements	1–29 days	25,000	—	At maturity	Sale of securities with agreement to repurchase at maturity at a stated price and rate
Commercial Paper	5–270 days 30–270 days 90–270 days	100,000 50,000 25,000	Nonmarketable	At maturity	Unsecured promissory note issued by a corporation to meet short-term cash needs
U.S. Treasury Bills	To 1 year	10,000	Marketable	At maturity	Short-term U.S. government obligation

Commercial Paper.   This term takes in a variety of unsecured, interest-bearing promissory notes issued by banks, finance companies, and other commercial concerns. Maturities begin at 1 day; more than 270 days is unusual. You can obtain commercial paper directly in return for a loan, or you can buy it through a broker. Here, too, the risk factor depends on the creditworthiness of the lender; higher risks should be reflected in higher interest rates.

Bankers' Acceptances.   A banker's acceptance is a draft drawn on a bank and accepted by it. The life of these drafts is usually somewhere between 30 and 270 days. For the most part, acceptances are used to finance transactions involving merchandise, where the drawer of the draft is the seller. A small fee is charged of the drawer. Bankers' acceptances are regarded as a shade more secure than promissory notes issued by a bank.

Bank Repurchase Agreements.   In this case you lend to a bank, taking as collateral money market securities. The bank agrees to buy back your loan at a set price in anywhere from 1 to 29 days. Your interest is the difference between the purchase price and the amount you advanced. These agreements are considered very secure investments.

Treasury Bills.   These instruments are short-term obligations of the U.S. government, non interest bearing and issued at a discount. The minimum purchase is $10,000, and maturities range from one week to one year. Treasury bills are considered to be one of the safest short-term investments; they are liquid and can be bought or sold through banks and stock and bond brokers.

Hints for Short-Term Investing.   Before you choose an investment, shop around; yields, even on comparable types of instruments, vary considerably. Also, since yields may be quoted on the face amount or current market price, make sure the yields of investments you are evaluting are expressed in the same terms. This is a matter of simple computation.

   Try to link your investing activities to financial forecasting so that, in your choice of investments, you can establish a schedule of maturities designed to give you cash when the forecast indicates you will need it. (Make sure that time of repayment is a fixed condition with every investment.) Do not go entirely by the forecast, however; that is, do not permit too wide a spread between maturity dates, regardless of forecast indications. Allow for the unexpected.

The Cash Budget

The cash budget, as distinguished from the operating budget (Chapter 3), represents a forecast of expected cash receipts and cash disbursements within the budget period. The receipts and expenditures are estimated on the basis of expected levels of activity, the anticipated rate of accounts receivable turnover, and any seasonal characteristics likely to affect cash flow.

Estimating Cash Receipts

A company's cash receipts greatly depend on the collection of accounts receivable—an activity fundamental to every business. Estimating collections is a more involved exercise for some firms than for others, but in all cases, the method used is essentially the same, because estimates must be based on budgeted sales and past collection experience. To project collections, you need the following information:

The budgeted sales figure for each month

The collection pattern; that is, the proportion of billings for which payment is received in successive time categories, such as the first month, the second month, the third month

The proportion of uncollectible accounts

Some companies sell on discount, others offer 90-day credit, and still others sell to prime accounts that almost invariably remit payment within 30 days. Although every business requires a slightly different approach, collections can be estimated with reasonable accuracy, provided they are constantly revised to reflect changes as they occur.

Generally, the relationship of collections to sales does not vary significantly from month to month. To illustrate this point, assume the following relationships between the collections and sales of a company, as determined by analysis of its records:

70.0 percent are paid within the discount period.

24.0 percent are paid within the month following the sale.

4.5 percent are paid in the second month following the sale.

0.9 percent are paid in the third month following the sale.

0.6 percent are uncollectible.

On the basis of this information, the estimate of collections for January 1982, is computed as follows:

Month of Sale	Sales	Collection in January	
		Percentage	Amount
October 19X1	$60,000[1]	0.9	$ 540
November 19X1	70,000[1]	4.5	3,150
December 19X1	90,000[1]	24.0	21,600
January 19X2	60,000[2]	70.0(98.0)[3]	41,160
Estimated collections for January 19X2			$66,450

1. Actual.
2. Budgeted.
3. After discount of 2 percent.

Your company may experience variations in collections for different months during the year. If so, you must analyze collection experience separately for each month and apply these percentages to the budgeted sales data. Take care in calculating percentages to avoid distortions due to unusual situations in past years, such as strikes and fires. Simply eliminate the affected period in determining the percentages to be used.

If your company has investments, schedule the anticipated income from them by months or by quarters. Do not forget to allow for the cash resulting from sale or redemption as well. Make an effort to anticipate receipts from miscellaneous sources. Admittedly, this kind of income is difficult to predict and not often significant. But where experience indicates that there will be such income, a conservative estimate is appropriate.

Estimating Cash Payments

The major portion of cash disbursements consists of payments for materials, labor, other expenses, capital improvements, and retirement of indebtedness.

Materials. In planning for estimated payments for materials, you should try to systematize your policies, item by item, in regard to time of payment and utilization of trade discounts. Your past practices should be applied to the appropriate items in the operating budget and to other cash requirements of the business. If you have been taking trade discounts whenever possible all along, your cash planning will be simplified because discounts are generally taken within 10 days, and if so, the operating budget is probably stated at net cash figures rather than at invoice cost.

Labor Costs. Labor costs usually represent a large portion of the cash requirements of a manufacturing company. Because the payroll must be met at specific times, the timing of labor costs is simplified. The figure to be used in planning cash requirements is the net cash payroll, since taxes and other items withheld from the gross payroll are not usually paid in the same period.

Other Expenses. Projected cash requirements for noncash items, such as depreciation, should not be in the operating budget schedules. For this purpose, expenses on the accrual basis, such as insurance and property taxes, are treated as noncash items. Instead, you should provide for meeting these expenses in the cash budget in the period in which they are paid. If, for example, all bills were paid on the tenth of the following month, there would be a month's lag between the incurring and the payment of the expenses.

Items not Under Profit and Loss. In addition to payments for materials, labor, and other expenses, you should provide for expenditures not included in the profit and loss accounts, such as payments of indebtedness, dividends, capital improvements, and all accrued items. Most of the large payments have specific dates of payment and can be determined easily.

The Three-Way Budget

Coopers & Lybrand has developed a cash budget that has been in use for many years. Known as the Three-Way Budget, Coopers & Lybrand's system is designed to enable small and middle-sized businesses to cope with liquidity problems and to plan and control month-to-month operations without great expenditure of time and money. The budget is built around the three basic aspects of cash management: operations, cash flow, and financial condition. Experience has shown that these items are so interdependent that they must be treated simultaneously.

Benefits. To the businessperson, the system is valuable because monthly he or she can:

1. Match actual operating results against forecasts and act on warning signals by taking corrective measures
2. Determine with reasonable accuracy when to borrow and how much
3. Monitor the company's financial strength on a regular basis

The system is also valuable to the banker, who can:

1. Compare anticipated income with prior years and, when actual results are available, with current performance as well
2. See when cash will be derived from company operations and when from credit grantors; when the cost of major projects will be paid; and when long-term loans, operating costs, and bank loans will be repaid
3. Determine, on a monthly basis, the company's financial position, including the value of the asset security pledged as collateral for loans and advances

Structure of the Budget.   The Three-Way Budget consists of:

A statement of objectives

A statement of assumptions on which the forecasts are based, covering such matters as:

> Expected line of credit available
>
> Gross profits and expense levels and trends
>
> Share of the market
>
> Major developments anticipated during the budget year, featuring projections of monthly:
>
> > Cost of sales
> >
> > Earnings
> >
> > Flow
> >
> > Profit and loss

Statements covering the same subjects as the above four projections, but comparing the monthly results of actual operations, for the elapsed portion of the current year with the previous year's projections.

Preparing the Three-Way Budget.   You start with an opening balance sheet and reports on the prior year's results in as much detail as you can reasonably achieve. You then estimate the expected sales level for the coming year and identify any anticipated changes from the previous year's levels. Now you are in a position to pinpoint revenues and expenses to specific months of the forthcoming year. On the basis of anticipated sales, and allowing appropriate lead time between sales and cash collections and between commitments and their eventual payment, you can determine the outlays needed to meet that level of sales.

Although the prior year's results are the principal point of departure for preparing the Three-Way-Budget, you should scrutinize these results for factors that may affect projections. For example, seasonal fluctuations in volume and product mix and additional output of new facilities can affect expenses, as can increases in raw material costs and new capital expenditures, such as added equipment or plant facilities.

When you break down expenses by months, you must pay careful attention not only to the magnitude of each item of expense but also to its quality. For example, net income and balance sheet items require the accrual basis of accounting, but in determining cash flow for items such as insurance, professional fees, licenses, commissions, and property, business, and income taxes, the cash basis is called for. Expenses related to sales promotions, production, utilities, advertising campaigns, maintenance, and vacation costs are subject to seasonal fluctuations. Interest and income taxes must be developed monthly because of their direct relationship to bank advances and earnings.

The procedures for preparing the Three-Way-Budget are relatively simple, and, for convenience, we summarize some principal points in the following sections. Although the finished statements are separate, they are closely interrelated and are prepared somewhat in tandem.

Everything flows from the basic sales projection and the assumptions as to how those sales will be met. Accordingly, by completing the cost-of-sales and earnings statements, you obtain major elements needed for the cash-flow statement and balance sheet projection.

Monitoring Performance.   Once you have completed the Three-Way Budget, you have a series of monthly projections for revenues, expenses, and account balances covering a 12-month period that will keep you continuously informed about your company's financial and operational condition. The statements will be sufficiently detailed to permit meaningful comparison with actual performance on a day-to-day basis, so that where disparities occur you can take prompt corrective action.

Taking Corrective Action.   Since a budget is no more than a statement of what will happen if observed trends continue and new plans materialize, you must expect variances and deal with them promptly when they arise.

Variations from the financial plan may be caused by any one of a number of unexpected factors, external or internal. External factors include market conditions, increases in property taxes, strikes, and plant shutdowns. Among the countless internal factors are abnormal maintenance and repairs, idle time, defective production, returned sales, and customer and supplier defaults. Whether they are favorable or unfavorable, controllable or uncontrollable, variations from plan demand your immediate attention.

Unfavorable developments that cannot be controlled can be met by protective measures or by negative revision of the plan. Favorable developments, on the other hand, can result in positive revisions in long-term plans, as well as in allocation of surplus cash to loan repayments, increased advertising expenditures, temporary investments, or even a totally new and ambitious marketing program.

Reviewing and Revising the Budget.   The same principles apply to reviewing and revising cash budgets as to the operating budget (see "Capital Budgeting" in this chapter).

Case Study Illustrating the Three-Way Budget

The following case study illustrates, step by step, the preparation of a cash budget on the three-way principle. Though the subject, which we call the Relentless Pursuits Company, is of course fictitious, the facts, figures, and events are a composite taken from actual client situations. You can use computerized models to facilitate the process illustrated in this study (see Chapter 3).

Objectives.   The Relentless Pursuits budget is based on an explicit set of objectives that anticipate a requirement for financing during periods of inadequate cash flow. These objectives, formulated with some care and summarized in a written statement, are as follows:

1. To continue increased market penetration
2. To expand physical facilities to meet increased product demand
3. To improve product quality without increasing unit cost

Assumptions.   Relentless Pursuits establishes a series of fundamental assumptions as a basis for assigning revenues, expenses, cash receipts, and expenditures to the appropriate periods. This process is highly deliberative and results from the owner–manager's evaluations and judgments in all areas including economic conditions, competition, employee relations, and banking relationships. The guiding principle is that a budget is only as good as the assumptions on which it is based. For purposes of this illustration, we will make the following assumptions:

A $120,000 mortgage loan commitment for a government development agency collateralized by a new building facility, payable $5,000 a month beginning in October

Construction costs to be paid in four equal monthly installments

A 30 percent sales increase on an annual basis

A 12.5 percent gross profit margin on sales on an annual basis

A 10 percent increase over prior year in total expenses, including interest expense

First quarter inventory buildup for peak summer sales season

Collection of accounts receivable anticipated to be 40 percent in month following sale, 50 percent in subsequent month, and 10 percent in third month

Payments for raw material purchases in January through September anticipated to be 75 percent in the first month following purchase and 25 percent in the subsequent months of that period; payments in October through December anticipated at 100 percent in the months following purchase

Labor costs and interest expense paid as incurred

Most other expenses in the following month after they are incurred

$1,200 a month set aside for estimated income tax payments

Preparing the Budget.   By applying all these assumptions to the basic sales expectations, Relentless Pursuits is able to complete the Three-Way Budget as three separate, projected monthly financial statements in the three basic categories: cost of sales, earnings and cash flow. These categories are shown in Figure 7.1 a, b, and c, respectively. In addition, Relentless Pursuits can use the information provided by these three basic statements to produce a balance sheet also broken down monthly. The balance sheet is shown in Figure 7.1d. The total presentation can serve as input to the bank for obtaining and maintaining assured financing.

The mechanics in preparing these four exhibits are described in the following lists. First you develop and record:

p 177
above

1. Statement of business objectives
2. Assumptions upon which the forecast is based

You next project cost of sales and operating statements as follows:

1. Estimate net sales by month (Figure 7.1b, line 1; in computerized models, this can be done by specific dollar or unit estimates or an

(a) PROJECTED STATEMENT OF MONTHLY COST OF SALES FOR THE YEAR ENDING DECEMBER 31 (IN DOLLARS)

	January	February	March	April	May	June	July	August	September	October	November	December	Total	
1 Inventory at beginning of month	668,000	110,000	157,000	189,000	210,000	195,400	178,200	148,600	120,200	99,300	92,800	85,400	68,000	1
2 Material purchases	78,500	86,400	72,200	62,300	38,100	49,900	49,600	41,500	32,600	42,800	37,100	36,200	627,200	2
3 Direct labor	3,600	3,600	3,600	3,600	3,000	1,100	1,100	1,100	1,100	3,000	3,600	3,600	32,000	3
Factory overhead														
4 Fuel	800	800	800	600	400	200	200	200	400	600	800	800	6,600	4
5 Insurance	400	400	400	400	400	400	400	400	400	400	400	400	4,800	5
6 Utilities	1,500	1,500	1,500	1,500	1,000	900	900	900	1,900	1,000	1,500	1,500	14,600	6
7 Maintenance and repairs	300	300	300	300	1,500	2,000	2,000	2,000	1,500	600	300	300	11,400	7
8 Property taxes	633	633	633	633	633	633	633	633	633	633	633	637	7,600	8
9 Trucks	400	400	400	400	200	50	50	50	150	300	400	400	3,200	9
10 Employee benefits	50	50	50	950	50	50	50	50	50	950	50	50	2,400	10
11 Depreciation	1,350	1,350	1,350	1,350	1,800	1,800	1,800	1,800	1,850	1,850	1,850	1,850	20,000	11
12	5,433	5,433	5,433	6,133	5,983	6,033	6,033	6,033	5,883	6,333	5,933	5,937	70,600	12
13	155,533	205,433	238,233	261,033	257,083	252,433	234,933	197,233	159,783	151,433	139,433	131,137	797,800	13
14 Inventory at end of month	110,000	157,000	189,000	210,000	195,400	178,200	148,600	120,200	99,300	92,800	85,400	80,200	80,200	14
15 Cost of sales	45,533	48,433	49,233	51,033	61,683	74,233	86,333	77,033	60,483	58,633	54,033	50,937	717,600	15

Figure 7.1. Relentless Pursuits Company: Key Reports in the Three-Way Budget

(b) PROJECTED STATEMENT OF MONTHLY EARNINGS OF SALES FOR THE YEAR ENDING DECEMBER 31 (IN DOLLARS)

	January	February	March	April	May	June	July	August	September	October	November	December	Total	
1 Sales	48,700	52,500	53,600	55,100	70,200	89,400	105,600	93,200	71,400	65,800	59,300	55,200	820,000	1
2 Cost of sale	45,533	48,433	49,233	51,033	61,683	74,233	86,333	77,033	60,483	58,633	54,033	50,937	717,600	2
3 Gross profit	3,167	4,067	4,367	4,067	8,517	15,167	19,267	16,167	10,917	7,167	5,267	4,263	102,400	3
Selling expenses														
4 Salaries and commissions	900	900	900	900	1,200	1,600	1,800	1,600	1,200	1,200	900	900	14,000	4
5 Advertising	100	100	100	100	300	600	800	600	300	200	100	100	3,400	5
6 Delivery and freight	150	150	150	150	300	650	850	650	350	200	150	150	3,900	6
7 Automobile	150	150	150	150	150	150	150	150	150	150	150	150	1,800	7
8 Depreciation	100	100	100	100	100	100	100	100	100	100	100	100	1,200	8
9	1,400	1,400	1,400	1,400	2,050	3,100	3,700	3,100	2,100	1,850	1,400	1,400	24,300	9
Administrative expenses														
10 Salaries	900	900	900	900	900	900	900	900	900	900	900	900	10,800	10

#	Item													Total	
11	Professional fees	125	125	125	125	125	125	125	125	125	125	125	125	1,500	11
12	Printing, postage, and so on	100	100	100	100	100	100	100	100	100	100	100	100	1,200	12
13	Telephone and telegraph	100	100	100	100	100	100	100	100	100	100	100	100	1,200	13
14	Business taxes and licenses	150	150	150	150	150	150	150	150	150	150	150	150	1,800	14
15	Sundry	50	50	50	50	150	150	150	150	150	150	50	50	1,200	15
16	Interest	200	575	1,090	1,555	1,705	1,665	1,620	1,400	1,080	860	750	700	13,200	16
17		1,625	2,000	2,515	2,980	3,230	3,190	3,145	2,925	2,605	2,385	2,175	2,125	30,900	17
18		3,025	3,400	3,915	4,380	5,280	6,290	6,845	6,025	4,705	4,235	3,575	3,525	55,200	18
19	Net profit before taxes	142	667	452	(313)	3,237	8,887	12,422	10,142	6,212	2,932	1,692	738	47,200	19
20	Income taxes	50	233	158	(109)	1,133	3,107	4,348	3,550	2,174	1,026	592	258	16,520	20
21	Net profit	92	434	294	(204)	2,104	5,770	8,074	6,592	4,038	1,906	1,100	480	30,680	21

Figure 7.1. (continued)

181

(c) PROJECTED STATEMENT OF MONTHLY CASH FLOW FOR THE YEAR ENDING DECEMBER 31 (IN DOLLARS)

	January	February	March	April	May	June	July	August	September	October	November	December	Total	
Cash receipts														
1 Receivable	47,350	47,580	50,000	52,560	54,090	60,990	76,370	93,960	99,020	85,720	71,340	63,760	802,740	1
2 Mortgage loan	30,000	30,000	30,000	30,000	—	—	—	—	—	—	—	—	120,000	2
3 Bank loans	—	26,000	48,000	36,000	23,000	—	—	—	—	—	—	—	133,000	3
4	77,350	103,580	128,000	118,560	77,090	60,990	76,370	93,960	99,020	85,720	71,340	63,760	1,055,740	4
Cash disbursements														
5 Raw material purchases	30,000	68,875	84,425	75,750	64,775	44,150	46,950	49,675	43,525	42,975	42,800	37,100	631,000	5
6 Direct labor	3,600	3,600	3,600	3,600	3,000	1,100	1,100	1,100	1,100	3,000	3,600	3,600	32,000	6
Factory overhead:														
7 insurance	—	—	—	—	—	—	4,800	—	—	—	—	—	4,800	7
8 property taxes	—	—	—	—	—	—	7,600	—	—	—	—	—	7,600	8
9 other, excluding depreciation	3,050	3,050	3,050	3,050	3,750	3,150	3,200	3,200	3,200	3,000	3,450	3,050	38,200	9
Selling expenses:														
10 salaries and comissions	900	900	900	900	1,200	1,600	1,800	1,600	1,200	1,200	900	900	14,000	10
11 other, excluding depreciation	400	400	400	400	400	750	1,400	1,800	1,400	800	550	400	9,100	11
Administrative expenses:														
12 professional fees	—	—	1,500	—	—	—	—	—	—	—	—	—	1,500	12

Item	1	2	3	4	5	6	7	8	9	10	11	12	Total	
13 business taxes and licences	—	—	1,800	—	—	—	—	—	—	—	—	—	1,800	13
14 salaries	900	900	900	900	900	900	900	900	900	900	900	900	10,800	14
15 interest	200	575	1,090	1,555	1,705	1,665	1,620	1,400	1,080	860	750	700	13,200	15
16 other	250	250	250	250	250	350	350	350	350	350	350	250	3,600	16
17 Income taxes	1,200	1,200	1,200	1,200	1,200	1,200	1,200	1,200	1,200	1,200	1,200	1,200	14,400	17
18 Plant addition	30,000	30,000	30,000	30,000	—	—	—	—	—	—	—	—	120,000	18
19 Long-term debt repayment	—	—	—	—	—	—	—	—	—	5,000	5,000	5,000	15,000	19
20 Bank repayment	—	—	—	—	—	6,000	6,000	32,000	45,000	27,000	12,000	5,000	133,000	20
21	70,500	109,750	127,315	119,405	77,180	60,865	76,920	93,225	98,955	86,285	71,500	58,100	1,050,000	21
22 Cash over (short)	6,850	(6,170)	685	(845)	(90)	125	(550)	735	65	(565)	(160)	5,660	5,740	22
23 Cash balance at beginning	—	6,850	680	1,365	520	430	555	5	740	805	240	80	12,270	23
24 Cash balance at end	6,850	680	1,365	520	430	555	5	740	805	240	80	5,740	18,010	24
25 Bank loan at beginning	—	—	26,000	74,000	110,000	133,000	127,000	121,000	89,000	44,000	17,000	5,000		25
26 Loans (repayments)	—	26,000	48,000	36,000	23,000	(6,000)	(6,000)	(32,000)	(45,000)	(27,000)	(12,000)	(5,000)		26
27 Bank loan at end	—	26,000	74,000	110,000	133,000	127,000	121,000	89,000	44,000	17,000	5,000	—	—	27
28 Accounts receivable	58,350	63,270	66,870	69,410	85,520	113,930	143,160	142,400	114,780	94,860	82,820	74,260	74,260	28
29 Inventories	110,000	157,000	189,000	210,000	195,400	178,200	148,600	120,200	99,300	92,800	85,400	80,200	80,200	29
30	168,350	220,270	255,870	279,410	280,920	292,130	291,760	262,600	214,080	187,660	168,220	154,460	154,460	30

Figure 7.1. (continued)

(d) PROJECTED MONTHLY BALANCE SHEETS FOR THE YEAR ENDING DECEMBER 31 (IN DOLLARS)

	Opening	January	February	March	April	May	June	July	August	September	October	November	December	
Current assets														
1 Cash	—	6,850	680	1,365	520	430	555	5	740	805	240	80	5,740	1
2 Accounts receivable	57,000	58,350	63,270	66,870	69,410	85,520	113,930	143,160	142,400	114,780	94,860	82,820	74,260	2
3 Inventories	68,000	110,000	157,000	189,000	210,000	195,400	178,200	148,600	120,200	99,300	92,800	85,400	80,200	3
4 Prepaid expenses	—	—	—	1,125	2,200	1,925	1,650	6,544	5,236	3,928	2,620	1,312	—	4
5	125,000	175,200	220,950	258,360	282,130	283,275	294,335	298,309	268,576	218,813	190,520	169,612	160,200	5
Fixed assets														
6 Cost	158,700	188,700	218,700	248,700	278,700	278,700	278,700	278,700	278,700	278,700	278,700	278,700	278,700	6
7 Accumulated depreciation	40,000	41,450	42,900	44,350	45,800	47,700	49,600	51,500	53,400	55,350	57,300	59,250	61,200	7
8	118,700	147,250	175,800	204,350	232,900	231,000	229,100	227,200	225,300	223,350	221,400	219,450	217,500	8
9	243,700	322,450	396,750	462,710	515,030	514,275	523,435	525,509	493,876	442,163	411,920	389,062	377,700	9

	1	2	3	4	5	6	7	8	9	10	11	12	13	
Current liabilities														
10 Bank loans	—	—	26,000	74,000	110,000	133,000	127,000	121,000	89,000	44,000	17,000	5,000	—	10
11 Accounts payable	40,000	88,500	106,025	93,800	80,350	53,675	59,425	62,075	53,900	42,975	42,800	37,100	36,200	11
12 Accrued liabilities	3,700	5,008	6,316	7,249	8,532	9,415	11,148	5,350	4,950	4,150	4,350	3,700	3,700	12
13 Income taxes	—	(1,150)	(2,117)	(3,159)	(4,468)	(4,535)	(2,628)	520	2,870	3,844	3,670	3,062	2,120	13
14	43,700	92,358	136,224	171,890	194,414	191,555	194,945	188,945	150,720	94,969	67,820	48,862	42,020	14
15 Long-term debt	—	30,000	60,000	90,000	120,000	120,000	120,000	120,000	120,000	120,000	115,000	110,000	105,000	15
16 Shareholders' advances	45,000	45,000	45,000	45,000	45,000	45,000	45,000	45,000	45,000	45,000	45,000	45,000	45,000	16
17 Capital stock	5,000	5,000	5,000	5,000	5,000	5,000	5,000	5,000	5,000	5,000	5,000	5,000	5,000	17
18 Retained earnings	150,000	150,092	150,526	150,820	150,616	152,720	158,490	166,564	173,156	177,194	179,100	180,200	180,680	18
19	243,700	322,450	396,750	462,710	515,030	514,275	523,435	525,509	493,876	442,163	411,920	389,062	377,700	19

Figure 7.1. (continued)

185

initial estimate and a growth percentage for each subsequent period).

2. Apply lead-time assumptions to establish monthly estimate of:

   a. Inventory levels required to service projected sales

   b. Production required to meet projected sales and inventory needs

   c. Raw material purchases needed to meet projected production needs

3. Estimate monthly inventory levels, considering the period of inventory buildup to meet the peak season sales (Figure 7.1a, lines 1 and 14).

4. Estimate overhead items and direct labor costs based on the projected production schedule (Figure 7.1a, lines 3–12; note assumptions made for payment of expenses).

5. Compute the monthly cost of sales figure (Figure 7.1a, line 15) using the most recent gross profit information available. If gross profit tends to fluctuate by season due to the sales mix, then a monthly percentage will be needed.

6. In Figure 7.1a, add line 14 to line 15 to arrive at line 13. This permits computation of line 2, monthly material purchases, thereby completing Figure 7.1a (line 13 minus lines 1, 3, and 12).

7. Review Figure 7.1a, noting the reasonableness of expense allocations and the material content of cost of sales compared with prior experience and in light of current projections.

8. Giving consideration to the timing of payments, transfer the appropriate information on Figure 7.1 from a to c and d as follows:

Item	Line	Figure 7.1c	Figure 7.1d
Inventory	14	–	Line 3
Direct labor	3	Line 6	–
Insurance	5	Line 7	–
Property taxes	8	Line 8	–
Fuel, utilities, maintenance and repairs, trucks, and employee benefits	4, 6, 7, 9, and 10	Line 9	–

9. Complete lines 4–15 of Figure 7.1*b* by estimating selling and administrative expenses.

10. Prepare the first month's estimate for the following items:

  Figure 7.1*b*
Line 16	Interest expense
Line 20	Income taxes

  Figure 7.1*c*
Line 15	Interest payments
Line 17	Income taxes

11. Again, considering the timing of payments, transfer the appropriate information on Figure 7.1 from *b* to *c* as follows:

Item	Line	Figure 7.1c
Salaries (selling)	4	Line 10
Salaries (administrative)	10	Line 14
Professional fees	11	Line 12
Business taxes and licenses	14	Line 13
Printing and postage	12	⎫
Telephone and telegraph	13	⎬ Line 16
Sundry	15	⎭
Interest	16	Line 15

12. Applying the appropriate assumptions for receipts and disbursements (Figure 7.1*c*), allocate information for lines 1, 2, 5, 10, 11, 18, and 19.

13. Complete Figure 7.1*b* for the month, and determine if it appears realistic in light of all assumptions. Then complete Figure 7.1*c*, estimating either bank loans (line 3) or bank repayments (line 20).

14. Complete the first month for the following items:

Line 1	Cash
Line 2	Accounts receivable

Line 10   Bank loans

Line 13   Income taxes

Line 16   Shareholders' advances

Line 17   Capital stock

You then perform the remaining steps for the balance sheet, Figure 7.1d, as follows:

15. Net fixed assets, line 8, should agree with beginning amount, less depreciation expense (Figure 7.1a, line 11, and Figure 7.1b, line 8), plus plant additions, if any (Figure 7.1c, line 18).

16. Accounts payable, line 11, should agree with the beginning balance plus liabilities incurred (Figure 7.1a and b) *less cash payments (Figure 7.1c)*.

17. Long-term debt balances, line 15, should change in accordance with Figure 7.1c, line 19.

18. Retained earnings, line 18, should change by the income on Figure 7.1b.

19. Apply accrual accounting techniques used in cost-of-sales and earning statements to expense payments of Figure 7.1c to compute lines 4 and 12.

20. Complete Figure 7.1d for the first month, and determine if it is reasonable in light of all assumptions.

21. Adjust first-month statements as determined necessary.

22. Repeat the procedure for each of the remaining 11 months of the year.

Cost-of-Sales Statement (Figure 7.1a). The cost-of-sales statement clearly reflects the seasonal factors inherent in the changing sales pattern and the company's productivity and vacation cycle.

Insurance and property taxes (lines 5 and 8) are level throughout the year. Material purchases clearly reflect the inventory buildup during the first four months of the year, and the seasonal factor clearly shows up in the summer months (lines 3, 4, 6, and 9). Direct labor and related factory overhead costs are substantially lower, and maintenance and repair costs (line 7) are definitely higher during the same period when maintenance will least interfere with production.

Cost of sales per month is one of the principal factors in projecting monthly earnings. The amount of detailed support needed for this projection is dependent on the extent of product lines and the product mix implicit in the sales projections.

Earnings Statement (Figure 7.1b). The earnings statement shows the rising and falling curve of monthly sales expected for the year with the heaviest month, July, more than twice the lightest month, January. Because of staggering the cost of sales, the gross profit spread is even larger, ranging from $3,167 in January to $19,267 in July.

As would be expected, selling expenses rise dramatically for the May–October period, and administrative expenses are highest during the March–September period because of heavy interest charges.

Earnings for the year show a healthy overall picture, with gross profit running at the targeted 12.5 percent and net profit before and after taxes running about 6 percent and 3.5 percent, respectively.

Cash-Flow Statement (Figure 7.1c). In calculating the timing of a bank loan, the cash-flow statement is critical. This statement shows that because of the heavy expenses entailed in the inventory buildup to meet summer sales, Relentless Pursuits would be seriously short without the bank loans (line 3). Even with the advances, the company will be cash poor in February and very tight through November. The statement thus serves as both an indicator of the right timing for the bank loan and as an early warning to management that if actual performance were to fall below the expected level, the company might have problems.

The importance of the cash-flow statement as a tool for monitoring operations can be shown in several examples. Thus if sales for a given month—or cumulative sales through that month—are significantly below budget, management is forewarned that receivables for the following months will be lower than anticipated and that liquidity problems may develop unless action is taken. Management has adequate lead time because the customer-payments assumption realistically provides for a pattern of staggered payment ranging from 30 to 90 days. Similarly, any substantial departure from the anticipated pattern of cash collections can be a warning. The modest cash balances anticipated for the April–November period indicate that the company would be wise to establish a procedure each month to review its collections and the collectibility of outstanding balances for possible follow-up.

Balance Sheet (Figure 7.1d).   Breaking down the balance sheet for each month rounds out the picture for both management and lending agencies. By itself, the balance sheet shows an increase in total assets from the opening balance of $243,700 to the closing December balance of $377,700. In conjunction with the other statements, it provides both a broad and a detailed profile of projected company operations for the year, enabling both management and lending agencies to assess the year's prospects clearly and confidently.

Monthly Reporting of Actual Performance.   Up to July, monthly reports show a reasonable relationship between budget and actual results, but in that month, significant differences develop, suggesting the need for operational changes. To illustrate this, the accompanying Figure 7.1e, f, g, and h presents the results of operations for seven months of the period ending in July.

The exhibits show that sales had been 3 percent higher than anticipated prior to July but that July sales themselves were considerably under forecast. The deficiency resulted from external factors, primarily a number of strikes in a highly industrialized area, which reduced consumer purchasing power.

Although raw material purchases declined in July, when sales decreases became apparent, the purchase slowdown did not match the sales decrease. As a result, Relentless Pursuits's management must consider action to deal with the effects of decreased accounts receivable, increased inventories, increased bank loans, and decreased payables. With inventories already excessive, purchasing according to projections would aggravate the imbalance further. A prolonged strike would make it difficult for the company to maintain the market that would justify projected buying and payment levels. Furthermore, cash collections in August and September will be automatically lower because of the reduced sales level already experienced.

Although cash flow for the year to date has been in step with the budget, the company must expect problems during August and September, unless remedial action is taken. The ending cash balances for these months in the original budget (Figure 7.1c) were small, and thus, to avoid significant deficits for both, the company must cut back cash outlays. This cutback may include cancellation of all purchases of raw materials for August, thereby reducing inventories and payables by $41,500. Peak collections on receivables previously anticipated for August will not be realized. The cancellation, however, of August purchases, combined with moderate cutbacks of purchases in July, would reduce payments on raw material purchases by $8,400 in August and $33,925 in September.

Although the company may have some minor cash problems in August, prompt action should restore stability by September. It should be noted here that, in the absence of a budgeting system, Relentless Pursuits might well have observed the sales decline and considered some kind of remedial action. Nonetheless, the owner–manager probably could not have acted on a timely basis and might have had to resort to a more drastic move—such as drawing up an emergency analysis of his financial position, evaluating it, and then weighing what action might be required. As a practical matter, the company could be enmeshed in serious financial problems before corrective measures could be taken.;

Reviewing the actual results of operations, as shown (Figure 7.1e to h), we can see that other variances are not material (aside from the departure from the sales budget). Also, the reasons for being off course are not related to any chronic condition likely to influence future sales or cost expectations. Accordingly, preserving the basic budget with appropriate reservations as to conditions influencing the summer months would be preferable to making budget revisions. Essentially, the budget must be seen for what it is—a practical guide to cash control.

Key Information Generated.   From the completed budget, the company obtains four critical items of information:

The year's profit is expected to be $30,680.

Cash-flow deficits call for a loan of up to $133,000 during the period February–May.

The loan can be repaid during the year, with all suppliers paid and sufficient cash left to retire the balance of estimated income tax liability.

There is adequate security to justify loans, such as a first mortgage on the new building from the Government Development Agency, and accounts receivable and inventories.

(e) STATEMENT OF COST OF SALES FOR THE SEVEN MONTHS ENDED JULY 31 (IN DOLLARS)

	Month				Year to Data			
	Projected	Actual	Over (Under) Difference	Comments	Projected	Actual	Over (Under) Difference	Comments
Inventory at beginning of period	178,200	181,700	3,500		68,000	68,000	—	
Material purchases	49,600	38,400	(11,200)	Down due to sales decrease.	437,000	440,900	3,900	Increased purchases due to increased sales; offset by July decrease.
Direct labor	1,100	900	(200)	Production down due to decreased sales and inventory buildup.	19,600	19,900	300	Increased production to meet increased sales prior to July.

Factory								
Fuel	200	200	—		3,800	3,650	(150)	Mild winter.
Insurance	400	450	50	Rate adjustment re new addition.	2,800	3,150	350	Rate adjustment re new addition.
Utilities	900	1,000	100	Increased power consumption because of heavy repairs.	8,800	9,050	250	Increased production to June plus July repairs.
Maintenance and repairs	2,000	2,600	600	Employee carelessness caused equipment burnout.	6,700	7,100	400	Fewer repairs during increased production to June.
Property taxes	633	667	34	Increased mill rate.	4,431	4,669	238	Increased mill rate.
Trucks	50	50	—		1,900	1,940	40	
Employee benefits	50	50	—		1,250	1,300	50	
Depreciation	1,800	1,800	—		10,800	10,800	—	
	6,033	6,817	784		40,481	41,659	1,178	
	234,933	227,817	(7,116)		565,081	570,459	5,378	
Inventory at end of period	148,600	165,950	17,350	Sales volume down.	148,600	165,950	17,350	
Cost of sales	86,333	61,867	(24,466)		416,481	404,509	(11,972)	

Figure 7.1. (continued)

(f) STATEMENT OF EARNINGS FOR THE SEVEN MONTHS ENDED JULY 31 (IN DOLLARS)

	Month				Year to Data			
	Projected	Actual	Difference Over (Under)	Comments	Projected	Actual	Difference Over (Under)	Comments
Sales	105,600	72,200	(33,400)	Industrial community riddled	475,100	452,850	(22,250)	Sales volume up approximately
Cost of sales	86,333	61,867	(24,466)	with strikes; consumers have	416,481	404,509	(11,972)	3% over projections prior
Gross profit	19,267	10,333	(8,934)	decreased buying power.	58,619	48,341	(10,278)	to July.
Selling expenses								
Salaries and commissions	1,800	1,600	(200)	Decrease in sales.	8,200	8,190	(10)	Varies with sales.
Advertising	800	800	—		2,100	2,150	50	
Delivery and freight	850	750	(100)	Decrease in sales.	2,400	2,350	(50)	Varies with sales.
Automobile	150	150	—		1,050	1,075	25	
Depreciation	100	100	—		700	700	—	
	3,700	3,400	(300)		14,450	14,465	15	

Administrative expenses								
Salaries	900	900	—		6,300	6,300	—	
Professional fees	125	125	—		875	875	—	
Printing, postage, and so on	100	145	45	Increased postal rates.	700	845	145	Increased postal rates.
Telephone and telegraph	100	120	20		700	700	70	
Business taxes and licenses	150	150	—		1,050	1,050	—	
Sundry	150	180	30		650	730	80	
Interest	1,620	1,635	15	Higher loan balance.	8,410	8,460	50	Higher loan balance.
	3,145	3,255	110		18,685	19,030	345	
	6,845	6,655	(190)		33,135	33,495	360	
Net profit before taxes	12,422	3,678	(8,744)		25,484	14,846	(10,638)	
Income taxes	4,348	1,287	(3,061)		8,920	5,196	(3,724)	
Net profit	8,074	2,391	(5,683)		16,564	9,650	(6,914)	

Figure 7.1. (continued)

(g) STATEMENT OF CASH FLOW FOR THE SEVEN MONTHS ENDED JULY 31 (IN DOLLARS)

	Month				Year to Data			
	Projected	Actual	Difference Over (Under)	Comments	Projected	Actual	Difference Over (Under)	Comments
Cash receipts								
Receivables	76,370	77,840	1,470	Increased sales to June.	388,940	397,380	8,440	Increased sales to June. July decrease will reflect in decreased collections in August and September.
Mortgage loan	—	—	—		120,000	120,000	—	
Bank loans	—	—	—		133,000	133,000	—	
	76,370	77,840	1,470		641,940	650,380	8,440	
Cash disbursements								
Raw material purchases	46,950	48,360	1,410	Increased purchases to June.	414,925	428,795	13,870	Increased purchases to June.
Direct labor	1,100	900	(200)		19,600	19,900	300	Refer to cost of sales.
Factory overhead:								
Insurance	4,800	5,400	600		4,800	5,400	600	Refer to cost of sales.
Property taxes	7,600	8,000	400		7,600	8,000	400	Refer to cost of sales.
Other, excluding depreciation	3,200	3,200	—		22,300	22,190	(110)	
Selling expenses:								
Salaries and commissions	1,800	1,600	(200)		8,200	8,190	(10)	
Other, excluding depreciation	1,400	1,400	—		4,150	4,275	125	

Administrative expenses:							
Professional fees	—	—	—		1,500	1,500	—
Business taxes and licenses	—	—	—		1,800	1,800	—
Salaries	900	900	—		6,300	6,300	—
Interest	1,620	1,635	15		8,410	8,460	50
Other	350	350	—		1,950	2,150	200
Income taxes	1,200	1,200	—		8,400	8,400	—
Plant addition	—	—	—		120,000	120,000	—
Long-term repayment	—	—	—		—	—	—
Bank repayment	6,000	4,000	(2,000) Increased purchases.		12,000	5,000	(7,000) Increased purchases.
	76,920	76,945	25		641,935	650,360	8,425
Cash over (short)	(550)	895	1,445		5	20	15
Cash balance at beginning	555	(875)	(1,430)		—	—	—
Cash balance at end	5	20	15		5	20	15
Bank loan at beginning	127,000	132,000	5,000		—	—	—
Loans (repayments)	(6,000)	(4,000)	2,000		121,000	128,000	7,000
Bank loan at end	121,000	128,000	7,000		121,000	128,000	7,000

Figure 7.1. (continued)

(h) BALANCE SHEET FOR THE SEVEN MONTHS ENDED JULY 31 (IN DOLLARS)

	Projected	Actual	Difference Over (Under)	Comments
Current assets				
Cash	5	20	15	
Accounts receivable	143,160	112,470	(30,690)	July sales down.
Inventories	148,600	165,950	17,350	Purchases slowdown did not match sales decrease.
Prepaid expenses	6,544	6,956	412	
	298,309	285,396	(12,913)	
Fixed assets				
Cost	278,700	278,700	M	
Accumulated depreciation	51,500	51,500	—	
	227,200	227,200	—	
	525,509	512,596	(12,913)	
Current liabilities				
Bank loans	121,000	128,000	7,000	
Accounts payable	62,075	52,105	(9,970)	Purchases slowed because of sales decrease.
Accrued liabilities	5,350	6,045	695	
Income taxes	520	(3,204)	(3,724)	Decreased earnings.
	188,945	182,946	(5,999)	
Long-term debt	120,000	120,000	—	
Shareholders' advances	45,000	45,000	—	
Capital stock	5,000	5,000		
Retained earnings	166,564	159,650	(6,914)	
	525,509	512,596	(12,913)	

Figure 7.1.   (concluded)

Summary

A cash budget furnishes management with a basis for control of a company's cash position. When properly prepared and maintained, the budget will serve as a frame of reference for evaluating the financial consequences of operating decisions and will provide advance indication of financial weaknesses before they have a chance to impact profitability. Cooper's & Lyband's Three-Way Budget is based on operations, cash flow, and financial condition. The system is designed to facilitate revision of assumptions in the light of changing conditions. It is readily adaptable to computerized projection modeling.

INVENTORY MANAGEMENT

Chances are you will have to maintain an inventory of the products you intend to sell. Few operations can produce entirely to order. Typically, customers expect quick delivery; inability to oblige them means loss of orders. Even if you can do almost entirely without an inventory of finished products, you will probably need to maintain stocks of parts and materials. To the extent that you stock any item unnecessarily, you will suffer a drain on your resources—that is, the interest cost on the capital invested plus carrying charges, which together can often run more than 25 percent. On the other hand, insufficient stock can mean reduced customer services or, in the case of materials and parts, curtailment of production—with consequent impairment of customer service.

Underlying Principles

The appropriate or optimal level for an item of inventory is a function of numerous factors, such as rate of turnover, time needed for replacement, and purchase price as a proportion of total inventory investment, including carrying cost. As a consequence, you cannot expand or contract inventory as a unit; you must apply different multiples to each distinct item or group of items. For example, if you decide to reduce your inventory to raise cash and cut all items uniformly, that is, by the same percentage, the faster-moving items would be depleted first. Since these items account for a high proportion of total volume, pressure on customer service would be disproportionately high in relation to the number of these items. Faced with mounting customer complaints, you would have little choice but to put through a series of rush orders. This action could not fail to have some disruptive effect on existing production schedules. Before you could get the situation back under control, your production would probably have dipped sharply and your customer service with it.

Even if you avoid this kind of across-the-board manipulation, your inventory will develop imbalances unless there is some kind of control based on assessment of the factors that influence inventory. The reason is that these factors are constantly changing quantitatively. For example, sales of a particular item may be rising, or the item's cost may be falling.

Danger Signs

The following conditions are symptomatic of inventory problems:

Inventories are climbing faster than sales.

There is noticeable shifting in inventory mix.

There are sharp disparities between actual stock and accounting records.

Write-offs for obsolete materials are increasing in proportion to inventory investments.

Established reorder points and order quantities are more than one year old.

Back orders and lead times are increasing significantly.

There are frequent customer complaints about back orders and missed deliveries.

Interruption of production schedules is frequently required to expedite specific orders.

Interruption or cessation of production is frequently required because of lack of needed materials.

Machine setup costs are increasing at a significant rate.

Machine downtime exceeds the norm derived from past experience.

Inventory turnover rates are generally below average for the industry.

Scrap costs are higher than past averages.

Material costs are rising at rates faster than overall product costs. The portion of cost of sales attributable to materials exceeds that of the industry in general.

Distribution costs exceed industry norms and are rising at a faster rate than overall product costs.

Analysis and Control

Strictly speaking, inventory control should be continuous. It is possible, however, to achieve a degree of control through periodic analysis.

Control Based on Periodic Analysis

In the periodic approach, a diagnostic analysis is carried out, and then certain routine controls are applied. Under the Coopers & Lybrand method, the analysis is constructed around two parameters: usage distribution and turnover. Usage distribution relates inventory movement (in terms of dollar value) to inventory investment, annually and cumulatively. Turnover shows the supply on hand of each item in terms of weeks or months available, calculated at the current annual rate of usage. For each of these parameters, four tabular reports are prepared: two dealing with maintenance and spare parts or raw materials and the other two with finished goods.

Inventory Analysis. The results of a typical Coopers & Lybrand inventory analysis are shown in Figures 7.2 and 7.3, which deal with finished goods. In the turnover report (Figure 7.2), the various coded items are ranked in descending order of coverage, defined as the number of months supply on hand (column 6). Coverage is computed by dividing inventory on hand in units or dollars (columns 7a and 7b) by monthly usage, either units into units or dollars into dollars. (Allowance must be made for rounding off in the figures.) Monthly usage (in units or dollars) is computed by dividing annual usage in units or dollars (columns 4a and 4b) by 12. Notice that annual usage is shown as a cumulative percentage of dollar usage (column 5) as well as item by item (columns 4a and 4b).

The segment covered in this report demonstrates a clear need for a drastic overhaul of inventory management practices. For many items, the

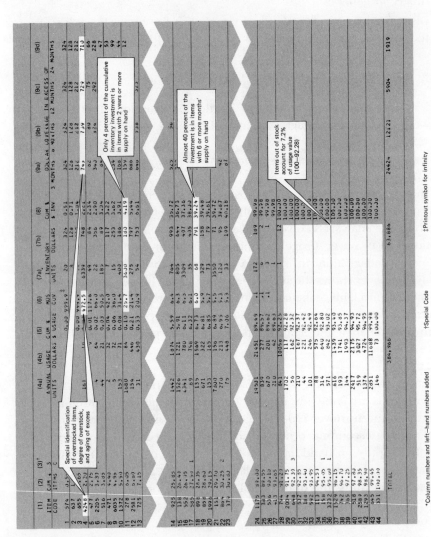

*Column numbers and left-hand numbers added.

†Special code.

††Printout symbol for infinity.

Figure 7.2. Inventory analysis, finished goods turnover report.

202

Figure 7.3 — Inventory analysis, finished goods usage distribution report.

(1) ITEM CODE	(2) CUM % ITEMS	(3)† C	(4a) ANNUAL USAGE UNITS	(4b) DOLLARS	(5) CUM % $ USAGE	(6) MOS COV	(7a) INVENTORY UNITS	(7b) DOLLARS	(8) CUM % $ INV	(9a) 3 MONTHS	(9b) 6 MONTHS	(9c) 12 MONTHS	(9d) 24 MONTHS
1863	0.55		7667	30668	7.97	.2	136	544	0.85				47
976	1.10		2315	29628	15.67	.4	172	896	2.25				
1175	1.65		1901	21453	21.23	.1		1105	2.55				
423	2.20		1385	20082	26.45	.6	66	963	4.06				
542	2.75		24234	16964	30.86	.7	1341	939	5.53				
874	3.30		3371	16260	35.08	2.1	670	2812	9.93				
645	3.85		2851	11688	38.12				9.93				
659	4.40		1175	11041	41.00	.9	91	853	11.26				
1831	16.50		446	2673	70.85	1.2	46	274	33.53				
2314	17.05		202	2610	71.53	2.0	33	425	34.19				
778	17.60		192	2560	72.19	2.5	40	542	35.04				
1089	18.15	1	912	2553	72.86	5.1	386	1082	36.74				
484	18.70		792	2534	73.52	5.1	334	1068	38.41				
1162	19.25		365	2338	74.12	.6	17	108	38.58				
518	19.80		2417	2175	74.69				38.58				
882	20.35	1	882	2116	75.24	20.3	3	45	38.65	2978	2461	1427	
163	20.90		689	2068	75.78	3.3	1165	3495	45.00	44	44		
554	21.45		573	2064	76.31		156	560	45.00				
365	22.00		144	1993	76.83				45.20				
969	22.55		152	1921	77.31	.9	12	153	45.23				
3073	54.45		90	604	94.36	6.9	52	349	80.84	198			
828	55.00		402	602	94.51	2.6	129	129	81.05		47		
2254	55.55		45	602	94.57	7.7	28	107	81.21				
839	56.10		36	600	94.83	7.7	23	383	81.81	233	83		
847	56.65		62	590	94.98	1.4		67	81.92				
113	57.20		88	575	95.13				81.92				
905	57.75		75	568	95.28	6.9	43	326	82.43				
1447	58.30		161	564	95.42	17.5	235	824	83.72	184	42		
721	58.85		262	550	95.56	2.9	64	135	83.93	643	542	260	
1359	59.40	2	147	543	95.71	1.8	22	82	84.06				
178	96.70		27		99.99	18.7	42	33	97.52	28	23	12	47
516	97.25		44					89	97.66	84	79	68	710
4248	97.80		161					748	98.83	743	739	729	66
657	98.35	5						84	98.96	82	80	75	212
5	98.90								99.29	212	212	212	324
574	99.45							324	99.80	324	324	324	128
637	100.00							128	100.00	126	128	128	
TOTAL				384,966				63,886	100.00	24424	12121	5906	1919

Callout: Slightly more than 4 percent of the items account for 41 percent of the dollar usage but this is covered by only 11 percent of the inventory investment

Callout: 75 percent of the usage supported by 38 percent of the inventory

Callout: An aging of the total inventory investment in this merchandise category, $24,424 of the total $63,886 is in excess of 3 months' supply; $12,121 is in excess of 6 months'.

*Column numbers and left-hand numbers added.

†Special code.

Figure 7.3. Inventory analysis, finished goods usage distribution report.

203

supply is overwhelmingly excessive. The quantity of the item in entry 4, for example, will suffice at the present usage rate for 472 months—almost 40 years! To compute that excess in monetary terms, we begin with the cost of the item, which is 11.8 cents (19 in column 4b divided by 161 in column 4a). There are 6,339 units on hand (column 7), which when multiplied by cost per unit, works out to a dollar value of $748. We can evaluate the excess amounts for future periods by subtracting from $748 the number of months usage we need to maintain for customer service. The results for four points in the future are shown in columns 9a–9d.

Other imbalances are pointed out on the report itself. Column 8 shows the percentage of total inventory that each item, plus all preceding items, accounts for.

The turnover report highlights the slow-moving or stationary items. The usage distribution report (Figure 7.3) is designed to emphasize the faster-moving items, which may also account for considerable excess inventory. The breakdown in this report is the same as in the turnover report, but the items are ranked in descending order of dollar usage.

In the usage distribution report, we find that slightly more than 4 percent of the items account for 41 percent of the annual dollar usages. This lopsidedness is not unusual, especially with diversified manufacturers. Those fast-moving items are supported by less than 11 percent of the inventory investment, indicating a very poor balance. In general, the cumulative investment for the fast-moving items should be much closer to the items' cumulative dollar usage. Moving down to the slower-moving items, we see (in entry 16) that 38 percent of the total investment supports 75 percent of the total usage; the other 62 percent of the investment supports only 25 percent. Clearly, this is the area of inventory investment to focus on for potential reduction.

Corrective Measures. The information from the diagnostic analysis can be applied to realize immediate inventory reduction caused by overages and excess quantities. Also, it can help you plan to institute routine controls such as the following:

On slow-moving items: (1) purchasing controls to prevent unnecessary buildup, and (2) disposing of obsolete items

On fast-moving items, manual controls to ensure timely purchasing of items in economic quantities

Continuous Inventory Control

Continuous control monitors inventory on a daily basis. The same historical usage information used in the diagnostic surveys is used prognostically to arrive at demand projections for each item. (The accuracy of the projections can be monitored by comparing levels of both inventory and inventory investment actually realized over a period with the levels predicted for the period.) In relation to projected demand, the factors relevant to optimal inventory levels are mathematically processed to determine the size of individual orders (taking into account quantity discounts), reordering schedules, and stock levels—that is, levels that provide maximum defense against depletion of stock in relation to cost of funds tied up.

The information and control systems associated with the continuous approach can be independent of preexisting control systems or may be linked to them. One sophisticated feature of continuous inventory control is that it generates data from which it is possible to evaluate the effect of alternative methods of control on inventory investment.

Liquidating Inventory

Essentially, there are four methods to liquidate inventory. The first of these is sale. If you sell to a regular customer, the chances are that you will get a better price than if you attempt to unload goods in bulk on the market. Bulk sales should be a last resort when it is doubtful the item can be disposed of by any other means. Your sales effort should be aimed at inducing your customers to buy and stock items that they previously relied on you to stock. In essence, you try to get them to take earlier delivery. Special deals can also be offered as incentives to customers. One device that often proves effective is the spare parts package: the customer is offered the right to purchase a number of constituent parts together with the completed product at reasonable markup over the price of the product alone.

A second method of disposition is returning stock to the original vendor. You may be surprised to discover how often this is possible. Even when the supplier will not grant full credit, he or she may be willing to take back merchandise in return for an allowance or on a restocking fee arrangement.

The remaining two basic methods of disposal are conversion and trade. Some of your surplus items may be convertible into other more needed items at no great expense. Often a surplus part can be used in the same way as an out-of-stock item of lower quality. If this is so, overall savings might be achieved by using the surplus part before reordering the standard one. The importance of trading as a method of disposition has risen in recent years with the appearance of companies that offer various services in return for inventory items. They often take items at full value. The range of services these companies offer is broad, and chances are you will be able to find something you can use. The use of their services, however, may be limited by the fact that they tend to prefer consumer or standard-industrial products.

Administering an Inventory Reduction Program

If your periodic analysis or continuous control process determines excess inventory levels, you might need to plan an inventory reduction program. It is important to exercise firm control over a planned disposal program for inventory. Your most effective approach is to designate a team of managers if your operation is small, a single manager, to serve as liquidation supervisors. Each member of the team should be responsible for categorizing items according to the method or methods of disposal as well as for negotiating with company salespersons or outside contacts. Make sure the supervisors keep careful records, and require them to report regularly on their progress. In addition, it is advisable to establish targets in order to evaluate the performance of individual managers in disposing of inventory.

Where the inventory is limited in volume and variety, these arrangements can be more or less informal. Otherwise, a formal approach is preferable to ensure effective reduction of inventory levels. Your assignments to supervisors should be in writing, and their reports to you should be written and follow a prescribed format. If you have more than three or four supervisors, you would be well-advised to hold regular scheduled meetings to monitor progress.

The discipline of such a formal program might well surprise you in terms of inventory reductions achieved. Remember that each dollar of inventory reduced (without reduced sales levels) cuts carrying costs by 25 cents or more.

CAPITAL BUDGETING

Capital budgeting is essentially a matching of available sources of funds with appropriate uses of those funds. The concept gives us a common basis on which to evaluate alternative uses: capital expenditures.

A capital expenditure is an outlay that is intended to benefit more than one fiscal year. The value received for the outlay may be tangible, such as equipment or even a complete facility, or the replacement or repair of a facility, for production, distribution, or provision of a service. It may also be an intangible as research and development, public relations or a patent.

The starting point for capital budgeting is the gathering of proposals for capital expenditures. You should encourage all employees to contribute any idea they think worthwhile. The use of a basic format for proposals is effective in ensuring that the person initiating the request has at least considered such key factors as estimated costs, operating cost benefits, and timing.

Evaluating Budget Proposals

Evaluation of proposed capital expenditures should cover such factors as the relationship between anticipated returns or benefits and costs for a specific project and the relative net effect of various alternatives. Methods of cost–benefit analysis are described in the following subsections.

Cost–Benefit Analysis

A cost–benefit analysis is an integral part of the evaluation process. You may dispense with it only when the proposed expenditure is for an item needed to maintain production (for example, replacing the burned-out motor that operates several essential machines or replacing a leaking roof) or to stay in business (i.e., installing equipment to satisfy a pollution abatement order). The analysis is based upon a standard economic model where benefits minus cost equals cash flow. It involves comparing two factors: one external—the cost of capital—and one internal—your anticipated return on the investment. Essentially, the return should exceed the cost, or the investment is not worthwhile.

Cost of Capital   The cost of capital may be calculated in different ways, always on the basis of the interest rate. In a practical sense, for most small businesses, the cost of capital is the marginal cost of borrowing through the best available vehicle, often the cost of borrowing from a bank. For a closely held company, the effective capital cost might also be viewed as "opportunity cost"—what the funds might earn (or save) if management used them elsewhere.

Return on Investment.   Return on investment is calculated from the anticipated annual net aftertax savings that will result from the capital expenditures. These net savings, also termed net cash flows, are the net benefits connected with the acquisition and its subsequent use. In the case of a machine bought to replace an outdated model, the initial cash flows would be the purchase outlay less any proceeds from sale or disposition of the old model. Over the life of the machine, there would be additional outlays and costs.

The outlays could take the form of building modifications necessary to install and use the machine or the cost of inventory or repair parts required to keep it running efficiently. Likely benefits would be investment tax credit (recognized in the first year), cash savings realized from the increased efficiency of the production process, income tax saved by additional depreciation deductions throughout the life of the machine, and the expected salvage value of the machine at the end of its useful life. Figure 7.4 shows the derivation of net aftertax savings (or loss) for a particular item. For simplicity, only the more important cash flows are used.

Only incremental cash flows related to the investment are considered in the capital budgeting process. Overhead costs are not considered unless they are specifically attributable to the project and different from those that would be experienced if the project were not undertaken. For an example of an includable overhead cost, consider the impact of purchasing a gadget that would modify a machine currently in use and raise annual output from 100,000 to 125,000 units but would also raise direct costs from $0.90 to $1.00. Assume also that the product sells for $1.50, that no other costs are affected, and that the machine could continue to be used without alteration. The benefits to be considered in the cash-flow analysis would be computed as follows:

	Current Equipment	Current Equipment with Gadget
Units produced	100,000	125,000
Sales value of units produced	$150,000	$187,500
Direct cost of units produced	$90,000	$125,000
Gross margin	$60,000	$62,500
Annual benefit (expected effect on gross margin)		$2,500

In this case, installation of the gadget would result in an incremental annual benefit of $2,500 over the machine's remaining life. Because there is a factor of risk in every cash-flow projection, you might wish to discount the aftertax savings accordingly. This exercise is illustrated in Table 7.2. The discount factor, expressed by a multiple, is of course judgmental.

Type of Cash Flow	Year:	1	2	3	4	5	6–10	11–15
1. Incremental sales								
2. Incremental cash savings or expenditures								
a. Maintenance								
b. Operation								
(1) Labor								
(2) Materials								
(3) Equipment downtime								
3. Other incremental cash savings or expenditures								
4. Total before-tax effect								
5. Tax effect								
6. Subtotal								
7. Tax effect—depreciation								
8. Investment tax credit								
9. Salvage value								
Net aftertax cash savings								

Figure 7.4.   Work Sheet for Estimating Aftertax Savings

Table 7.2
DISCOUNTING OF CASH FLOWS TO ADJUST FOR RISK

	Project A—Fairly Certain			Project B—Moderately Risky			Project C—Very Risky		
Year	Cash flow	Risk discount factor	Risk adjusted cash flow	Cash flow	Risk discount factor	Risk-adjusted cash flow	Cash flow	Risk discount factor	Risk-adjusted cash flow
1	$40,000	1.00	$ 40,000	$50,000	1.00	$ 50,000	$50,000	0.90	$ 45,000
2	50,000	1.00	50,000	70,000	0.90	63,000	80,000	0.75	60,000
3	50,000	1.00	50,000	60,000	0.80	48,000	90,000	0.60	54,000
4	30,000	1.00	30,000	40,000	0.70	28,000	100,000	0.35	35,000
5	20,000	1.00	20,000	40,000	0.60	24,000	70,000	0.20	14,000
			$190,000			$213,000			$208,000

Two Methods of Comparison.   There are two methods for comparing cost of capital and return on investment. Under the internal method, the two rates are computed separately; under the present-value method, the rates are computed together. With both methods, return on investment is calculated on the principle that money received in the future has less value than money received now. Money has a time value in terms of its opportunity cost (cost at which it could be invested elsewhere). The discounted or present values of the future aftertax savings are obtained from tables that give, for any rate and any number of years, a factor or multiple based on one dollar.

The application of these two methods is illustrated in Tables 7.3 and 7.4. These tables are based on an investment of $100,000 covering the cost of a hypothetical facility and of establishing an inventory in connection with it. This $100,000 is net of the salvage value of discarded equipment that the new facility replaces. The anticipated net aftertax savings resulting from the investment are as follows:

End of Year	Savings
1	$ 50,000
2	60,000
3	30,000
4	20,000
5	20,000
6	30,000
	$210,000

The cash savings for the sixth year include the proceeds of liquidating the inventories and scrapping the equipment.

The internal method is illustrated in Table 7.3. It involves determining the rate of compound interest required to discount future earnings—that is, net aftertax savings—from the purchase in such a way that they add up to the investment required now—that is, $100,000. At that rate compounded, the present—that is, discounted—values of the future savings could be invested today for periods corresponding to the number of

Table 7.3

ESTIMATING THE INTERNAL RATE OF RETURN

Year	Cash Flow	i = 20%		i = 40%		i = 30%		i = 35%		i = 33%	
		Factor	Present Value	Factor	Present Value	Factor	Present Value	Factor	Present Value	Factor	Present Value
1	$50,000	0.83333	$ 41,667	0.71429	$35,715	0.76923	$ 38,462	0.74074	$37,037	0.75188	$ 37,594
2	60,000	0.69444	41,666	0.51020	30,612	0.59172	35,503	0.54870	32,922	0.56532	33,919
3	30,000	0.57870	17,361	0.36443	10,933	0.45517	13,655	0.40644	12,193	0.42505	12,752
4	20,000	0.48225	9,645	0.26031	5,206	0.35013	7,003	0.30107	6,021	0.31959	6,392
5	20,000	0.40188	8,038	0.18592	3,719	0.26933	5,387	0.22301	4,806	0.24029	4,608
6	30,000	0.33480	10,047	0.13281	3,984	0.20718	6,215	0.16520	4,956	0.18067	5,420
Total present value			$128,424		$90,169		$106,225		$97,589		$100,883

Table 7.4

**COMPUTATION OF PRESENT VALUE
(BASED ON INVESTMENT OF 15%)**

Year	Flow	Discount Factor	Present Value
1	50,000	0.86957	$ 43,479
2	60,000	0.75614	$ 45,368
3	30,000	0.65752	$ 19,726
4	20,000	0.57175	$ 11,435
5	20,000	0.49718	$ 9,944
6	30,000	0.43233	$ 12,970
	Total present value		$142,922

years before each saving is realized, and the aggregate result would be equal to the total projected future savings—that is, $210,000.

The rate is found by a technique known as intrapolation: the next aftertax savings are discounted at different rates until a close approximation of the true rate is arrived at. In Table 7.3, the rate is 33 percent, found after successive trials with four other rates. If this percentage is higher than the cost of capital, the expenditure is evaluated in comparison with other investment opportunities. If you have such alternative investment possibilities, you can rank them by applying the internal-rate-of-return method to each. Those ranked highest receive priority in use of available funds.

In the present-value method (Table 7.4), you discount future earnings by the amount of your estimated cost of capital and compare the totaled result with the expenditure called for. If the total discounted future earnings surpass the expenditures, the investment is justifiable in terms of cost of capital. The rate used is often called a "cut-off rate" since it eliminates projects below that rate. To rank projects, you divide the present value of future earnings by the initial investment. The higher the resultant ratio is (1.43 in Table 7.4), the more secure the proposed expenditure is as an investment.

Do not forget that future cash flows are uncertain and risks are involved. For really risky projects (such as a new product line), consider using a cut-off rate of two or three times your cost of capital.

Evaluating Your Capital Budget Practices

The following conditions are symptomatic of a deficiency in capital budgeting, either in the process itself or in the basic management information system.

Assets acquired without knowledge of top management

High incidence of budgetary oversights, especially the failure to allow for significant factors

Estimated income not being realized

Estimated cost savings not being realized

Status of approved expenditures not reported to top management

Permanent decline rate in level of return on assets after capital expenditures

Continuing need to refine cost data

Serviceable plan or equipment not in use (especially recently acquired items)

Poor feedback from company personnel, in regard to ideas for improvements or changes

Chronic lag behind competition in introducing new ideas

Monitoring

Once you have made a capital investment, it is essential that you keep track of how that investment is performing. If an item is not fulfilling expectations, the sooner you know it the better. It is a question not only of taking remedial steps—which in drastic cases could consist of reversing the investment, that is, withdrawing it from service and trying to recoup costs—but also of being able to apply the knowledge gained to future investments.

Tracking and Postaudits

There are two ways of monitoring the performance of capital items: keeping track of operating costs, and holding periodic audits. The documentary basis for the tracking of costs is a series of reports produced at scheduled intervals, showing the operating costs connected with individual items. These reports permit item-by-item analysis of variances between budgeted and actual costs.

The Postaudit.   The periodic operating cost analysis will not give you all the information you need to evaluate the performance of the capital item. The total performance picture, including certain factors that cannot be readily "dollarized," can be presented only in a broad evaluation or audit. The frame of reference for the audit is your original scheme of estimates covering every aspect of performance, such as operating and other costs and effect on sales volume, unit output, and labor costs. The audit should consider changes in such key factors as sales prices, labor rates, and fuel costs.

Postaudits may be held several times during the life of the capital item. A favorite time for the first audit is the year beginning 90 days after either the completion of the installation or the time at which the asset was predicted to become significantly productive.

CHAPTER
EIGHT

ACCOUNTING SYSTEMS AND INTERNAL CONTROLS

egardless of your company's size, its accounting system will be the vehicle by which the basic data you need to manage the business is gathered, stored, and reported. In this chapter, we outline, in general terms, some basic accounting concepts and describe in a general way how data flow through your company's books and records. We also discuss how internal controls can minimize the risk of inaccurate, incomplete, or misrepresented data. We include a sample set of financial statements and a sample internal control checklist.

Our intention is not to equip you to be an accountant but rather to sensitize you to certain accounting concepts and to the need to implement controls to protect your investment. Every business needs strong financial management. This comes from a combination of the owner–manager's talent, a competent financial person, such as a controller or chief financial officer, and an independent accountant. The outside accountant, especially one from a recognized firm, lends credibility to financial statements, serves as a "sounding board" for ideas, and provides creative advice.

BASIC CONCEPTS OF ACCOUNTING

The American Institute of Certified Public Accountants defines accounting as "the art of recording, classifying and summarizing in a significant manner and in terms of money, transactions and events which are, in part at least, of a financial character, and interpreting the results thereof." In its broadest sense, accounting has been defined as the "language of business."

The most obvious function of accounting is to keep track of assets and liabilities through continuous recording of changes in such items as cash, accounts receivable, inventory, capital equipment, accounts payable, and debt. In performing this function, accounting generates information for assessing a business's financial position and performance, that is, through the balance sheet and statements of profit and loss and cash flow; for meeting operational requirements, such as maintaining desired inventory levels or preserving the continuity of customer service or production; and for systematic assessment of performance in many key areas.

The following three premises are inherent in the concept of accountancy as understood today:

The Entity. A business undertaking is treated for accounting purposes as a separate entity distinct from the parties that provide the funds or capital for the operation. (In business operations, planning, and formulating goals, however, the owner–manager and the business are inseparable.)

The Going Concern. In the absence of evidence to the contrary, a business is treated as continuing in operation indefinitely. (Otherwise, assets would be valued at liquidation value rather than cost.)

The Matching of Revenues and Costs. Depending on the accounting principles in effect, income must be recognized when earned or collected. (Accounting principles used for managing a business need not always be the same as those used for income tax purposes.)

Cash versus Accrual Basis Accounting

When accounting is on a cash basis, no revenue is recognized from sales until collections are received, and expenses are recorded as costs in the period in which payments are made. Collections received for services to be rendered in the future are regarded as revenue during the period in which they are received, even though nothing has been done to earn the revenue. No depreciation expense is recognized under the cash method of reporting because the purchase price of fixed assets is frequently charged to operations in the period the cash payment is made. Similarly, no bad-debt expense is recorded under this method since no earnings are recorded until the receivable is collected.

The cash basis of reporting is generally not meaningful for any business that has material amounts of sales on account, inventories, prepaid expenses, revenues collected in advance, fixed assets, or accounts payable. Financial statements prepared on this basis do not usually represent an entity's actual financial position or results of operations; their only usefulness is to summarize cash flow, which is necessary but should not be the sole or primary focus of an accounting system.

The accrual basis of accounting is the most widely used in business today. Under this approach, revenue is recognized as earned in the period in which sales were made or services performed—regardless of when payment is received—and expenses are regarded as applicable to the period in which they were incurred—regardless of when paid. Under the accrual method, it is often necessary to make estimates (accruals) in order to match revenues and expenses of the accounting period.

ACCOUNTING SYSTEMS

Accounting is a concept; an accounting system is the body of records and procedures that implement that concept. The basic records for a manual or computerized accounting system include journals, ledgers, and registers. From these are compiled operating financial statements as well as specialized reports such as sales by region or by person, profitability by product or division, backlog, production variances, and other important data.

Standard Procedures

Accounting is usually thought of as a record-keeping activity; as such, it is distinct from the activities it records. The modern concept of an accounting system, however, tends to override this distinction. Thus, for example, ordering of merchandise and dispensing of funds are considered accounting system procedures even though these activities are not of a record-keeping nature.

The following record-keeping procedures are standard in both manual and computerized systems.

Preparing, checking, and processing forms, such as sales orders and invoices, in connection with business transactions

Recording transactions in books of original entry, such as voucher register, sales journal, and payroll register

Posting to the general ledger

Conforming general ledger balances to subsidiary ledgers or registers

Preparing a trial balance of the general ledger

Preparing statements from the trial balance that reflect the results of operations for the period and the financial position of the enterprise

Preparing special management reports using statistics or other specific data

Accounting Cycles

To understand accounting systems, it is convenient to think in terms of groups of related functions that are basic to the operation of a business. Among these are purchasing goods or services, selling to and collecting from customers, controlling production and inventory, and paying salaries. These functions, of which there are others besides the preceding, are often termed *cycles* because they are carried out continously and each depends on a particular set of procedures that must be performed in a certain sequence.

In a typical personal service enterprise, the accounting cycles would be:

Billing and cash collections
Project control and payroll
Purchases and cash disbursements

In a typical retail or wholesale business, the accounting cycles would be:

Sales and cash collections
Purchases and cash disbursements
Payroll

The accounting cycles of a typical manufacturing company are:

1. Sales and Cash-Collection Cycle.   This cycle includes:
   a. Sales order and credit control
   b. Sales distribution
   c. Billing and accounts receivable
   d. Cash receipts

2. Purchase and Payment Cycle. This cycle includes:
   a. Purchase order and receiving report
   b. Purchase and expense distribution
   c. Vouchers payable; accounts payable
   d. Cash disbursements

3. **Payroll Cycle.**   This cycle includes:
   a. Employment
   b. Timekeeping
   c. Payroll disbursements
   d. Labor distribution

4. **Production and Cost Cycle.**   This cycle includes:
   a. Production order
   b. Inventory control
   c. Cost accounting

The accounting system should result in a monthly operating statement that is timely (generally prepared by the fifteenth working day of the succeeding month) and accurate and that includes the important data needed to manage the business.

A sample monthly operating statement for a manufacturer is presented in the Appendix to this chapter, in Exhibit 8.1. It must, of course, be tailored for each specific circumstance. All of the data for this report should come directly from the accounting records or should be easily obtainable. The key indicator report at the outset of this report and the two graphs at the end are in themselves good indications of the direction the business is going.

Specialized Reports

The monthly three-part financial reporting package—balance sheet, income statement, and statement of cash flow—is necessarily broad in scope. For a close-up view of specific aspects of your business, you must rely on specialized reports. These reports need not be lengthy or costly. For the most part, you will find the data you need for them in the records of your basic accounting support systems. The following subsections describe the subjects most often covered in these important aids to management.

Profitability.   An analysis by individual products or lines of business can shed light on "off-target" areas that need attention. For example, a product may be less profitable because of obsolescence, softness in demand, price competition, or manufacturing inefficiency. Pinpointing the cause permits evaluation of changes in order to improve profitability or may indicate a need to terminate the product.

Accounts Receivable. Accounts receivable is a critical barometer, not only of cash flow but also of satisfaction with the company's products. Behind every disputed account may lurk a more serious problem. Simple aging analyses, combined with systematized response to and resolution of disputed accounts, can keep a debt from going bad or avert customer ill-will (see Chapter 7, Part 1).

Inventory. Understanding inventory position is not easy. Overall balance sheet amounts should be broken into significant segments. The inventories can then be aged, thereby permitting a review of slow-moving items. Lastly, the balance of inventory levels against stock-outs can be tested and reported. With this information, meaningful decisions on stock disposition and overall inventory management can be made (see Chapter 7, Part 2).

Cash. Daily, weekly, and monthly monitoring is essential. Naturally, a forecast of cash inflow and anticipated needs must be available (see Chapter 7, Part 1). A major element of such a forecast would be a purchase commitment report—that is, a detailed record of commitments to suppliers for future purchases, including, of course, the contract prices. (Cash should never be left unproductive; any excess should be invested.)

Payroll, Production, and Cost Variances. Weekly payroll analyses, production reports, or variance analysis of standard versus actual costs all cover subjects relevant to the efficiency of a business. If job costs are used as the basis of the analysis, progress reports on unfinished jobs may provide other critical data (see Chapter 3).

Sales Backlogs. A sales backlog report can serve as a guide to monitoring purchase and production staffing schedules. A schedule of shipments showing promised or order-received dates compared to actual shipping dates can serve as a measure of customer service.

Labor Turnover. A high labor turnover may be related to low shop morale; it may also explain excessive operating costs. Remember that a new employee costs a good deal before he or she approaches normal efficiency.

Projections. By extrapolating from the monthly financial reports going back at least six months, it is possible to construct a hypothetical series for each report extending several months into the future. Using these projections, management can identify weaknesses that will presumably develop if not corrected in advance. Examples are a shortfall, as revealed in a cash-flow forecast, for which the necessary funds might have to be raised by additional borrowing or improvements in inventory turnover or receivable collections.

Checklist for System Performance

To test the efficiency of your accounting system, ask yourself the following questions:

Is financial data available on a timely basis?

In your experience, has this data been reasonably accurate?

Does this system ensure that orders are approved and processed timely?

Are shipments billed timely, and is data generated to ensure an adequate collection follow-up effort?

Do records provide you with production information, especially:

Receipts of inventories?

Slow-moving or obsolete items?

Movement of goods through the production process?

Shipments?

Backlog?

Can you obtain information about:

Performance of individual salespersons?

Sales by location, region, bureau, or division?

Product profitability and relationship to sales commissions?

Sales forecasts?

Does the system ensure that vendor discounts are taken, and is the priority of a payable readily established?

Is cash information readily available?

Do the reports generated by the system answer more questions than they raise?

If the answer to any of these questions is no, radical corrective actions are probably necessary.

INTERNAL CONTROLS

Theoretically, malfunction is possible in any action or process. In a business operation, however, there are certain actions or processes in which the possibility of malfunction poses particular dangers. Examples are the granting of credit, where the danger lies in accepting bad risks; billing, where the danger lies in the failure to bill an occasional shipment; and handling of cash receipts or disbursements, where the danger lies in misappropriation through manipulation of documents or defalcation. To counteract these dangers, it is necessary to set up special safeguards, called internal controls. An internal control system is "the plan of organization and all of the coordinate methods and measures adopted within a business to safeguard its assets, check the accuracy and reliability of its accounting data, promote operational efficiency and encourage adherence to prescribed managerial policies."

Accounting versus Administrative

Two types of internal controls may be distinguished: accounting and administrative or operational. Accounting controls relate directly to a company's financial and accounting departments. They are designed to supply reasonable assurance that

Only authorized transactions are recorded.

All assets are accounted for.

Financial statements are prepared in accordance with generally accepted accounting principles.

Only authorized employees have access to assets.

Records are compared periodically with assets, and differences, if any, are investigated and corrected.

Administrative or operational controls are concerned with business functions outside the financial and accounting departments; examples are matters associated with the delivery of products and services (minimum acceptable sales orders, product pricing, and so on), hiring practices, employee training, warehouse security, and organization of inventories.

There is some overlap between these two classes of controls; that is, the same control can affect accounting and operations, but for most purposes they are distinct.

Representative Control System

Let us examine how accounting controls work in just one accounting cycle: purchasing and paying (see "Accounting Cycles" in this chapter).

Order Placing

The initial procedure deals with placing an order for goods or services. The order may come through department managers or corporate officers or under blanket purchase orders. An important control on the ordering and receiving process is the requirement for centralization. Only certain designated employees should be permitted to authorize a purchase. Other controls are concerned with either the purchasing or receiving process. Controls on purchasing include:

Imposition of order criteria; that is, that the price is the lowest available for the quality or type of goods purchased, that the quantity ordered is economical (a three-year supply of paper clips at a bargain price being no bargain), and that the purchase is affordable (within the company budget). To implement these controls, a purchase order form that specifies the quantity, price, and all other relevant data should be used.

Systems for ensuring that purchases of components or subassemblies for a product do not significantly exceed the sales forecast for that product. These systems should be sophisticated enough to consider lead times for delivery and alternative sources of supply.

A special function (for which a single person might be held responsible) for following up orders that were not received.

The most important control on receipt is checking the goods for conformity with the purchase order in respect to quantity, quality, and type. This control is generally implemented by requiring a prenumbered receiving report with provision for the foregoing data to be completed and signed by a designated employee. Copies of the "packing slip" can sometimes be used as receiving reports if they are numerically controlled.

Purchase and Expense Distribution; Vouchers and Accounts Payable

The second and third procedures in the purchasing and paying cycle involve:

Vouching (recording) and processing the vendor invoices

Entering the vouchers—as they may now be called—in a payable system, verifying the mathematics on the invoice or voucher, and then checking them for approvals

Entering the vouchers in a summary or register for distribution in the general ledger

Processing a vendor invoice requires procedures to ensure that payment is correct in amount, is made only once and not before the preplanned date (considering invoice terms, cash discounts, and cash availability), and is for goods and services actually received and authorized. Such procedures might involve comparing the invoice with the receiving report, noting that prices and quantities agree with those on the authorized purchase order, and verifying the mathematics. The paid invoice should be cancelled, preferably by a perforating stamp to prevent duplicate payment. Payments should not be made on the basis of a duplicate invoice.

When entering the vouchers in the payable system, there must be controls to ensure that all items were recorded. Vouchers can be prenumbered sequentially and a designated employee made responsible for periodically accounting for missing numbers.

Distributing vouchers for summarization in the general ledger means assigning the account numbers to each transaction. This procedure should ensure that a salesperson's credit card bill is included in travel and entertainment expenses and in accounts payable rather than in some inappropriate account.

Cash Disbursements

The final procedure in the purchasing and paying cycle is the issuance of a check in payment of the amount due. The signature on the check is itself a control, but it is a good idea to have the voucher package attached to the check for review by the check signer. Once in a while, you might catch an error or defalcation that has slipped by your prior controls. Discrepancies that have been picked up in this way include duplicate payments, payments for the wrong amount, absence of regular payments, and excessive payments to one vendor—the latter a possible indication of fraud covered by false invoices.

Instituting and Evaluating Controls

In many cases, putting in an internal control is a routine matter, involving a small adaptation to a sequence of activities. In some cases, however, the required adaptation is more complicated. In these cases, there may be several possible approaches that vary in cost and in their effect on other operations.

To take a simple example, selling for cash only would eliminate the risk of credit losses, but it would also restrict sales potential and perhaps increase the risk of cash misappropriation as well. Before resorting to this extreme form of protection, you should consider establishing credit evaluation policies, requiring accountability for credit decisions and establishing follow-up collection procedures. Similarly, you could reduce the risk of failing to invoice a customer for goods shipped or services provided by hiring an employee whose sole responsibility is to monitor and document all shipments, match them against invoices, and compare the invoice price with catalogues or a published price list. A less expensive and equally effective procedure would be to match prenumbered shipping documents and production forms, as well as freight bills, with invoices, making sure that all discrepancies are investigated on a timely basis.

Sources of Assistance

If your company's financial statements are audited by an outside accounting firm, you should expect, as part of their procedures, to receive, in written form, their comments and suggestions relating to your company's system of internal accounting controls. In addition, since it is unreasonable to expect that periodic services rendered in connection with an audit can make it unnecessary for you to be knowledgeable in the area of internal controls, we suggest some basic reading on the subject. Particularly useful is *Evaluating Internal Controls: Concepts, Guidelines, Procedures Documentation* by Kenneth P. Johnson and Henry R. Jaenicke.*

Questionnaire for Evaluation

Exhibit 8.2 in the Appendix to this chapter is a portion of a questionnaire designed to help evaluate a company's system of internal accounting controls. The complete questionnaire was developed by Coopers & Lybrand and is reproduced in its entirety in *Evaluating Internal Controls*. The questions are related to specific control objectives listed at the head of each sequence. The flowchart referred to in the column heading is a graphic depiction of an accounting system in which each significant step and each control is identified. The numbers in the column indicate the step number in the flowchart that depicts the control cited. Obviously, only "yes" answers will have an entry in this column.

Even if all the answers to the questionnaire are in the affirmative, you have no absolute assurance that an error will not be made or a misappropriation will never take place. Accounting literature points out that errors can result from "misunderstandings of instructions, mistakes of judgment, and personal carelessness, distraction or fatigue." Controls can be overridden by management or circumvented by collusion. Furthermore, controls that are effective today may become inadequate tomorrow as circumstances change. On the other hand, the internal controls questionnaire is unsurpassed as a tool for a rapid, substantially reliable evalaution of a company's control system. It helps identify weaknesses and points the way to alternative approaches.

*New York, John Wiley & Sons, 1980.

APPENDIX

Exhibit 8.1

SAMPLE MONTHLY OPERATING STATEMENT FOR A MANUFACTURER

1. MONTHLY KEY INDICATOR REPORT

Month of _____

	Two Months Ago	Last Month	This Month
Cash on hand	$ _____	$ _____	$ _____
Receivables	_____	_____	_____
Inventories	_____	_____	_____
Payables	_____	_____	_____
Sales	_____	_____	_____
Sales order backlog	_____	_____	_____
Purchase orders outstanding	_____	_____	_____

Three-Month Moving Averages

	Last Month	This Month
Incoming order value	$ _____	$ _____
Order backlog value	$ _____	$ _____
Open purchase value	$ _____	$ _____

Key Ratios

	Last Month	This Month
Current ratio	_____	_____
Receivable turnover	_____	_____
Collection period	_____	_____
Inventory turnover	_____	_____
Days sales in inventory	_____	_____

2. BALANCE SHEET

——————————— ——, 19———

Assets

Current assets:

Cash		$ ———————
Accounts receivable		———————
Inventory:		
Parts	$ ———————	
Work in process	———————	
Finished goods	$ ———————	———————
Demonstration	$ ———————	———————
Prepaid expenses		———————
Total current assets		———————
Property and equipment:		
Machinery and equipment	———————	
Office furniture and equipment	———————	
Leasehold improvements	———————	
Accumulated depreciation and amortization	(———————)	———————
Other assets		———————
Total assets		$ ═══════

3. BALANCE SHEET

——————————— ——, 19———

Liabilities and Stockholders' Equity

Current liabilities:

Notes payable— First National Bank		$ ———————
Accounts payable—trade		———————

Accrued commissions   _____

Accrued interest   _____

Accrued payroll and payroll taxes   _____

Notes payable—stockholders   _____

Accrued taxes on income   _____

Other current liabilities   _____

Total current liabilities   _____

Long-term debt

    Bonds payable $ _____

    Notes payable—stockholders   _____   _____

Total liabilities   _____

Stockholders' equity

    Common stock $ _____

    Paid-in capital   _____

    Retained earnings   _____

    Current year income   _____

Total liabilities and
stockholders' equity $ _____

4. STATEMENT OF OPERATIONS FOR THE MONTH OF _____ AND THE _____ MONTHS ENDED _____, 19___

	Current Month						Year to Date				
	Plan		Actual				Actual		Plan		
	Percent	Amount	Percent	Amount			Amount	Percent	Amount	Percent	
Sales	100.0%	$	100.0%	$			$	100.0%	$	100.0%	
Cost of sales											
Gross margin											
Administrative											
Marketing											
Income from operations											
Research and development											
Interest											
Other income (expense											
Income before provision for income taxes											
Provision for income taxes											
Net income	___%	$	___%	$			$	___%	$	___%	

234

5. SCHEDULE OF MANUFACTURING VARIANCES FOR THE MONTH OF _____ AND THE
_____ MONTHS ENDED _____ __, 19__

Current Month
Actual

$ _____	Materials price variance	$ _____
_____	Overhead variance	_____
_____	Materials usage variance	_____
_____	Cost of sales adjustment	_____
_____	(Over) underapplied labor (from schedule of manufacturing costs)	_____
$ ══════════	Total variances	$ ══════════

6. SCHEDULE OF MANUFACTURING COSTS FOR THE MONTH OF _____ AND THE _____ MONTHS ENDED _____, 19___

	Current Month		Year to Date	
	Plan	Actual	Actual	Plan
Direct labor:				
Salaries and wages	$ _____	$ _____	$ _____	$ _____
Payroll taxes	_____	_____	_____	_____
Insurance and benefits	_____	_____	_____	_____
Subtotal direct labor	_____	_____	_____	_____
Labor applied to inventory	(_____)	(_____)	(_____)	(_____)
(Over) underapplied labor	$ _____	$ _____	$ _____	$ _____
Manufacturing overhead:	$ _____	$ _____	$ _____	$ _____
Indirect labor				
Supplies and equipment rental	_____	_____	_____	_____
Travel and entertainment	_____	_____	_____	_____
Other operating costs	_____	_____	_____	_____
Professional services	_____	_____	_____	_____
Allocated occupancy expenses	_____	_____	_____	_____
Depreciation and amortization	_____	_____	_____	_____
Subtotal manufacturing overhead	_____	_____	_____	_____
Manufacturing overhead applied	(_____)	(_____)	(_____)	(_____)
(Over) underapplied overhead	$ _____	$ _____	$ _____	$ _____

236

7. SCHEDULE OF RESEARCH AND DEVELOPMENT FOR THE MONTH OF _____ AND THE _____ MONTHS ENDED _____, 19___

	Current Month		Year to Date	
	Plan	Actual	Actual	Plan
Project labor:				
Direct labor applied	$ _____	$ _____	$ _____	$ _____
Materials and parts	_____	_____	_____	_____
Outside engineering costs	_____	_____	_____	_____
Total project costs	_____	_____	_____	_____
Research and development overhead:				
Salaries and wages	_____	_____	_____	_____
Payroll taxes and benefits	_____	_____	_____	_____
Labor applied to manufacturing	(_____)	(_____)	(_____)	(_____)
Supplies	_____	_____	_____	_____
Rental equipment	_____	_____	_____	_____
Dues and subscriptions	_____	_____	_____	_____

237

238

7. SCHEDULE OF RESEARCH AND DEVELOPMENT FOR THE MONTH OF _____ AND THE _____ MONTHS ENDED _____, 19___

	Current Month		Year to Date	
	Plan	Actual	Actual	Plan
Freight				
Equipment depreciation				
Travel				
Entertainment				
Telephone and communications				
Professional services				
Miscellaneous				
Allocated occupancy expenses				
Materials and parts				
Total	$	$	$	$

8. SCHEDULE OF MARKETING EXPENSE FOR THE MONTH OF _____ AND THE _____ MONTHS ENDED _____, 19___

	Current Month		Year to Date	
	Plan	Actual	Actual	Plan
Salaries and wages	$	$	$	$
Payroll taxes and benefits				
Casual labor				
Total salaries and benefits				
Supplies and equipment rent				
Travel and entertainment				
Commissions expense				
Professional services				
Advertising				
Trade shows				
Demonstration expense				
Bidding				
Other operating expenses				
Allocated occupancy expenses				
Total	$	$	$	$

9. SCHEDULE OF OCCUPANCY EXPENSE FOR THE MONTH OF _____ AND THE _____ MONTHS ENDED _____, 19__

	Current Month		Year to Date	
	Plan	Actual	Actual	Plan
Occupancy:				
Rent	$	$	$	$
Repairs and maintenance				
Property taxes				
Utilities				
Miscellaneous				
Subtotal				
Allocation of occupancy expenses:				
Manufacturing	[ ]	[ ]	[ ]	[ ]
Research and development	[ ]	[ ]	[ ]	[ ]
Marketing	[ ]	[ ]	[ ]	[ ]
General and administrative	[ ]	[ ]	[ ]	[ ]
Total allocated expenses	[ ]	[ ]	[ ]	[ ]
(Over) underallocated occupancy expenses	$	$	$	$

240

10. SCHEDULE OF GENERAL AND ADMINISTRATIVE EXPENSES FOR THE MONTH OF _____ AND THE _____ MONTHS ENDED _____,
19__

	Current Month			Year to Date	
	Plan	Actual		Actual	Plan
Salaries and wages	$ ____ $ ____			$ ____	$ ____
Payroll taxes and benefits	____ ____			____	____
Total salaries and benefits	____ ____			____	____
Supplies	____ ____			____	____
Rental equipment	____ ____			____	____
Dues and subscriptions	____ ____			____	____
Postage	____ ____			____	____
Office equipment and depreciation	____ ____			____	____
Vehicle expense	____ ____			____	____
Travel and entertainment	____ ____			____	____

10. SCHEDULE OF GENERAL AND ADMINISTRATIVE EXPENSES FOR THE MONTH OF _____ AND THE _____ MONTHS ENDED _____ 19__

	Current Month		Year to Date	
	Plan	Actual	Actual	Plan
Telephone and communications				
Insurance				
Professional services				
Taxes and licenses				
Continuing education				
Donations				
Amortization of leasehold improvements				
Miscellaneous				
Allocated occupancy expenses				
Total	$	$	$	$

242

11. SCHEDULE OF OTHER INCOME AND EXPENSE FOR THE MONTH OF _____ AND THE _____ MONTHS ENDED _____, 19___

	Current Month		Year to Date	
	Plan	Actual	Actual	Plan
Income:				
Interest income	$_____	$_____	$_____	$_____
Other income	_____	_____	_____	_____
Subtotal	_____	_____	_____	_____
Expense:				
Interest expense	(_____)	(_____)	(_____)	(_____)
Subtotal	(_____)	(_____)	(_____)	(_____)
Net total	$══════	$══════	$══════	$══════

Thousands of Dollars

12. SALES AND COST OF SALES

—— Sales
· · · · Standard cost of sales
- - - - Total cost of sales

105
100
95
90
85
80
75
70
65
60
55
50
45
40
35
30
25
20
15
10
5
0

APR MAY JUN JUL AUG SEP OCT NOV DEC JAN FEB MAR APR MAY JUN JUL AUG SEP

Thousands of Dollars

—— Target
· · · · Actual

13. SHIPMENTS MONTH OF _____

80
75
70
65
60
55
50
45
40
35
30
25
20
15
10
5
0

1 2 3 4 5 6 7 8 9 10 11 12 13 14 15 16 17 18 19 20 21 22 23 24 25 26 27 28 29 30 31

Day

Exhibit 8.2
INTERNAL CONTROL QUESTIONNAIRE[a] FOR CASH DISBURSEMENTS
(PURCHASES AND PAYMENTS CYCLE)

Control Objective

1. Control should be established over goods and
   services received as a basis for:
   a. Determining and recording the liability for goods
      and services received but not entered as accounts
      payable
   b. Where required, posting the items to detailed
      inventory records

Questionnaire	Flowchart Ref.	Yes	No

Initial recording of receipt of goods and services

  a. Are the following checked by suitable methods (for
example by counting or weighing and inspecting
goods received) and the results recorded at the
time of their receipt for subsequent checking with
the related invoices:

    (i) Nature, quantity, and condition of goods
received (including property, plant and
equipment, and major supplies such as fuel
and stationery)?

    (ii) Major services received (to the extent
practicable)?

  b. Are the receiving records (a) controlled in such a
way that it can subsequently be established
whether all the related transactions have been
accounted for (for example, by sequentially
prenumbering receiving reports or by entering
receipts in a register), in respect of:

  (i) Goods [a(i)]?

  (ii) Major services [a(ii)]?

Liability for unprocessed invoices

  c. Are there adequate records of goods and services
received which have not been matched with the
related suppliers' invoices, in respect of:

    (i) Goods [a(i)]?

    (ii) Major services [a(ii)]?

  d. Where sequentially prenumbered forms are used (b)
are all numbers accounted for as part of the control

procedure over unmatched receipts (c) in respect
of:
- (i) Goods [a(i)]?
- (ii) Major services [a(ii)]?

e. Are unmatched records of goods and services
received (c) reviewed on a regular basis, such as
monthly, to determine the reasons for any such
receipts that have not been matched within a
reasonable period of time, in respect of:
- (i) Goods [a(i)]?
- (ii) Major services [a(ii)]?

f. Are the results of the procedures in (e) reviewed
and approved by a responsible official?

Control Objective

2. Invoices and related documentation should be
properly checked and approved as being valid before
being entered as accounts payable.

Questionnaire	Flowchart Ref.	Yes	No

Detailed checking of documentation
a. Are invoices for goods received checked as to:
- (i) Quantities and conditions of goods received (to
receiving records)?
- (ii) Nature and quantities of goods ordered (to
purchase orders)?
- (iii) Prices and other terms (to purchase orders or
suppliers' price lists)?

b. Are invoices for services received compared with
the underlying documentation (such as records of
receipts [1.a.(ii)] completion reports, leases, records
of meter readings) or if such documentation is not
available, approved by a responsible official?

c. Are the following functions performed by separate
individuals:
- (i) Preparation of purchase orders?
- (ii) Preparation of receiving records?
- (iii) Checking of purchase invoices (2.a and 2.b.)?

d. Are credit (or debit) memoranda checked to
confirm that:
- (i) They agree with the original record of the
goods returned or claims made?

    (ii) Where applicable, the prices agree with the
        original invoice?

  e. Are the extensions and additions of invoices and
     credit (or debit) memoranda checked to an
     adequate extent?

  f. Do the invoices and credit (or debit) memoranda
    bear adequate evidence that the checking (2.a., 2.b.,
    2.c. to 2.e) has been carried out?

Approval of documentation

  g. Are invoices and credit (or debit) memoranda
    subject to final written approval by a responsible
    official prior to entry as accounts payable?

  h. Are adjustments to suppliers' accounts properly
    documented?

  i. Are the adjustments and related documentation
    (2.h) reviewed and approved by a responsible
    official prior to entry in the accounts payable
    records?

Control Objective

3. Payments in respect of wages and salaries should be:
  a. Made only to company employees at authorized
    rates of pay
  b. Where required, in accordance with records of
    work performance
  c. Accurately calculated

Questionnaire	Flowchart Ref.	Yes	No

Standing payroll data
  a. Are the following authorized in writing:
    (i) Employees added to payrolls?
    (ii) Employees removed from payrolls?
    (iii) Rates of pay and changes in rates of pay?
    (iv) Payroll deductions other than the compulsory
      deductions (specify below)?

  b. Do persons other than those who prepare the
    payrolls provide the authorizations required in 3.a.?

  c. Are there adequate controls designed to ensure
    that the payroll reflects all authorized standing data
    (3.a.) and only such authorized data?

Transaction payroll data

d. If employees are paid on the basis of time worked:
   (i) Is the payroll based on adequate time records?
   (ii) Where applicable, are the time records checked to supporting records of time spent (for example, time charges to jobs)? [3.d.(i)]
   (iii) Are the time records [3.d.(i)] approved?
   (iv) Do the time records [3.d.(i)] indicate that overtime has been properly authorized?

e. If employees are paid on the basis of output, are the payments based on output records that are reconciled with production records that are under accounting control?

f. If salaried or other employees not included in 3.d. or 3.e. are paid for overtime, is the payroll based on time records that indicate that overtime has been properly authorized?

g. If employees receive commissions on sales, are the commissions based on sales records that are reconciled with sales (less, where applicable, returns) recorded in the books?

Payroll preparation

h. Is there a check on the calculation of gross pay (for example, by agreeing in total with predetermined control totals or with cost records, or by sufficient checking of individual amounts), in respect of:
   (i) Employees paid for time worked (3.d.)?
   (ii) Employees paid for output (3.e.)?
   (iii) Employees paid for overtime (3.f.)?
   (iv) Employees paid commissions (3.g.)?

i. Are the calculations and additions of payrolls and payroll summaries checked to an adequate extent?

j. Do payrolls bear adequate evidence that the procedures in 3.h. and 3.i. have been completed?

k. Are payrolls subject to the final written approval of a responsible official before they are paid?

Payments to employees

l. If employees are paid in cash:
   (i) Is cash withdrawn only for the net amount of the payroll?
   (ii) Do persons other than those who prepare the payroll physically control cash until it is distributed to employees?

(iii) Are unclaimed wages promptly recorded and controlled by persons other than those who prepare the payroll?

Control Objective

4. Payroll deductions should be correctly accounted for and paid to the third parties to whom they are due.

Questionnaire	Flowchart Ref.	Yes	No
Initial control over deductions			
a. Are all payroll deductions recorded in separate control accounts?			
Checking of amounts to be paid to third parties			
b. Are payments of payroll deductions to third parties agreed to the related payrolls?			

Control Objective

5. Reimbursements of imprest and similar funds (such as postage and other franking meters, payroll deduction stamps) should be made only for valid transactions.

Questionnaire	Flowchart Ref.	Yes	No
Overall control of funds			
a. Are imprest and similar funds:			
(i) Maintained at a reasonable balance in relation to the level of expenditure?			
Expenditures from funds			
b. Are all disbursements from imprest and similar funds:			
(i) Supported by adequate documentation?			
(ii) Approved where appropriate?			
c. In the case of cash funds, are there reasonable limits on:			
(i) The size of individual disbursements?			
(ii) The extent to which personal checks of employees are cashed?			
(iii) Loans and advances such as for wages made from such funds?			

Requests for reimbursement of funds
- d. Are all reimbursements made on an imprest basis?
- e. Are requests for reimbursement accompanied by details of expenditures and supporting vouchers?
- f. Are the reimbursements approved by an official who is not the custodian of the funds?

Control Objective

6. Disbursements from bank accounts should be made only in respect of valid transactions

Questionnaire	Flowchart Ref.	Yes	No

Preparation of checks and bank transfers
- a. Are checks and bank transfers prepared by persons other than those who initiate or approve any documents that give rise to disbursements for:
  - (i) Payments of accounts payable?
  - (ii) Payrolls and payroll deductions (control objectives 3 and 4)?
  - (iii) Reimbursements of imprest and similar funds (control objective 5)?
- b. Are checks and bank transfers prepared only on the basis of evidence that the validity of the transactions has been confirmed in accordance with the company's procedures, in respect of:
  - (i) Payments of accounts payable?
  - (ii) Payrolls and payroll deductions (control objectives 3 and 4)?
  - (iii) Reimbursements of imprest and similar funds (control objective 5)?
- c. Are checks and bank transfers for transactions that, because of their nature, do not pass through the normal approval procedures as referred to in 6.b. (such as purchase of investments, payment of dividends, repayment of debt), initiated only on the basis of proper documentation of the validity of the transactions?
- d. Is the documentation in 6.c. reviewed and approved in writing by a responsible official before checks and bank transfers are initiated?

Signing of checks

  e. Are checks signed by officials other than those who approve transactions for payment in respect of:
    (i) Payment of accounts payable?
    (ii) Payrolls and payroll deductions (control objectives 3 and 4)?
    (iii) Reimbursement of imprest and similar funds (control objective 5)?
    (iv) Other payments (6.c.)?

  f. At the time of signing checks and bank transfers, does each signatory examine:
    (i) Original supporting documents (for example, invoices, payrolls, or imprest cash records) that have been checked and approved in accordance with the company's procedures (control objectives 2, 3, 4, and 5 and Question (6.c.)?
    (ii) Substitute documents (such as remittance advices or check requisitions) that provide adequate evidence of the validity of the related transactions?

  g. Are the supporting documents effectively cancelled by, or under the control of, the signatories to prevent subsequent reuse?

  h. If a mechanical check signer is in use, is there adequate control over the custody and use of the signer and the signature plates?

Control of checks and bank transfers after signing

  i. After signing, are checks and bank transfers forwarded directly to the payees (or to the bank with the bank transfer lists) without being returned to the originators or others who are in a position to introduce documents into the cash disbursements system?

Control Objective

7. General ledger entries arising from the payments cycle should be accurately determined.

	Flowchart		
Questionnaire	Ref.	Yes	No

Classification of expenditures

a. Is the coding of the following transactions for posting to general ledger accounts checked to an appropriate extent:

   (i) Invoices and other supporting documentation related to the payment of accounts payable?

   (ii) Payrolls?

   (iii) Reimbursements of imprest and similar funds?

   (iv) Disbursements from bank accounts not covered in (i) to (iii) above?

   (v) Depreciation of property, plant, and equipment?

CHAPTER
NINE

BUYING A COMPUTER

Once your accounting system has developed to the point that the procedural cycles are more or less continuous operations or your present data processing equipment is nearing the end of its useful life, you should begin to think about the possibility of investing in a small computer. As your business continues to grow, it is not unlikely that your present system will begin to show strain. Even before that happens, you may find that you cannot get information to help manage important operational matters such as inventory control, product line profitability or data needed to improve customer service.

Technological advances and attractive prices mean that the point of considering a computer or changing equipment comes earlier in a company's life cycle.

THE VALUE OF A COMPUTER TO YOUR BUSINESS

The modern business computer has the ability to:

Carry out, quickly and accurately, such simple tasks as price or wage calculations

Store and display a tremendous quantity of information

Transfer common data among different systems (for example, to feed sales order information directly through a production planning and stock system to the general ledger)

Relieve employees of routine mathematical or record-keeping tasks

In practical terms, these capabilities can translate into impressive benefits. Some examples are:

Order Processing. This provides quicker deliveries and more accurate order statistics.

Accounts Receivable. This gives faster routine billing and collection.

Inventory. This allows for reduced investment and improved availability.

Purchasing. This provides better cash management and improved purchasing history.

Payroll. This gives faster calculations and wider analysis of costs.

General Ledger Accounting. This allows for more timely management summaries.

Production Planning. This provides better use of manned production facilities.

EVALUATING YOUR COMPUTER NEEDS

Initially, you will have two questions to answer in connection with automation: first, Do I need it? and second, If so, how much, and what kind? These questions are not easy to answer; they require study and, unless you have a good knowledge of computerized accounting, a certain amount of expert assistance. If you act hastily, you run the risk of committing a potentially costly blunder, such as:

Computerizing systems that would be better processed by improved manual or semimechanized methods

Choosing a computer system that is unnecessarily expensive or complex or that cannot be expanded to accommodate additional work

Delegating systems development to a staff that lacks the proper technical skills or business understanding

Choosing a computer or software with poor vendor support or inappropriate processing techniques

To help the nontechnical owner–manager avoid these pitfalls, we will discuss:

The types of computers available and their costs

How to select the right system

The installation process

Preliminary Survey

Before you begin a detailed investigation of your computer needs, you should undertake a kind of preliminary survey, identifying:

The reasons for considering computerization

The overall objectives, taking into account your overall corporate objectives, and the expected benefits

The application areas to be examined

The cost justification for the system

The third of these steps involves identifying high priority areas, such as invoicing and sales analysis, and considering all applications related to these areas. The importance of this step lies in the fact that one of the major advantages of computers is their ability to integrate separate clerical tasks and reduce the duplication of information. For instance, once sales invoices are processed, the data can be reused for sales accounting and sales analysis without reinputting the information. If all the priority areas are not identified before the computer is installed, the accounting system can outgrow the equipment as more opportunities for linking with other areas are discovered.

Feasibility Study

If the preliminary survey turns up no decisive reason for postponing action, your next step would be to determine whether computerization is technically and economically feasible. Your feasibility study should include:

An analysis of the present systems, highlighting strengths and weaknesses

A sufficiently detailed outline design showing how the proposed systems will work so that other managers can understand and agree to the implications of the proposals

An analysis of current and projected data volumes

A proposed implementation timetable

Estimates of the costs and benefits of the new systems

In carrying out the study, bear in mind the following points:

Never replace an existing procedure with a computer system until you have carefully considered whether the same benefits could be more cheaply obtained in other ways. Sometimes, improving existing systems and procedures such as forms, filing systems, and clerical procedures; the layout of offices; or the pattern of work flow can render computerization unnecessary. Consider also use of a service bureau as an alternative to installation of a computer.

Seek the advice of computer salespersons only after you have a good understanding of your requirements. If you need expert advice in obtaining that understanding, use an independent consultant. It is only natural for computer salespersons to recommend an approach that demonstrates the best features of their own equipment—equipment that may not be the best for you.

TYPES OF COMPUTERS AND COSTS

If a decision is made to proceed, you can, in general, take two approaches: install your own in-house computers, or use a computer service bureau.

In-House Computers

If an in-house computer is chosen, three types of computers are suitable for smaller organizations: the small business computer or minicomputer, the microcomputer, and the programmable accounting machine.

Small Business Computers

The development of small business computers was led by a generation of computer manufacturers whose original work was in the scientific and educational fields. These firms developed a range of inexpensive processors geared to users working via multiple terminals. These processors were simple to operate and program and did not require special environmental conditions. They became known as minicomputers, and as a result of their adaptability to commercial data processing, versions of the basic models were packaged for the commercial market.

These computers, referred to as small business computers, incorporate the minicomputer concept of simplicity of systems development and operation. The computers are designed:

For the direct entry and checking of data and for immediately updating transactions and filing inquiries

For operation in an office with user staff, instead of a special computer operations staff, entering data and controlling the operation

To be capable of forming part of a computer network communicating with remote terminals and a large central computer

Small business computers offer on-line systems that allow each transaction—for example, a customer order—to be processed as soon as it is received. The latest equipment is typically based on multiple microprocessors, and thus the distinction between microcomputers and small business computers is disappearing. At the same time, the power and facilities of small business computers have increased dramatically.

Typical small business computer configurations include processors with either:

48,000 characters of memory, two keyboards and screens, 10 million characters of disk storage, and a printer operating at 180 characters per second (as low as $15,000)

128,000 characters of memory, four keyboards and screens, 20 million characters of disk storage, and a printer operating at 300 lines per minute (as low as $35,000)

The larger configuration could support an operation wherein a sales clerk is entering orders, an accounts clerk is posting cash to sales ledgers, a third clerk is making an inventory inquiry, and a fourth is initiating a batch payroll system, all simultaneously.

The attraction of small business computers is that they bring the facilities of powerful computers into the office. Instead of completing input forms, sending them to a remote central computer department for processing, and then receiving an error report many hours later listing data errors, the user can control the computer by entering data on a keyboard and having it checked immediately for errors. The processing then takes place on individual transactions and causes an immediate response. Systems can thus be designed in which, for example, an order for goods entered by a sales clerk can cause packing and dispatch instructions to be printed immediately on a remote printer in a separate area.

Microcomputers

A typical microcomputer for business use consists of:

A microprocessor with 48,000 characters of memory

Dual exchangeable floppy disk drives giving immediate access to one million characters of information (equivalent to about 8,000 to 10,000 stock records)

A printer operating at 60 characters per second

A visual display screen and keyboard.

The purchase price for this system would be about $6,500.

Microcomputers are suitable for a wide variety of tasks. On the equipment just described, a typical system covering order entry, inventory, sales analysis, and general ledger accounting could be implemented for a distributor with 5,000 items 500 customers, and 200 orders a day. The equipment can be used as a terminal that provides local processing capability and is linked via telephone lines to a larger central computer. Alternately, keyboard terminals can be installed at remote sites to capture data on cassette tapes for periodic transmission to a central computer.

The limitation of this type of equipment, at present, is that the volumes of work are effectively limited to the maximum number of transactions that can be entered via one keyboard (say, 500 per day) and can be supported by the maximum amount of disk storage possible (about 1 to 2 million characters). Growth beyond these volumes can be covered only by acquiring a second microcomputer or by moving up to a larger capacity computer. If this expansion is expected soon, it will be more sensible to start with a machine at the bottom end of the small business computer range. A machine with similar capabilities that can be enhanced by the addition of multiple keyboards, display screens, and larger disks can be purchased for about $9,000.

Programmable Accounting Machines

Programmable accounting machines (PAMs) have been popular over the last 10 years because they provide significant improvement in performance over normal accounting machines at a relatively low price. In the simplest form, they consist of

A programmable processor

A ledger card printing device and a separate forms printer

A keyboard

This type of configuration will cost about $15,000.

The speed of operation of a programmable accounting machine can be improved by using ledger cards with a magnetic stripe on which important information can be recorded, such as customer name and address and the balance outstanding. A PAM fitted with a magnetic stripe ledger card reader can be used on applications involving 500–1,000 transactions a day. It is normally impractical to base an order entry system, requiring instant access to product and credit control information, on a programmable accounting machine. Nevertheless, various enhancements have increased the versatility of PAM's, and it is now possible to add cassette tapes (similar to those used in stereo equipment) for recording sales analysis data during ledger posting.

PAMs became popular in office environments where they presented significant improvements over normal accounting machines. By comparison, modern microcomputers and small business machines can give constant access to information via display screens and allow greater throughput and system flexibility through the use of magnetic disk storage.

As programmable accounting machines no longer enjoy a cost advantage, it is normally difficult to justify their use in a new application unless a particular application package is available that results in a cost savings, or handling and circulating ledger cards throughout the company is an advantage.

Service Bureaus

Until recently, small organizations requiring computer facilities normally used a computer service bureau. The majority of service bureaus developed by offering basic batch processing services. For example, copies of invoices and cash receipts for a week would be grouped into batches and taken to the service bureau for data preparation and sales ledger processing. The service bureau would then return a series of printed reports, including customer statements, an aged debtors list, and a complete listing of the ledger. Another group of service bureaus offered remote computing services accessed by telephone using remote terminals; these became known as time-sharing bureaus and were used mainly by engineers and financial analysts for mathematical calculations requiring a brief time on a powerful computer. Over the last few years, the facilities offered by the two types of bureaus have tended to coalesce. In order to respond to the challenge of the small business computer, most service bureaus now offer a variety of remote data capture and communications capabilities. These include the installation:

In a user organization—of a terminal that allows users to undertake their own data preparation, transmit it periodically to the bureau, and have the resulting reports printed on the terminal

In a user organization—of an "intelligent" terminal (in effect, a minicomputer with disk storage linked by telephone line to the bureau) that allows data to be entered and checked and limited processing to be carried out before the data are transmitted for further processing

Of display screens, keyboards, and printers connected by telephone lines to the bureau

Many service bureaus claim they can offer users levels of operational convenience, performance, and inquiry facilities similar to those of the small business computer described earlier. Whether this claim is valid will depend on individual circumstances.

Because communication costs have not fallen as fast as processor costs, equipment costs alone tend to favor the installation of a small business computer. However, since a major cost in the total computer package relates to systems and program development, a service bureau might offer a special service based on software packages that have been proven in operation and that may not be available on a small business computer. It is not unusual for a company to use a service bureau for this type of application, even though it may install its own small computer for day-to-day processing requirements.

THE SELECTION PROCESS

You have now determined the system and general type of computer facility that you require and have also made a choice between an in-house computer and a service bureau. Your next step is to invite a selection of suppliers to present their proposals.

Inviting Supplier Proposals

To avoid misunderstandings and to provide a consistent basis for comparing proposals, you should give the suppliers a written statement of requirements. This should contain:

A brief description of the company, the existing processing systems, and the environment in which the system must operate

A description of the main purpose and features of each system required

An indication of the volume and content of each of the input documents and output reports you intend the system to produce and, where necessary, a description of the intermediate processing steps to clarify the logic of any complex requirements

Current and projected data volumes

An itemized statement of the information on costs, time frames, maintenance, experience, and staffing that suppliers must include in their proposals

The range of choice in suppliers is wide, making the job of selecting the best combination of features and price somewhat difficult. Here too, consider getting independent expert advice.

Many electronic data processing (EDP) suppliers handle both equipment and software. These firms, known as system houses, will either undertake the necessary systems and programming or supply applications software off the shelf. Currently, however, the trend is toward using nonsupplier specialists in the form either of employees—equivalent to acquiring a permanent in-house software capability—or of management consultants. There are, of course, advantages in dealing with only one contractor, but many businesses have found that the supplier of the best hardware is frequently lacking in the skills and experience necessary to understand the business's particular systems requirements. For this reason, many computer manufacturers do not offer systems development support and thus refer customers to systems houses.

Evaluating Proposals

You should give suppliers a reasonable time in which to submit their proposals. In assessing the proposals, ask yourself the following questions:

Can the proposed equipment process the current and planned workload within defined time limits?

Are the proposed terminal response times adequate?

Can the components of the equipment be expanded to handle increased workloads?

How versatile, reliable, and easy to use are the computer programs (systems software) supplied with the equipment to control its operation?

How well do the bidders understand the application system requirements, and how sound is their approach to system design?

What is the user history of the proposed application packages?

How reliable is the equipment and the quality of engineering maintenance?

Selecting a Service Bureau

The recommended procedure for selecting a computer bureau is essentially the same as for buying the equipment or software: several bureaus should be asked to quote against defined requirements. The criteria for evaluation are also the same, except that with service bureaus you must consider ability to provide efficient day-to-day operational service. The extent to which an outfit can be relied on to keep your computerized operations going in emergencies, such as mechanical breakdowns and fires, is also a consideration. The measure of reliability is not only the capacity to provide the emergency services but also the willingness to undertake contingency commitments.

INSTALLING THE COMPUTER

Once you have chosen your EDP system and your contractors, you are ready to enter the development phase of computerization. This is a difficult period not only in a technical but also in a human sense. EDP interfaces with people, and in certain circumstances, people have trouble getting used to it. It is important, therefore, to proceed cautiously; obstacles that arise in this period tend to be difficult to remove later.

The Development Plan

Your first step should be to appoint an automation manager, giving him or her overall responsibility for the development phase. (Most large consulting and accounting firms have on hand people with the necessary qualifications for this job.) Have the automation manager, in consultation with you, your department heads, and your contractors, draw up a detailed development plan and address the following:

Specification of user requirements in each of the areas to be computerized   .

Agreement to and acceptance of the specification by the users

Design of supporting clerical procedures

Production of a system and program specifications

Preparation of computer programs

Preparation of user instructions

Site preparation and installation of facilities such as:

Communications systems

Air conditioning

Electrical connections and cabling

Fire prevention and safety equipment

Security systems

Computer room furniture

Installation of computer equipment

Equipment acceptance testing

Training of user staff

Preparation of computer operating instructions

Systems testing and analysis of systems test results

Creation of computer master files

Pilot and parallel running of each system and checking of results by users

Systems acceptance by users

Post-implementation review

The chart in Figure 9.1 summarizes the major steps you should consider in introducing automation in your business. Remember, with careful planning you can avoid costly mistakes.

Controls

One of the major challenges you will have to face when you automate is the problem of setting up controls to curb errors in, and fraudulent manipulation of, your automated procedures.

A small business computer system requires more specific controls than does a large one. Like their counterparts in middle-size and large organizations, smaller systems often incorporate integrated applications with on-line—that is, directly linked to the computer—input, processing, and update of data files. Yet typically, the atmosphere of a small operation is informal, making it difficult to keep unauthorized persons away from the computer. In addition, small operations seldom have much in-house technical capability, so they cannot rely on ad hoc investigations to police their automated activities to the same degree as better-staffed, larger operations can.

The American Institute of Certified Public Accountants identifies two major types of controls relevant to all EDP installations: integrity or general controls and application controls.

Integrity Controls

Generally, integrity controls are aimed at the prevention or detection of fraud, direction of computer resources, and concentration of functions in EDP. This kind of control is inherent in the plan of organization and operation of the EDP activity and in the procedures for documenting reviewing, testing, and approving systems or programs. Other integrity con-

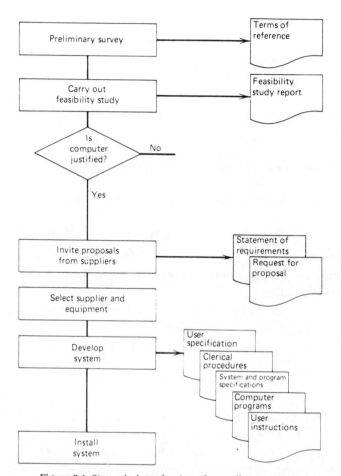

Figure 9.1. Stages in introduction of a small computer.

trols include those built into the equipment, those over access to equipment, and certain others concerned with data or procedures and affecting overall EDP operations. The following discussion focuses on integrity controls that are especially relevant to the needs of small businesses.

Controls on Access. These controls include:

Restricted access to terminals through use of key locks, badge readers, and so on

Lockup of terminals when not in use

Safe storage and periodic change of locks and keys

Password requirement for sign-on to a terminal

Periodic change in passwords

Controls Supporting User Dependence on the System. These controls include:

Adequate fallback procedures fully documented

Controls on EDP Personnel. These controls include:

A formal organizational structure within the EDP department

Thorough checking of new employee references

Prohibition on programmers and analysts working in other areas of the organization

Involvement of management, users, and auditors in new systems design and in system maintenance activities

Continuous logging of computer processing

Application Controls

Application controls relate to specific tasks performed by EDP. They are designed to provide reasonable assurance that the system is recording, processing, and reporting data completely and accurately. Application controls are often categorized as input controls, processing controls, or output controls. A checklist of items to consider in defining application controls for a small business computer system is as follows:

Input Controls. These controls include:

Requirement for approval of all source documents

Procedures for unauthorized forms

Batching and totaling source documents

Continuous logging of batches entered

Required initialing of source documents

Design of programs to: (1) validate all input data extensively; (2) require error correction before proceeding; and (3) accumulate totals during processing

Data entry instructions for all functions

Instructions for abnormal termination of processing

Review of audit trails and logs

Processing Controls.   These controls include:

Periodic balance of file controls against manually calculated totals

Verification of processing date in month-end and year-end processing programs

Checklist of functions to be performed

Procedures for timely handling of suspense items

Output Controls.   These controls include:

Schedules for preparation of reports

Verification of report totals against manually calculated totals

Incorporation of appropriate printing control techniques in reports

Checklist for report distribution

Procedures to prevent "spooled" reports from remaining in the system too long

Password requirement for access to inquiry screens

Other Controls

In addition to integrity and application controls, there are other basic controls that you should not overlook when you install your automated system. Most of these are concerned with physical security—a broad category that includes protection of equipment, software, and records (the latter largely from premature destruction). Provisions for contingencies (maintaining service in adverse circumstances) also comprise a category of controls.

CHAPTER
TEN

FRINGE BENEFIT PLANS

Retirement Plans
    Qualified versus Nonqualified
    Pension Plans
      Defined Benefit Plans
      Defined Contribution Plans
   Other Plans
    Floor Plans
    Combination of Pension and Profit-Sharing Plans
    Keogh Plans
    Thrift Plans
    Cash or Deferred Compensation Plans
    Stock Ownership Plans
    Individual Retirement Accounts
    Tax-Sheltered Annuities
    Simplified Employee Pension Plans
   Health and Welfare Plans
    Accident and Health Insurance
    Uninsured Medical Reimbursement Plans
   Funding Arrangements
    Individual Insurance Policies
      Applicability

Group Insurance Contracts
Banks and Savings and Loan Institutions
Individual versus Group Life Insurance
Summary

Fringe benefit plans can make a significant contribution to the security of employees and owner–managers and provide substantial tax advantages at the same time. For employers, the benefits, which include pension and welfare plans as well as executive perquisites, are important tools for attracting and retaining personnel. Not to establish, or at least consider establishing, a pension or profit-sharing plan can be a bad mistake. For one thing, as owner–manager, you may be able to make youself the principal recipient of program benefits. For another, if the plan qualifies for special tax treatment, you can use it to shelter income. Finally, as a management tool, fringe benefit plans can have a positive effect on employees attitudes toward themselves and the goals of the company and often result in improved productivity and a more reliable workforce.

Retirement and other "income security" plans present the most interesting and challenging decisions to the owner–manager, and it is with these that we will deal primarily in this chapter. We will also cover several kinds of health and welfare plans.

BASICS OF A WELL-DESIGNED PROGRAM

The following conditions are characteristic of a well-designed benefit program:

The level of benefits is high enough to attract and hold key employees, but the program is not designed to provide an incentive for key employees who become ineffective to continue working, making their termination difficult.

Plans are coordinated with one another and with government benefits—including Social Security, Medicare, unemployment insurance, and worker's compensation insurance—to preclude overlapping. For example, where there is a long-term disability insurance policy in force, as well as a retirement plan, no disability benefits are paid out under the latter until benefits under the former expire. Similarly, the benefit under the disability program is reduced (or offset) by some or all of the Social Security payable on disability. Thus, it should be possible for a younger worker earning less than the company average who becomes disabled and eligible for Social Security never to receive a benefit from the employer's plan, because the Social Security benefit exceeds what the company plan would have provided.

All the significant hazards that an employee is reasonably likely to face are considered.

Benefits are funded on an economical basis, with resulting tax savings.

Benefits are allocated, within allowable limitations, to the employee groups that are most important to the organization.

Benefits are related to the objectives of the organization.

Need for Experts

The whole area of benefits planning is highly complex. To accommodate the many needs of even a modest-size organization with a single plan would be difficult enough without the myriad of applicable government regulations covering taxation and security of benefits. In developing your benefit package or evaluating your existing one, you must work with at least one professional—a benefits consultant or an actuary—and often it is also advisable to have a lawyer. This chapter is designed to give you the basic understanding you will need to evaluate their recommendations properly.

RETIREMENT PLANS

A retirement plan is a plan that pays out benefits to the employees primarily, but not exclusively, on retirement. The term takes in a variety of arrangements, of which we will discuss the most important. Retirement plans may be distinguished according to whether they are qualified or nonqualified.

Qualified versus Nonqualified

The Internal Revenue Code of 1954 and the regulations issued under this body of law by the IRS establish rules for retirement plans covering minimum participation, vesting, minimum funding, and so forth. If a plan meets these requirements, it is deemed "qualified" and is subject to favorable tax treatment. It is unusual to preclude qualification. (Plans that are so designed are generally set up to provide particular benefits to a limited number of top executives.) For this reason, you may assume that plans discussed in this chapter are qualified unless we state otherwise.

The major advantages of a qualified plan are as follows:

An employer contribution to a qualified retirement plan is tax deductible. Thus, the federal government contributes a portion of the plan's cost.

The investment income and capital appreciation of the plan's assets are not taxed until distributed to plan participants or their beneficiaries.

Company contributions do not become taxable income to an employee until the employee receives benefit payments.

Lump-sum distributions of plan assets and investment income receive special tax treatment if the employee meets certain requirements. The treatment takes the form of a 10-year forward-averaging provision, whereby the distribution is divided by 10 and the tax on this result is computed using the tax rate for a single individual with no exemptions. This result is then multiplied by 10 to get the total tax due, which will usually be substantially lower than the tax on the aggregate distribution at the graduated rates.

Qualified plans also have some notable disadvantages. For example:

They usually require a current cash outlay in the form of an annual contribution. (This is an expense item, however, and thus decreases reported income.)

Employees with short service may be rewarded. Under current rules and regulations, the vesting schedules often require a plan to provide an employee terminating service after 4 years with 40 percent of the funds accumulated for him or her under a retirement plan. Some vesting schedules require 100 percent after 10 years.

Administrative expenses, including the cost of in-house paperwork and fees to lawyers, actuaries, and accountants, can be significant.

A qualified plan cannot discriminate in favor of shareholders, owners, and other highly compensated individuals. The Employee Retirement

Income Security Act of 1974 and numerous regulations issued by the IRS specifically address this point. For purposes of this antidiscrimination provision, all employees of all corporations that are members of a controlled group of corporations are considered to be employed by a single corporation. Therefore, years of service with any of the corporations must be counted for participation and vesting purposes, and the limitations on benefits and contributions apply as though the employees were participants under one plan.

A plan that is terminated within 10 years after inception without a valid reason may be denied qualified status retroactively to its inception. In that event, employer income tax deductions for contributions to the plan will be disallowed for all open tax years. In addition, the benefits of the 25 most highly paid employees may be scaled down if the plan's benefits are not fully funded.

With the assistance of an expert benefits consultant, you can usually minimize the impact of at least one, and often most, of these drawbacks.

Pension Plans

Pension plans generally fall into one of two categories: defined benefit and defined contribution.

Defined Benefit Plans

In a defined benefit plan, the employer undertakes to contribute the necessary amount to provide a specific benefit. The benefit is generally payable monthly and is stated as a sum of money, a percentage of average compensation, or a percentage of compensation times years of service.

A typical benefit might call for lifetime payments beginning upon retirement of $1,000 a month or 50 percent of average salary. The benefit is usually a function of at least one, and sometimes all, of the following factors:

Age at which benefits commence

Service accumulated at termination of employment, often including service before the adoption of the plan

Salary earned during employment or during a shorter period, such as 5 or 10 years, before retirement

The amount of the employer contribution is actuarially determined on the basis of these factors together with the expected investment return on plan assets and the probabilities of termination of employment due to all causes, including death and disability. There are six mathematical models, called actuarial cost methods, that may be used in determining the annual pension costs. Regardless of which of these methods is used, the maximum annual retirement benefit that can result in 1982 is the lesser of either $136,425 or 100 percent of the average annual income for whatever three consecutive years have the highest total income. To qualify for this maximum, an employee must have at least 10 years of service credit. This dollar limitation has been adjusted upward every year in accordance with the change in the national average wage.

Beginning in 1983, the maximum dollar limit will be reduced to $90,000 for defined benefit plans. The change is intended to scale back the benefits derived by highly paid individuals from qualified plans. The new dollar limitation will remain in effect through 1985 and will be adjusted for cost of living increases for later years according to the Social Security benefit index formula then in effect.

Sometimes the employer's contribution will be defined in terms of an interval ranging from the miminum funding amount required by ERISA to the maximum contribution that will be tax deductible. If the employer contributes in excess of the minimum funding requirement, the excess amounts build up a credit that may be used in future years to offset that requirement. The credit can grow to the point at which it equals an entire year's minimum required contribution. Not all actuarial cost methods provide this feature, so it is important to discuss the choice of method with your actuary at the time you decide on the plan you want.

A Tool for the Employer Manager.   It is possible for an owner–employee to allocate a large portion of the contribution to a defined benefit plan to him- or herself under the following conditions:

The owner–employee has long service, is older than 45 (approximately), and is highly paid.

Other employees have short service, are young, and are at the lower end of the pay scale.

These conditions are exceptional, but that does not mean that you cannot design a defined benefit pension plan to favor yourself, to some degree at least, without forfeiting other key plan objectives.

Beginning 1984, new restrictions will apply to plans that are considered to favor key employees, i.e., so-called "top-heavy" plans. Under the new law, a defined benefit plan is considered top heavy if the present value of accrued benefits of key employees exceeds 60 percent of the present value of accrued benefits of all planned participants. Considered as key employees are officers, 5-percent owners, 1-percent owners earning more than $150,000, and employees owning the ten largest interests in the employer. Top-heavy plans are subject to special rules affecting vesting, contributions, and benefits.

Although the new rules will generally increase costs for employers maintaining top-heavy plans, the benefits for key employees will still be substantial in most situations. Top heavy plans will continue to provide immediate deductions for contributions, tax free accumulations of trust earnings, and favorable income tax treatment for certain plan distributions.

Advantages and Disadvantages.   The following characteristics of a defined benefit pension plan are advantageous:

The plan provides a definite benefit that the participants can rely upon.

There may be a degree of flexibility in funding.

The plan can provide a benefit formula that automatically takes into account salary increases.

Benefits, at least in part, are insured by government through the Pension Benefit Guaranty Corporation.

Service prior to the effective date of the plan can be recognized.

The following characteristics are disadvantageous:

The plan usually requires a minimum annual contribution.

Administrative costs may be higher than they are in other plans because of the actuarial calculations required.

The company assumes the responsibility for the satisfactory investment performance of the plan's assets. If the investment yield is less than anticipated, the company's contributions may increase in future years to meet the promised benefits.

If the plan is terminated, the company may be liable to the government's Pension Benefit Guaranty Corporation for the excess of the present value of guaranteed benefits over the plan's assets, up to 30 percent of the net worth of the company.

Defined Contribution Plans

Defined Contribution Pension Plan.   One type of defined contribution plan is a defined contribution pension plan, also referred to as a money purchase pension plan. In this plan, the employer's contribution is fixed, but the benefits are not. The amount of contributions and investment income accumulated in the plan determines the level of benefits available for payment to participants. For each employee, there is an individual pension account to which the employer promises to contribute annually. The amount is almost always defined as a percentage of the participant's pay. The maximum contribution permitted is 25 percent of salary, up to $45,475 in 1982, for any one participant. As with defined benefit plans, the dollar limitation has been annually adjusted upward in accordance with the change in the national average wage. Investment earnings, including realized and unrealized gains and losses are also allocated to individual participant accounts. At retirement, the employee withdraws funds from his or her account to satisfy retirement needs.

Beginning in 1983, the maximum dollar limit will be reduced to $30,000 for defined contribution plans, and that limit will remain in effect through 1985. In 1986 and later years, this dollar limitation will be adjusted for cost-of-living increases according to the Social Security benefit index formula then in effect. Also, beginning in 1984, the new top-heavy plan rules will apply to defined contribution plans. A defined contribution plan is top heavy if more than 60 percent of the account balances have been accumulated on behalf of key employees.

The annual defined contribution is reduced by any amounts forfeited by employees who terminate and are not 100 percent vested. Thus, there is no flexibility in funding.

A defined contribution pension plan favors the owner–employee under the following conditions:

The owner–employee is young and has little or no service.

The company's income expectations for the periods the plan will be in operation are solidly grounded.

Other employees, regardless of their age and service, are at a level of pay lower than that of the owner–manager.

The following characteristics of a defined contribution pension plan are advantageous:

The contribution can be easily determined.

Administration is simpler than it is for a defined benefit plan, and consequently administrative costs are lower.

There is no potential liability to the Pension Benefit Guaranty Corporation.

Contributions are allocated to individual accounts, which employees can easily understand.

The plan can be combined with a defined benefit pension plan for fewer restrictions on contributions (see "Combination of Pension and Profit-Sharing Plans" in this chapter).

The following characteristics are disadvantageous:

There is no flexibility in funding.

The employee bears the investment risk.

There is no promised retirement income that the employee can rely upon.

Service prior to the establishment of the plan cannot be effectively recognized.

The company must maintain records of individual employee accounts.

Profit-Sharing Plans. The other type of defined contribution plan is a profit-sharing plan. This plan can have a defined contribution feature, but the contribution is established in relation to some aspect of profitability, such as a percentage of pretax profit. Thus, in most profit-sharing plans, there would be no contribution in any year in which there were no profits, except for the contribution required under the rules for plan qualification. (In certain plans structured along profit-sharing lines, management does accept a contributory obligation not contingent on profits; see "Thrift Plans" in this chapter.) The rules for plan qualification call for a "substantial and recurring" contribution; *recurring* is usually construed by pension consultants as not less than once every three years, if there are profits.

More frequently, a profit-sharing plan can also be designed without *any* specified contribution; that is, the amount of the contribution, if any, is entirely at the discretion of management, subject, of course, to the above-mentioned regulatory requirement.

The maximum annual company contribution is limited to 15 percent of the *aggregate* compensation of all the plan members. As with a defined contribution pension plan, however, the maximum amount that may be allocated to any *individual's* account in any year is 25 percent of pay, up to $45,475 in 1982. Again, the dollar amount has been adjusted annually on the basis of national average wages; in 1983 it will be reduced to $30,000. Under a profit-sharing plan, any amounts forfeited by employees who terminate before they are 100 percent vested may be reallocated to the individual accounts of the remaining participants or used to reduce future company contributions.

A profit-sharing plan is ideal for a new business where the following conditions exist:

The owner–employee is young.

The company desires flexibility in funding.

There is rapid turnover of employees—advantageous because of the correspondingly high level of forfeitures that augment the interests of the remaining plan participants. (Forfeitures are, however, included with contributions in determining the maximum amount that may be allocated to any member's account.)

The advantages of defined contribution pension plans also apply in general to profit-sharing plans. The profit-sharing plan, however, has the major advantage of flexibility in determining the annual contribution. The chief drawbacks of profit-sharing plans are:

An owner–employee with long service cannot shelter as much income as under a defined benefit plan, especially if the other employees are younger and have short service.

There is no flexibility in funding when the contribution is specified in the plan (for example, by formula).

There is no promised retirement income that the employee can rely upon.

The employee bears the investment risk.

Service prior to the establishment of the plan cannot be effectively recognized.

The company must maintain records of individual employee accounts.

OTHER PLANS

Not all benefit plans fall neatly into one or another of the basic categories of retirement plans described in the preceding discussion. Certain plans partake of the characteristics of defined benefit and defined contribution or even of pension and profit sharing. Moreover, some plans have features that are distinct from any so far discussed. The following subsection deals with the more common of these benefit plan variants.

Floor Plans

A floor plan is a defined contribution pension plan or a profit-sharing plan with the added feature of a promised, defined benefit. At retirement, the employee receives the greater of the defined benefit or the amount that can be provided from his or her individual account balance. The principal advantages of floor plans are:

The contributions are allocated to individual accounts that employees can easily understand.

The plan can be designed to favor the owner–employee (within the constraints imposed by the new top-heavy rules).

There is a promised minimum retirement income on which the employee can rely.

Service prior to the effective date of the plan can be recognized.

The following conditions constitute the chief disadvantages of the plans:

There is a potential liability to the Pension Benefit Guaranty Corporation.

Each annual contribution must be supported by an actuarial valuation.

Records of individual employee accounts must be maintained.

The employer assumes downside investment risks, to the extent of the minimum benefits i.e., the floor.

Combination of Pension and Profit-Sharing Plans

Many organizations start out with pension plans and later add profit-sharing plans to increase retirement benefits and to provide incentives to younger employees. Conversely, many begin with a profit-sharing plan and later add a pension plan when fixed commitments can be safely undertaken. Finally, there are companies that have both types of plans at the outset.

The maximum deductible contribution allowed when a company combines a profit-sharing plan with a defined benefit or a defined contribution pension plan is 25 percent of the annual pay of the plan participants. If, therefore, the minimum contribution required to the defined benefit plan equals or exceeds 25 percent of pay, no additional contribution can be made to the profit-sharing plan. This limitation is not imposed on the combination of a defined benefit plan and a defined contribution pension plan, since these plans each require minimum contributions.

Keogh Plans

The Keogh, or HR–10, plan is a type of pension plan designed for partnerships, sole proprietorships, and corporations that elect to file their returns under Subchapter S of the Internal Revenue Code. Keogh plans have the favorable tax treatment afforded other plans, but contributions and the accrual of benefits have been more restricted. In 1982, the maximum contribution that could be made for an individual in a defined contribution Keogh plan is the lesser of either 15 percent of the participant's compensation or $15,000. By comparison, the maximum allocation on behalf of a participant in a money purchase pension or profit-sharing plan is either 25 percent of his or her compensation or $45,475, whichever is less.

Beginning in 1984, however, larger contributions and benefits will be permitted under Keogh plans. As a result of the Equity and Fiscal Responsibility Act of 1982, Keogh and corporate plans will be subject to the same deduction limits. The effect of this change is summarized in the following table.

Most Keogh plans are of the defined contribution type. Defined benefit plans are permitted, but because of restrictions on benefits, they have sel-

Limit	Defined Contribution	Defined Benefit
Old law	Lesser of 15% of earnings or $15,000.	Effectively limited by restrictions on accruals for self-employed.
New law	*Profit sharing plans— lesser of 15% of aggregate compensation or $30,000; *Money purchase plans— lesser of 25% of compensation or $30,000	Actuarially determined— same as corporate defined benefit plan limits.

*For self-employed individuals, earnings have been redefined so that these percentage limitations apply to net earnings less *all* deductible contributions to the plan.

dom offered any advantage over the defined contribution arrangement. Beginning in 1984, Keogh plans will be able to provide post-service benefits. Thanks to this change, there will be as much flexibility and latitude in the design of Keogh plans as there has been in the design of corporate plans.

Besides the restrictions on contributions and benefit accrual, there were special rules for qualification applicable to Keogh plans. These special rules have been repealed effective in 1984.

The repeal of the Keogh rules and the addition of top-heavy plan restrictions will effectively eliminate the differences in the rules applying to corporate and noncorporate plans. Only minor differences remain. As a result, in the future there will be no advantage for professionals to incorporate their practices to obtain greater retirement benefits.

Current Status of Professional Corporations. In addition to discouraging the formation of professional service corporations, the new law affects existing professional corporations. The IRS will be permitted to disregard the corporate tax status of certain personal service corporations in which substantially all of the services are performed by employee-owners for or on behalf of another corporation, partnership or entity (including related parties). This provision aims at individuals who have incorporated principally for tax advantages. In these situations, income, deductions, credits, exclusions, etc. of the corporation may be allocated to the employee-owners (i.e., more-than-10 percent owners of the outstanding stock).

This change may even encourage existing personal service corporations to liquidate. The law includes a transitional rule for 1983 and 1984 under which these corporations may complete a one-month liquidation (see Chapter 6) without risking taxation on unrealized receivables. Income represented by unrealized receivables will retain its character as ordinary income and will be recognized by the shareholder on collection or other disposition. The rules are effective for 1983.

Thrift Plans

Employee thrift plans or savings plans are retirement plans that call for employee as well as employer contributions. The plans are structured on the defined contribution principle: the employer's contribution is a function of the amount or rate of the employee's contribution—which is, of course, voluntary. For example, the employer may contribute 50 cents for every dollar from the employee. Thus, by limiting the amount of the employee contribution, management can limit its own contribution. A thrift plan may be of the pension or the profit-sharing type. (In the latter case, the plan would be one of the few profit-sharing plans with management's contribution not hinged on profits.) Besides providing employees with an incentive to save on a regular basis, thrift plans also offer them tax advantages. Neither company contributions nor fund earnings are taxable to the plan participants until distributed. Company contributions are tax deductible when made. A recent study indicated that more than half of the large industrial companies in the United States have thrift plans.

Cash or Deferred Compensation Plans

Employers may offer elective deferred compensation arrangements to employees—in other words, each employee can decide whether to receive cash or to have the same amount contributed to a qualified profit-sharing or stock bonus plan. These plans, referred to as 401K plans, must follow certain antidiscrimination rules. They provide that contributions by the company are deductible but will not be taxed to the employee until withdrawn from the plan.

Employers may offer the cash or deferred compensation choice to employees in a number of ways. One way is to offer an annual bonus; another is to offer a salary reduction plan, with taxable salary to be decreased by the amount deferred. Salary reduction plans may be especially attractive to employees now making nondeductible contributions to thrift or savings plans with aftertax dollars. This plan allows them to make an equivalent contribution with pretax dollars. Where employees agree to a salary reduction, the employer's outlay will be reduced as a result of lower Social Security to the extent that salaries are reduced below the maximum wage base of $32,400.

Stock Ownership Plans

There are several types of stock ownership plans that a company can adopt. Basically, the objective of these plans is to give employees a stake in the company through stock ownership. The contributions of the employer can be related to profits. Contributions are often made in stock, and benefits may be distributed in stock. For purposes of allocating the employer's stock, such plans are subject to the same requirements as a profit-sharing plan.

Employee stock ownership plans, known as ESOPs (plans structured as trusts are known as ESOTs) yield attractive tax advantages. The plans can also be used as a technique of corporate financing. The ESOP or ESOT obtains a loan from a financial institution for the purpose of acquiring company stock. The loan is guaranteed by the company, and the company can use the funds paid to it by the plan for its capital stock as it chooses.

Existing legislation provides for a specially designed ESOP or ESOT that allows the employer to elect an investment tax credit through 1982. The Economic Recovery Tax Act of 1981 amended, effective in 1983, the Tax Reduction Act ESOP (TRASOP) rules, so that the investment-related tax credit is replaced by a tax credit based on the compensation of plan participants.

The major disadvantage of the ESOP–ESOT is that the participant must be offered the right to be paid in stock. The impact of this feature is not usually felt until the plan is several years old, but if you fail to consider this factor at the time you formulate your plan, you may be saddled later with an ownership structure far from what you intended.

Individual Retirement Accounts

For the owner–manager who wants to avoid much of the cost and complexity involved in other programs, the individual retirement account (IRA), or individual retirement annuity, may be the best arrangement, particularly because, unlike other pension programs, IRAs, can be established for a select group of employees. The employer contributes to each employee's IRA accounts up to either $2,000 or 100 percent of earnings annually, whichever is less. The contribution is reported as ordinary income on the employee's W–2 tax form, but the employee, in preparing his or her return, deducts the employer's contribution as a personal contribution to his or her IRA account. As in other qualified plans, the income earned by the plan assets is not taxable until distributed. Substantial penalties are imposed, however, except in the event of death or disability, if withdrawals are made before age 59½.

Individual retirement accounts may be adopted by all individuals, including those who are active participants in other qualified plans.

Tax-Sheltered Annuities

Tax-sheltered annuities (TSAs) are similar to IRAs but are available only to employees of certain tax-exempt charitable, educational, or religious organizations, or to employees of a public school system or state or local educational institution.

Like IRAs, TSAs permit an employer to contribute funds to the TSA accounts of a select group of employees. The contribution is excluded from the employee's gross income for income tax purposes.

Simplified Employee Pension Plans

Simplified employee pension plans (SEPs) may be adopted by a corporation, a partnership, or a sole proprietorship. Such plans were authorized in the Tax Revenue Act of 1978. SEPs combine many of the features of Keogh and IRA plans. They do not, however, offer the favorable tax treatment on distribution characteristic of Keogh plans. Also, the SEPs must cover all employees who have attained the age of 25 and have completed three years of service. These features, plus the amount of administration and reporting to the government required by the plans (which, notwithstanding the intentions of the plans' designers, is frequently considerable) may explain why these plans have not come into wide use.

HEALTH AND WELFARE PLANS

Health and welfare plans generally consist of life and accident as well as health and disability insurance programs. These plans are popular among entrepreneurs because of the large coverage at a relatively low cost.

The benefit packages offered by various insurers in the health and welfare area differ widely in coverage and in cost. It is essential, therefore, to shop around before you adopt a particular plan. Assistance by independent experts in this area can help you evaluate various proposals.

Accident and Health Insurance

The major forms of accident and health insurance include hospital insurance, surgical and medical insurance, major medical, and disability income coverage.

Premiums paid by an employer for accident and health benefit plans are generally tax deductible as ordinary and necessary business expenses. In the absence of a plan, the employer may also deduct reimbursement to employees for medical expenses under limited circumstances. Amounts received by employees under employer-financed accident and health plans are generally excluded from gross income. Premiums paid by an employer for such coverage are similarly excluded from the employee's income. Thus, amounts received as reimbursement for medical care are not taxable.

Wage continuation plans cover payments for income lost from personal injury or sickness resulting in "permanent and total" disability. The amount excluded from income cannot exceed $5,200 per disabled spouse annually and is reduced dollar for dollar to the extent the employee's adjusted gross income exceeds $15,000.

Disability insurance premiums paid by an owner–employee outside of the corporation—that is, personally—are not deductible to the corporation or the individual. The benefits under such policies, however, are not taxable. Benefits under a company-sponsored wage continuation plan for the owner–employee with adjusted gross income in excess of $15,000 will be at least partially taxable. Therefore, when the benefits are to exceed $15,000, it would make sense to select the personally owned-and-paid-for policy. The cash needed to meet additional premium payments could be obtained from the corporation in the form of salary increases.

Uninsured Medical Reimbursement Plans

Besides being subject to the same limitations on excludability that are applicable to insured plans, uninsured medical plans must comply with special stringent nondiscrimination rules. Where amounts paid to "highly compensated employees" fail to satisfy these nondiscrimination rules, these amounts will be treated as excess reimbursements and will be taxable to those individuals. Highly compensated individuals include the five highest-paid officers, more-than-10-percent shareholders, and the highest-paid 25 percent of all employees.

FUNDING ARRANGEMENTS

The more common funding arrangements used for retirement plans and related administrative cost considerations are highlighted in the following subsections.

Individual Insurance Policies

Many retirement plans with 25 or fewer participants are funded with individual whole-life insurance policies and an auxiliary fund. The fund holds pension plan assets required over and above the cash values of the individual insurance policies. The company purchases for the plan whole-life insurance on the participants' lives at a guaranteed annual cost. These policies are owned by the retirement plan, and the company is allowed a deduction for the premiums paid. Often the insurance company agrees to assume most of the administrative burden connected with the plans at little or no charge.

Applicability

The chief drawbacks of this kind of funding are high commissions and the low yields realized under individual insurance policies. In most cases, group insurance outside the retirement program will give more benefits for the same level of contributions. In addition, group programs offer the participants major tax advantages over individual policies (see "Individual versus Group Life Insurance" in this chapter).

Group Insurance Contracts

For retiremènt plans that use contemporary group insurance contracts, there is a choice of two general types of contracts: the Deposit Administration (DA) contract, or the Immediate Participation Guarantee (IPG) contract. Funds are not allocated to individual participants under these contracts.

Under a DA contract, the insurer guarantees the rate of interest to be credited to the pension fund for a specified number of years. At the end of the specified period, the insurer may revise the interest guarantees on the basis of investment performance and actual expenses during the period. If the company refuses to accept the revised guarantees, it can opt out of the plan, but at a price—specifically, a penalty imposed for contract termination.

The IPG contract works much like an equity account in that the interest credited represents the actual investment result achieved by the insurance company. The actual expenses incurred are charged against the fund. Thus, there is no need for periodic revision of the rates based on experience. This type of contract is usually designed for plans with an annual contribution in excess of $50,000. Like DA accounts, IPG contracts have clauses designed to deter termination of the contract.

Banks and Savings and Loan Institutions

Banks and savings and loan institutions have many investment arrangements available. For small pension funds, banks usually recommend that a plan's assets be invested in one or more pooled funds, such as an equity fund, a fixed-income fund, a short-term fund, or a balanced equity and fixed-income fund.

Banks and savings and loan associations provide limited administrative services; for example, they will often allocate contributions to individual accounts under a defined contribution pension or profit-sharing plan. They do not provide actuarial services, however, so that you will probably need consultants to assist you in this and other administrative aspects.

Individual Versus Group Life Insurance

As previously mentioned, due to high commissions and low yields achieved by individual insurance policies, the premiums for group insurance are lower. Also, individual insurance policies do not permit, except indirectly, coordination with other benefits, including those provided by the employer and those stemming from the death and disability features of Social Security.

A major advantage of group insurance over individual life is that under the former, the cost of up to $50,000 of coverage is not taxable to the employee but the premiums are deductible by the employer. At death, the beneficiary has no reportable income. Further, through assignment, it is possible for the death benefits to be kept out of the insured's estate.

Nevertheless, individual insurance does have some applications, especially where large amounts are needed on only a few individuals. Some of these applications are:

Buy–Sell Agreements.   These agreements are used in partnerships or closely held companies and require that upon the death or disability of one of the owners (or partners) the remaining owners (or partners) will automatically buy out that owner's interest in the business. For this purpose, individual disability insurance can be as important as individual life insurance.

To Insure Key People.   Corporations whose success is contingent upon certain key individuals will purchase insurance to protect the company or tide it over during a period of transition upon such individual's death or disability.

To Ensure Liquidity for Estate Tax Purposes.   Individual life insurance affords an assured way of generating cash to meet estate taxes that arise on the death of individuals who have large estates.

Summary

Except in very special cases, failure to use at least one fringe benefit plan is incompatible with good business practice. There is no shortcut to benefits planning; you must work out the optimal arrangement for yourself and your employees in the light of your objectives, the annual cost, flexibility in funding, administrative costs, and taxation. A qualified benefits consultant is indispensable to this process.

CHAPTER
ELEVEN

TAX STRATEGIES AND TRAPS

I n our experience, many owner–managed businesses fail to take advantage of the wide variety of legitimate tax-planning devices available. To reduce income taxes, they often use simplistic methods, such as undervaluing inventory, that can actually result in economic losses. This chapter is not intended to enable you to dispense with competent and creative tax advice. What we try to do is lay the foundation for a knowledge of tax-saving mechanisms available so that you can work effectively with your tax counsel to ensure that all avenues—and pitfalls—have been considered.

We will cover such matters as hiring family members, medical reimbursement plans, travel and entertainment expenses, country club memberships, compensation, and inventory valuation. We will also cover tax traps relating to accumulated earnings, personal holding companies, losses and expenses among related parties, and collapsible corporations. Tax matters relating to the form in which a business operates, such as a corporation, Subchapter S, partnership, or proprietorship, are treated in Chapter 5; estate planning matters, in Chapter 12; and fringe benefit plans, in Chapter 10.

THE STRATEGIES

Hiring Family Members

Hiring retired parents or student children who have little or no taxable income can be an effective tax-saving strategy. The family member must really work, however, and the pay should be in line with what nonfamily employees would earn for similar work. (The IRS looks closely at intrafamily financial transactions.) You can even hire young children in your business. In a recent Tax Court ruling, wages paid to three children ages 7, 11, and 12 were allowed after it was shown that they actually performed services and that the compensation, ranging from $1,200 to $1,900 from 1972 to 1974 for the youngest child, was reasonable.

Children who are under the age of 19 or are full-time students during part of five calendar months can be claimed as dependents regardless of their earnings. You will, however, lose the $1,000 exemption for a dependent child if the child contributes more than half of his or her own support, even as a student, or if the child is over 19, earns more than $1,000, and is not a student. Social Security benefits for older family members may be reduced if earnings exceed $4,000 from ages 62 to 64, and $6,000 from ages 65 to 71. Also, both the company and the employee must make Social Security contributions, except where the employee is a child working in an unincorporated business owned solely by his or her parents.

Medical Expense Reimbursement

There are tax advantages in having your company reimburse you for all of your family's medical expenses, including those not covered by the company's medical insurance plan; examples are visits to the doctor and dentist, eyeglasses, deductibles (from coverage) under insurance plans, charges that exceed policy limits, and certain psychiatric expenses. There are three alternative plans for the company to fund this expense:

Purchase of Additional Insurance.   The insurance may be discriminatory; that is, it can cover any number of employees. The premiums will be deductible by your company, and the benefits will be tax free to you. "Administrative services only" plans, which provide that the premiums will equal the losses incurred plus a fee for processing the claim, generally will not qualify as insurance for this purpose.

Adoption of a Nondiscriminatory Self-Insurance Plan.   The plan must provide reimbursement by the company of the medical expenses of all employees over 25 who have at least three years of service. (Union members may be excluded if collective bargaining covers medical benefits.) The payments will be deductible by the company and tax free to the recipients.

Adoption of a Discriminatory Self-Insured Medical Reimbursement Plan.   The plan need cover only one or more officers. Usually, however, the payments will be deductible to the company and taxable to you.

Transportation, Travel, and Entertainment Expenses

There are few items of expense that give rise to more disputes than amounts claimed for transportation, travel, and entertainment. The usual controversy is over whether a particular item of expense is deductible, and if so, the actual amount of that item incurred. An understanding of the rules that the IRS plays by will minimize these challenges or will at least arm you for battle.

Transportation Costs

The costs incurred by your company in connection with owning or leasing an automobile for you or your employees are deductible for federal income tax purposes if the car is used in the pursuit of the business. Costs attributable to personal use, including commuting to and from work, are not deductible. If you own a second car, you should use it for personal transportation. If you have only one car and use it for both business and personal purposes, you must allocate the costs between the business and nonbusiness portions. Your company should be reimbursed for personal use on some basis, such as a stated amount per month or per mile. The allocation between business and nonbusiness use is usually based on the ratio of business miles to total miles. It is therefore esssential that you keep records of these two mileage figures.

Deductible automobile expenses include the cost of fuel, oil, repairs, maintenance, insurance, licenses, washing, automobile club memberships, and depreciation. This last item is most significant since an automobile is in the three-year property class for depreciation purposes. Under the accelerated cost recovery system (ACRS), a car purchased at any time during the taxable year and having a cost of, say, $16,000 is depreciated as follows:

	Amount	Percentage
Year of purchase	$4,000	25%
Year 2	6,080	38
Year 3	5,920	37
	$16,000	100%

In addition, the company is entitled to a 6 percent investment tax credit, or $960, in the year of purchase. Therefore, if you intend to buy a car around your tax year end, you should consider closing the deal prior to year end, thereby accelerating the tax deduction.

The depreciable basis of property placed in service in 1983 and thereafter is reduced by one-half of the investment tax credit claimed. Alternatively, the basis reduction can be avoided by electing to reduce the investment tax credit claimed by two percentage points. Therefore, in the foregoing example, the depreciable basis of the car, if purchased in 1983 or thereafter, is $15,520 ($16,000 less $480) if the full investment tax credit of $960 is claimed. If the $16,000 basis is used for depreciation purposes, then an investment tax credit of only $640 (4 percent of $16,000) is allowed.

If you use your own car for business, you may deduct the business portion of actual expenses (including a portion of the depreciation) less reimbursements from the company, or use the optional mileage method. In addition, when you claim the business portion of actual expenses, you may also be entitled to an allocable portion of the investment tax credit. Under the optional mileage method, a deduction of 20 cents a mile for the first 15,000 miles of business use and 11 cents a mile for any mileage over 15,000 miles is allowed. As with the actual expense method, the total deduction must be reduced by any reimbursements from the company. Under this method, you are not required to prove actual costs for operating an automobile, but you must keep records of actual business mileage. If the automobile is leased, only the portion of the lease payments that are attributable to business use of the car is deductible.

Other deductible transportation costs include bus, cab, train, and plane fares; parking fees; garage rentals; and tolls.

Travel Expenses

Travel expenses, as defined by the Internal Revenue Code, are the reasonable costs incurred by an employer or his or her employee while traveling away from home. Travel expenses incurred for personal activities are, of course, not deductible.

An employer may claim a deduction for travel expenses only to the extent that he or she has actually paid for, or is obligated to pay for, the expense and meets certain record-keeping requirements (see "Record Keeping and Substantiation" in this chapter). To the extent an employee is not fully reimbursed for the travel expenses he or she has incurred, the unreimbursed portion will generally be allowed as a deduction on the employee's personal tax return, but, again, only if the record-keeping requirements have been met. The most common type of travel expenses include:

Air, rail, and bus fares

Operation and maintenance of an automobile while away from home

Taxi fares or other transportation costs to and from airports, hotels, and so on

Baggage charges

Meals and lodging while away from home

Cleaning and laundry expenses

Telephone charges

Public stenographers' fees

Tips incidental to a legitimate travel expense.

"Ordinary and Necessary." *Reasonable*, in a travel-expense context, means "ordinary and necessary." An expense is ordinary if it is the type normal to your particular type of business; it need not be recurring. An expense is generally considered necessary if it is helpful in the production of income. Travel expenses deemed lavish or extravagant will be disallowed. What is lavish or extravagant is a question of judgment. An expense will not be considered lavish or extravagant merely because it exceeds a specified dollar amount or because it was incurred traveling first class, staying at a first-class hotel, or dining at a first-class restaurant.

Away from Home.   The travel expenses listed earlier must be incurred while "away from home." Generally, the metropolitan area where the principal or regular place of business or employment is located is considered home, regardless of the location of the individual's family residence. If you have no principal place of business, your home is the place where you maintain your family residence.

Away from home, for tax purposes, means away for a period longer than the normal workday. It does not necessarily mean away overnight, so long as you are away for a period long enough to require rest.

Business Purpose.   Travel expenses must be for business rather than for personal activities. If you are on a business trip—say, at a convention or making a sales call—and incur costs to go sightseeing or to visit friends, those costs are not deductible. If the travel is primarily personal, only those expenses that are directly related to business activities are deductible. This means that generally such items as air fare and hotel accommodations are not deductible when the trip is primarily personal.

Travel expenses incurred by a spouse or a friend on a trip that is otherwise primarily for business purposes are deductible only if the presence of these parties on the trip serves some "substantial" business purpose.

Record Keeping.   No matter how valid your travel-expense claims, they may not be honored unless you can substantiate compliance with all requirements. The key to substantiation is record keeping—the more detailed, the better. The type of records that must be maintained will be discussed later in this chapter.

Entertainment Expenses

Entertainment activities generally include the cost of recreation or amusement in connection with the active conduct of a business. The most obvious example is entertaining guests at nightclubs, restaurants, sporting events, theaters, or country clubs. Providing food and drink, a hotel room, or use of an automobile or private plane to a business customer or his or her family is also considered an entertainment activity.

In connection with means either directly related to or associated with. It is not necessary that the business benefit or that income result from a particular entertainment expense. Thus, for example, expenses incurred to generate goodwill are allowed unless the relationship of costs to future revenue is remote.

Direct Relation to Business.   For an entertainment expense to be considered directly related to the active conduct of your business, *all* of the following conditions must be met:

At the time of the expense, there was more than a general expectation of deriving income or some other specific benefit at some time in the future.

A business discussion was maintained with the person being entertained during the period (as later defined) when the entertainment was taking place.

The primary purpose of the combined business and entertainment meeting was to transact business.

The IRS presumes that expenses for entertainment that occur in a clear business setting are directly related to the business. Generally, the following situations are considered to be clear business settings:

Entertainment at a hospitality room at a convention

Entertainment of civic or business leaders at public events to obtain publicity

Entertainment where it is shown that no meaningful social or personal relationship exists between the person being entertained and the person entertaining

Where a clear business setting is not present, you may be required to show that the entertainment was directly related to the business. To do this, you will need to document that a substantial business discussion occurred during the entertainment. If the entertainment occurs at a place where there is little or no possibility of conducting a business discussion it will generally not be considered a "directly related" entertainment expenditure.

Associated with a Business.   Even if an expense is not directly related to the business, it will still be deductible if it is "associated with" it. To be associated with the business, the entertainment must have directly preceded or followed a bona fide business discussion. What constitutes a bona fide business discussion again is a facts-and-circumstances determination. The facts should indicate that the parties actively conducted a discussion, meeting, negotiation, or some other type of business transaction.

Generally, a business discussion will be considered to directly precede or follow entertainment if the discussion and entertainment took place on the same day. If the entertainment and business discussion do not occur on the same day, then a determination will be made based on the facts, including the place, date, and duration of the business discussions and whether the business associate or the person entertained is away from home, and if so, when he or she arrived and departed.

Other Criteria.   As with travel expenses, only those entertainment activities that are deemed ordinary and necessary, that are not lavish or extravagant, and for which proper records are maintained are deductible.

Entertainment Facilities Owned by the Taxpayer. Any property you own, rent, or use primarily for entertainment, amusement, or recreation will be classified as an entertainment facility. If a property is so classified, then the costs of nonentertainment—that is, business—activities held within the facilities are deductible, but the costs of operating or maintaining it are not deductible. (If the property is not an entertainment facility, entertainment activities are deductible under the principles described earlier: that is, "directly related" or "associated with.") Entertainment facilities include:

Yachts

Hunting lodges

Ski lodges

Fishing camps

Swimming pools

Beach cottages

Home at a vacation resort

Hotel suite

The Country Club. Country clubs and business luncheon clubs are often ideal places to entertain customers, suppliers, bankers, and others potentially beneficial to the business. Although, as noted earlier, you cannot deduct the cost of entertainment facilities, you can deduct dues and fees charged by country clubs or luncheon clubs if more than 50 percent of your use of the club is for business purposes, that is, directly related to or associated with the business. The proportion of business use is determined by comparing the number of days (not dollars) used for business purposes with total days used.

Record Keeping and Substantiation

Generally, no deduction will be allowed for an otherwise deductible transportation, travel, or entertainment expense unless the required records are maintained. The records must show:

The amount spent

The date and place

The business purpose

The business relationship of the person entertained to the person claiming the deduction

In order to substantiate travel or entertainment expenses, you should maintain an account book, diary, statement of expense, or other similar record. This type of record must also be supported by other documents, including receipts, cancelled checks, and/or credit card statements for each expenditure over $25. The entries in the diary or account book or on the expense statement should be made at or near the time the expenditure was incurred, since the IRS places little reliance on records that have been created long after an expenditure was incurred.

Of course, the most thorough record keeping will not result in a deduction if the amount claimed is based on an estimate or approximation or if it is deemed lavish or extravagant.

Owner's Compensation

If your business is doing well and its cash flow is adequate, you should consider whether increased salaries for the officer–stockholders are appropriate. Salaries are deductible, whereas dividends are not.

What is Reasonable?

The IRS can challenge compensation as excessive or unreasonable. Many owner–managers, however, are not receiving anywhere near enough to trigger this challenge. Of course, the maximum that the IRS will accept may not be the optimal level for you. That level should be determined by tax and other considerations. The following circumstances favor raising your salary:

Your salary may be used as a base-period amount if wage–price controls are ever imposed.

Your compensation sets the level on which retirement benefits will be based.

The company is faced with the possibility of a tax on its accumulated earnings (see "Tax Traps" in this chapter).

The following factors tend to weigh against salary raises:

The possibility that other executives will demand similar consideration, especially if their salaries are pegged to yours

The effect of reduced earnings and profits on lenders and on the
valuation of the company in the event you seek to sell it

That you are able to draw other forms of compensation such as bonuses, expense allowances, contributions on your behalf to retirement
plans, and dividends

Timing the Payments

If your company is an accrual-basis taxpayer using a calendar tax year,
you can declare a bonus in the current year but not pay it until the beginning of the following year. The bonus is a deduction to the company currently but is not taxable to you until the following year because individuals are generally on the cash basis. An accrual-basis taxpayer is one who
records revenue when earned, not when collected, and expenses when
incurred, not when paid. Cash-basis taxpayers record transactions when
the cash is collected, or when there was an unrestricted right to receive
the cash, and expenses are recorded when paid (see Chapter 8).

There are, however, certain hazards connected with payments of bonuses or other forms of compensation that are accrued in the current
year and paid subsequently to senior officers, especially if the officers are
also stockholders. If an officer has unrestricted authority to decide when
the payment is made, the IRS may contend that it was "constructively"
received—that is, received in fact though not in form—and thus should
be taxed in the current year. This risk can be minimized if the board of
directors decides that bonuses will be paid in the following January or
February and will be determined by a formula related to the current
year's financial results. This action must be taken early in the year; otherwise, the IRS may contend that bonuses to employee–stockholders are
really disguised dividends. The IRS is especially likely to take this position if the decision comes after it is apparent that profits will be better
than expected.

If you own more than 50 percent of the stock, accrued bonuses, or
other payments such as interest, must be paid within two and a half

months of the end of the company's tax year. If payment is made after that, the deductions for the payments will be disallowed to your company, not only in the year accrued but also in the year actually paid. In addition, the payments will be taxable to the shareholders on receipt. If your company does not have the cash for the payments, consider payment in the form of a note.

Perquisites

Certain benefits provided for the owner–manager by the company, and deductible to it, may be nontaxable to, or deductible by, the recipient. Most of these benefits are in the form of free services, known as perquisites. Examples are:

Low-interest or interest-free loans, (whose repayment schedule or due date and interest rate, if any, should be documented)

Professional assistance in personal finance and estate planning

Reimbursement of educational expenses, which must be for the purpose of maintaining or improving the job skills of the individual taking the classes or for meeting legal or regulatory requirements

Travel accident insurance

An annual medical examination with diagnostic tests

A physical fitness program

A payment of up to $5,000 to the spouse or children in the event of the executive's death

Dental or vision-care insurance

Professional assistance in tax planning and preparation of tax returns

The cost of professional dues

An educational assistance program or an educational benefit trust for the children of employees

Other Tax Strategies

There are many other tax strategies that might be right for you. The expedients in the following discussion were especially selected with emerging businesses in mind.

Research and Development Costs

Identify and separately account for research and development costs. Your company is entitled to a tax credit equal to 25 percent of the excess of certain research and development expenditures over the average amount the company spent in a base period (generally the three preceding years beginning in 1980) but never less than 50 percent of current year costs. A separate computation applies to performance of research outside the company under contract.

Income Shifting within Your Family

One way to reduce the tax burden on investment income is to transfer the income to one or more members of the family who are in low tax brackets. If, for example, you are supporting an elderly parent of modest income, you might give him or her bonds or other securities. The income would be taxed at low rates, and the securities could be returned to you or your children free from estate tax at the parent's death (assuming the latter's estate is modest). Annual transfers to minor children can be an excellent way to build a fund for college and graduate school. If the child has no other income, at least $1,100 in 1982 of investment income is tax free, and additional amounts will be taxed at rates as low as 12 percent in 1982 and 11 percent after that.

The transfer may be either temporary or permanent. If it is permanent, it may produce significant estate-tax savings and also reduce income taxes. The gift-tax consequences can be minimized with careful planning (see Chapter 12).

Methods for shifting income within the family include:

Direct gifts

Gifts to a custodian under the Uniform Gifts to Minors Acts.

Gifts to an irrevocable trust, with the income either distributed or retained and reinvested by the trustee

Gifts to a 10-year reversionary trust (often called a Clifford trust), under which securities or other assets are transferred to the trust and are to be returned when the trust expires, or at the beneficiary's death, if that occurs earlier.

Interest-free loans, repayable on demand. Courts have held that these loans do not incur any income or gift taxes, but the IRS continues to challenge them. With careful planning, the loan can be structured to minimize disputes with the IRS.

The effects of income shifting can be substantial. For example, suppose an individual owns property that produces taxable interest income of $10,000 per year. The following table shows how much will be left after federal income taxes if the income is transferred to other family members.

	Aftertax Income	
Recipient	1982	1983
Married individual in top bracket	$5,000	$5,000
Dependent child[1]	8,505	8,648
Parents, if both are 65 or over[1]	9,679	9,704
Trust[2]	8,157	8,333

1. This assumes no other taxable income and no itemized deductions.
2. Tax may be affected by distributions and certain other rules.

THE TRAPS

A tax trap is a seemingly valid approach to reducing taxes that is actually impractical or counterproductive. Sometimes, the approach represents the misapplication of a sound tax-planning principle.

Inventories

Owners of small businesses sometimes claim to have a hidden asset—undervalued inventories. The "undervaluation," which is, of course, designed to minimize taxable income, is usually contrived by creating liberal reserves for obsolescence or excess quantities. One risk is that intentional understatement of inventories constitutes fraud, and you and your officers could be subject to civil and criminal penalties. In addition, the hidden inventory is disadvantageous for several other reasons, among them:

It may not be insured under the company's property and liability insurance policy.

Banks will probably not lend against it.

Product pricing, ordering lead times, and warehouse requirements are all difficult to determine without reliable inventory data.

If may be difficult to receive full value for this inventory if you decide to sell your business.

To these drawbacks, add the possibility of shrinkage through theft or error. One company that undervalued inventories for many years by not counting the goods in portions of certain designated warehouse areas, finally decided to count physically the entire inventory. When the count was taken, management was shocked to find that the cupboard was bare. Much of the "hidden" items had been lost, stolen, or misplaced. All this does not mean that there are not significant tax-planning opportunities with inventories.

Last-In, First-Out Valuation

An effective method for minimizing taxable income is to value inventory on the basis of last-in, first-out (LIFO). Under this method, the units in ending inventory are valued on the basis of the oldest costs, and, therefore, current costs are expensed as part of cost of sales. Consequently, in times of rising prices, the current more-expensive "widgets" are included in cost of sales, whereas the older less-expensive ones are included in inventory for valuation purposes.

Two methods for calculating LIFO are the dollar-value and the unit, or quantitative, method. Under the dollar-value method, the increase in the LIFO inventory in any year is determined by comparing the total dollar value of the beginning and ending inventory (calculated by multiplying quantities times first-year LIFO prices or base prices) and developing an index, which is then applied to the current year's increase. The unit method, on the other hand, requires specific inventories to be valued in order of acquisitions, whether or not specifically on hand. Once you have selected the method—and the dollar-value method is much more common—you can elect to use prices in effect at the beginning or end of each year or the average prices during the year to value incremental quantities.

The beginning inventory for the year that LIFO is elected (the base year) consists of the ending inventory cost for the preceding year.

You can elect to adopt LIFO when you file your return, but upon audit the IRS must approve the specific method of application. A change from LIFO or a change in the method of application requires permission from the IRS. If you use LIFO for tax purposes, you must also use it for financial reporting purposes.

The following features of LIFO are advantageous:

In times of rising prices, income is lower, and, therefore, federal and state income taxes are deferred. (Before adopting LIFO, consider the likelihood over the long term of future inventory prices falling below base-year prices.)

Income tax payments, quarterly or total, are reduced.

Lower income taxes translated into greater cash flow and therefore reduced borrowings.

The following features are disadvantageous:

The financial statements going to the bank will reflect lower earnings. (Supplemental disclosures, however, may reflect earnings and net worth on a FIFO or current-cost basis).

Sale, merger, or public offering could be adversely affected by the lower earnings that are reported.

Inventory writedowns below cost, made at the end of the year preceding the one in which the election to adopt LIFO is made, must be added back to inventory.

Performance comparison with non-LIFO companies is not meaningful.

Over a period of several years, the difference between current inventory prices and the LIFO price can be quite substantial. This difference times the company's income tax rate equals the amount of income taxes deferred. Furthermore, unlike covertly written-down inventory, this difference can be shown in the company's financial statements and hence can serve as loan collateral, is eligible for insurance, and can be controlled and managed effectively.

First-In, First-Out Valuation

Under the first-in, first-out (FIFO) method of inventory valuation, units purchased most recently are treated as making up the ending inventory, and older purchased parts are treated as sold. In times of falling prices, FIFO is tax beneficial for the same reason that LIFO is beneficial when prices are rising. Thus, in recent years, certain high-technology industries, such as manufacturers of computers and telecommunications equipment, would probably find it advantageous to use FIFO.

Change in Inventory Method

Undervaluation of inventory is not acceptable for tax or accounting purposes. To change your method of inventory valuation to an acceptable one, a request must be filed with the IRS. Under IRS regulations, any income that results from this change can be spread over a period of up to 10 years, depending on circumstances.

Earnings and Compensation

Compensation is taxable at up to 50 percent. Dividends are not deductible to a corporation but are taxable to the shareholder. During periods of high interest rates, earnings retained in the business can be invested at attractive yields. Accordingly, it might seem like good tax planning to distribute no more than personal needs dictate. After all, if earnings are left in the company, they are not taxed until paid out. As in the case of inordinately high compensation, however, the IRS has weapons to attack this expedient.

The Accumulated Earnings Tax

If your corporation accumulates earnings beyond its reasonable needs, it could be subject to a tax of 27.5 percent on the first $100,000 of the amount deemed to be excessive—"accumulated taxable income"—and 38.5 percent on the remainder. Normally, the IRS will consider only liquid assets in determining the amount in excess. To impose the tax, the IRS must demonstrate that the amount in question was accumulated solely to avoid income taxes. You can rebut this contention by showing that you have sound reasons for the retention of earnings. Acceptable reasons include:

The existence of significant debt or other liabilities that must be paid

Plans for expansion, documented by sketches, architectural designs and board minutes

Litigation threatened or underway

A requirement to redeem shares of a deceased shareholder

It is essential that you continually evaluate your earnings situation. If a quantitative analysis suggests the possibility of an accumulated earnings tax penalty, consider these steps:

Electing Subchapter S status (see Chapter 5)

Planning business transactions during the year to get the best possible results under the IRS formulas used to test for accumulated taxable income

Planning, documenting, and implementing programs requiring use of funds

Reducing taxable income through various tax-deferral techniques, such as installment sales or changes in inventory accounting methods

Increasing compensation to stockholder–officers, if possible

Amending your retirement plan to provide increased benefits

Raising dividends

Becoming a member of a consolidated group.

Unreasonable Compensation

When considering an increase in compensation to avoid accumulated earnings, care must be exercised that the amount is not excessive. If the IRS considers your salary to be too high, it will disallow a deduction to your corporation for the excess portion and treat this excess as a dividend. In determining whether your compensation is unreasonably high, the IRS will consider the following:

The extent of your involvement in the business

The importance of your contribution to the success of the company
Salary levels of similar individuals in comparable companies

A modest dividend paid by the company may be a convincing argument
against an IRS contention that a portion of an employee's salary is a dividend.

The Personal Holding Company Tax

Closely held corporations receiving a sizable amount of passive investment income, such as dividends, interest, and rent, may be taxed on that
kind of income if they are deemed personal holding companies. For a
company to be classified as a personal holding company, at least 50 percent of the value of its stock must be owned directly or indirectly by not
more than five shareholders at any time during the last half of the taxable
year (Chapter 6). The risk of being so classified is heightened for
companies that hold investments during periods of high interest rates.

If your company is in danger of being treated as a personal holding
company, consider these alternatives:

Postpone investment income to a future year

Enhance operating rather than passive income

Manage and evaluate transactions with related companies; perhaps
file consolidated returns

Reassess the distribution of stock ownership

Select investments to avoid or postpone taxable investment income

Review dividend policy prior to year end, especially where rental income is significant

If personal holding company status cannot be avoided, it is probably advisable for your corporation to pay dividends in amounts sufficient to
avoid having the income taxed a second time at the personal holding
company rate. Of this income, an amount equivalent to 20 percent of the
dividends paid in the year the income was earned can be paid in the first
two and a half months of the next year and still be credited against that
income.

Interest Expense

Interest expense is generally a deductible item. Under certain conditions, however, your interest deduction may be limited. Thus:

You cannot deduct interest on money borrowed to purchase or maintain investments in municipal or other tax-exempt obligations. If a municipal bondholder has interest expense deductions, the IRS is likely to challenge the deductions unless the money was borrowed on a home mortgage or to invest in an actively managed business.

Prepaid interest is generally deductible not in the year of payment, but rather in the year incurred.

Individuals can deduct interest on loans whose proceeds they use to make or maintain investments, to the extent of $10,000 plus the amount of their "net investment income." Net investment income includes income from rents, dividends, interest earned, and net short-term gains, less the expenses incurred in producing these income items. Any nondeductible amounts may be carried over to future years. More liberal rules apply to debt incurred to acquire a more-than-50-percent interest in a corporation or partnership.

Capital Gains that Are Not Capital Gains

Ordinarily, where certain property is held for more than 12 months and then sold at a gain, the seller will realize a long-term capital gain, taxable at a rate lower than that of ordinary income. The property must be in the nature of a "capital asset"—a category that in an entrepreneurial business generally includes all property owned by the business, with the notable exceptions of inventories and accounts receivable. (Technically, real estate and depreciable assets are not capital, but gains from their sale will usually qualify for capital-gain treatment under another Internal Revenue Code provision.)

Under the rate schedule currently in affect, the tax rate on long-term capital gains for a corporation whose taxable income is over $100,000 is 18 percent lower than the tax on ordinary income (28 percent versus 46 percent). For an individual, only 40 percent of a net long-term capital gain is taxable, and therefore, since the maximum tax rate is 50 percent, the maximum capital-gains rate is 20 percent (40 percent times 50 percent). In many cases, you can plan sales of capital assets so that the proceeds will qualify as long-term capital gain instead of as ordinary income. There are, however, a number of approaches that appear likely to accomplish this, but that in fact do not. The reason is that the Internal Revenue Code specifically denies long-term capital-gain status when these approaches are used. Some of these expedients are discussed in the following subsections.

Collapsible Corporations

Among the most complex of Internal Revenue Code provisions, Section 341 attempts to deny capital-gain treatment where an enterprise is sold before it has realized a substantial portion of the income from the business activity for which it was originally organized. For example, a corporation is organized to construct a building, and the shareholders, after holding the shares for more than 12 months, during which time the building is erected, sell the shares to another owner or operator of the facility. Under the collapsible-corporation provisions, the gain on the sale would be treated as ordinary income, on the theory that such gain is construction profit, not capital appreciation.

Collapsible Partnerships

Certain provisions, relating to sale of partnership interests or dissolution of partnerships, are designed to deny capital-gains tax treatment. If you sell a partnership interest, all or part of the gain on the sale will be ordinary income to the extent that the gain represents appreciation in property owned by the partnership that would have produced ordinary income had that property been sold by the partnership. Therefore, if a partnership owns "substantially appreciated inventory" or has "unrealized receivables," all or part of the gain on the sale of an interest by a partner will be treated as ordinary income.

Transactions between Related Parties

Various Internal Revenue Code provisions define the nature and degree of the relationships that represent "related parties." The definition of the term *related* differs with the context of the various provisions in which it is mentioned. Virtually all of the provisions have one aspect in common, however: the concept of constructive ownership. Under this concept, an individual, corporation, or other entity is treated as owning stock that it does not actually own if there is a close relationship among the actual owners.

Assume, for example, that Mr. Jones owned 100 percent of Ace Corporation and that Best Corporation was owned 51 percent by Jones's daughter and 49 percent by her husband. By virtue of the father–daughter relationship, Jones is deemed to own the shares actually owned by his daughter and therefore to be in control of both corporations—control being defined as 50 percent ownership of the value or voting power. If Jones were to sell all or part of his shares in Ace to Best, the gain would generally be treated as a dividend taxable at ordinary rates. Jones would thus be in the distressing tax position of having received a dividend from a corporation in which no shares are actually owned by him.

The lesson for taxpayers is clear: any contemplated transaction involving the sale of property must be reviewed not only with a view toward the relationship of the parties in the transaction but also for the possible applications of the constructive-ownership provisions.

Reallocation of Income and Expense. The IRS has the power to reallocate items of income and of deduction between related parties. The theory is that these parties must deal with one another as they would if unrelated; stated another way, all transactions must be at "arm's length." (Unfortunately, this theory has not been easy to implement, and the body of law covering it is copious and growing.)

The arm's-length standard applies to sale of goods, services, rentals, and licensing agreements. It can apply to interest on loans between affiliates; for example, if a lender is deemed to be charging insufficient interest to a borrower affiliated with the lender, additional income may be imputed to the lender. This could have adverse results if the additional income to the lender is taxed at a higher rate than the tax benefit of the corresponding interest deduction to the borrower.

This power of reallocation is often applied to dealings between domestic entities and their foreign affiliates. In many foreign countries, the rates of tax are substantially below those in effect in the United States. If a

U.S. manufacturer organizes a subsidiary in a low-tax country to act as a local distributor of the company's product, there is nothing to stop him or her from setting the selling price to the affiliate at a level that would minimize the profit to the U.S. company and maximize the income of the affiliate. In these circumstances, the IRS has the power to step in and reapportion the total income so that a larger part is attributed to the U.S. company. The IRS has the same power over domestic entities.

Sale of Depreciable Property. All or part of the gain on the sale of real estate or depreciable fixed assets may qualify for capital-gain treatment. The taxable gain is the excess of selling price over the adjusted basis—generally, cost less depreciation—of the asset sold. Under the recapture rules, that portion of the gain attributable to depreciation will be taxed at ordinary rates, since when originally claimed, it offset ordinary income. The excess of the gain generally qualifies for capital-gain treatment.

There is, however, a provision of the Internal Revenue Code by which, if you sell depreciable property to a party related to you, the entire gain will be treated as ordinary income. Among the categories of related parties are an individual and his or her 80-percent-or-more-owned corporation or two corporations 80 percent owned by the same individual. The rationale for this treatment is that the purchaser would otherwise be able to take ordinary-income deductions on the purchase price in the form of future depreciation, whereas the seller would have a capital gain on the same property.

Sale of Stock. If you are conducting a business through two or more corporations that you control—for example, one corporation to own land and buildings and another to operate the business housed in the buildings—you cannot sell all or part of the stock of one corporation to the other and be eligible for the same favorable long-term capital-gain treatment as you would be if the shares had been sold to an unrelated purchaser. The transaction would be treated as a distribution from the purchasing corporation to the shareholder—that is, *you*—with the usual result that the gain will be treated as a dividend in the amount of the total selling price. Thus, if Jones, the owner of all of the shares of both Ace Corporation and Best Corporation, were to sell part of his Ace shares, which cost him $10,000, to Best for $30,000, Jones, instead of having a

$20,000 long-term gain, would most likely be taxed on the receipt of a $30,000 dividend from Best.

Equity versus Debt

In general, as much of the capital of the company as possible should be in the form of debt, especially where much of the capital is provided by owner–managers. When a loan you made is repaid, only the interest is taxable, and that interest is deductible by the company. When equity capital is returned to you, you either are subject to tax on the appreciated value of the shares or have dividends taxable in their entirety to you and not deductible by the company.

In maximizing debt over equity, you must anticipate the possibility of challenge by the IRS. Any of the following conditions may be taken as evidence that the indebtedness should be treated as equity capital:

There is no written obligation to pay a specified amount on demand or on a specified date.

The obligation does not bear a fixed interest rate.

The debt-to-equity ratio is too high.

The relationship between the percentage of the debt held by each stockholder is the same as his or her percentage of stock ownership.

The debt is convertible into the stock of the corporation.

Failure to plan the capitalization of your company properly can cost the company the loss of an interest deduction and rule out repayments to you on a tax-free basis.

Other Tax Traps

A brief listing of other potential tax problem areas will conclude this chapter.

Subchapter S Corporations

Often corporations elect Subchapter S status as a technique for avoiding income taxes at the corporate level (see Chapter 5) and either fail to qualify or, more seriously, lose their status because of failure to meet one or more of the conditions imposed under the law. To protect your Subchapter S status, you should annually review your shareholder composition and the type of income being realized. Distribution to shareholders must also be carefully planned in order to avoid double taxation to shareholders and other adverse consequences.

Utilization of Net Operating Loss from an Acquired Business

Quite often, a growing enterprise will seek to expand by acquiring other companies. In many cases such target companies may possess unused loss or credit carry-overs. Without proper planning, these tax-saving attributes may be incompletely utilized or lost.

Tax-Free Exchanges

It is often possible to sell or exchange assets of, or shares in, a corporation in such a way that taxation on the transaction is either deferred or avoided entirely. The conditions for nontaxability are complicated and exacting, however, and the number of possible fact patterns is virtually unlimited. One of the better-known pitfalls is that an otherwise tax-free exchange of shares of a selling company for those of the acquiring corporation can become taxable in whole or in part if the seller receives "boot," that is, property other than that permitted for tax-free treatment.

Some Final Words

Taxation, particularly for people in business, is a complicated maze—a maze, furthermore, that is continuously changing as the laws, regulations, and interpretations that define it are modified or superseded. There is no substitute, therefore, for competent tax advice. On the other hand, you should have enough tax knowledge to formulate ideas and strategies that are fundamentally practical taxwise. Otherwise, your tax consultant's job, which is to adapt your ideas to the realities of tax law, will be that much harder, and your decision-making process will be that much slower and less efficient.

The most effective tax-planning devices may be quite impractical for reasons unrelated to taxation. For example, hiring family members to shift income to lower-tax-bracket taxpayers may cause significant dissension among other employees. Similarly, it may be possible to shift income to elderly parents by means of gifts that can be recovered after their death—by inheritance and free of estate tax—but such gifts have been known to create serious differences between spouses. Clearly, effective tax planning requires consideration of matters that go beyond the possible tax savings, and, in certain circumstances, it may be necessary to forgo tax benefits for nontax and even nonbusiness reasons.

CHAPTER
TWELVE

ESTATE TAX PLANNING

The primary objective of estate planning is to make sure that your will and other documents accomplish what you want them to accomplish. Other objectives are:

To minimize estate and income taxes

To provide funds to pay debts and estate taxes

To arrange for capable management of assets

DESIGNATING YOUR ASSETS

Estate planning begins with an understanding of the assets that make up your estate. The following lists of the major categories of personal assets are designed to help you prepare an inventory. Personal property includes:

Interest in a business (sole proprietorship, partnership interest, or stock)

Life insurance policies

Stocks and bonds held for investment

Tax shelter investments (usually limited partnership interests)

Deferred compensation

Bank accounts

Automobiles

Jewelry

Art objects and collectibles

Household furnishings

Deferred compensation may include:

1. Unpaid salary or bonus as of date of death. A carefully planned company death benefit may be excluded from your taxable estate provided you had no access to, or control over, it during your lifetime.

2. Payments received under a qualified pension and profit-sharing plan, to the extent that they represent a return of your contribu-

tions to the plan. Employer contributions to the plans are not included in your taxable estate unless the funds are paid in a lump sum and the recipient elects to treat the lump-sum payment as if it were received over a 10-year period.

Real property includes:

Home (principal residence)
Vacation home
Investment real estate

Where an asset is insured, make sure that the insurance policy agrees with the ownership. Otherwise, the assets may be included in the estate of the insured rather than that of the owner.

Jointly Held Property

The joint holding of property by spouses is widely prevalent but is not necessarily advantageous from an estate-planning standpoint. Normally, property transferred as part of an estate is valued at fair market value, at the time of death or six months later, rather than at cost. When the surviving spouse later sells the asset, the fair market value at which he or she received the property from the estate is the basis on which gain or loss on the sale is reckoned. To the extent this value exceeds the original cost, the taxable gain will be lower. With jointly held property, however, 50 percent of the cost basis is included in the estate of the decedent and accordingly is excluded from the survivor's basis. (Property held jointly is treated as owned one-half by each spouse regardless of how much each contributed to the purchase price.) Therefore, the taxable gain on sale will not be reduced by as much as it would have been if the property were originally owned entirely by the deceased.

ESTATE AND GIFT TAXATION

The rules governing the taxation of gifts and estates are highly developed. The recommendations in this discussion are premised on a knowledge of a few rules that can be briefly summarized.

Valuation

Transfers by gift or by bequest are taxable: gifts, to the giver; bequests, to the estate. In general, the value of an item for gift-tax purposes is the market value at the time the gift is made; the value for estate-tax purposes is the value at time of death or, electively, six months from date of death. With gifts of life insurance policies, the equivalent of market value is replacement value—that is, replacement cost—at the time of transfer. This also applies to transfers of the policies by bequest, which, strictly speaking, can take place only when the insured is not the decedent.

Deductions and Exemptions

All transfers of property between spouses are allowed a 100 percent marital deduction. Gifts to anyone are subject to an exemption for each recipient, and there is an additional one-time exemption (in the form of a credit) based on the aggregate of the estate and total lifetime gifts.

The Marital Deduction

Virtually everything you leave your spouse, whether outright or in the form of a legal life estate or trust, will be free of federal estate taxes. There is one catch; your spouse's estate will be subject to estate tax on his or her death. Furthermore, unless the spouse remarries, there will be no marital deduction on that estate. This means that if the largest part of your spouse's estate came from your bequest—and that estate did not diminish appreciably in his or her hands—the tax on your spouse's estate might well be larger than the tax was on yours, even if your estate, including distributions to your other beneficiaries, was considerably larger. Community property is eligible for the marital deduction as well as a qualified terminable interest life estate (see "Testamentary Trusts" in this chapter).

The unlimited marital deduction applies to tax years beginning in 1982. You cannot get this deduction unless your will provides for it explicitly. Furthermore, this proviso or codicil, whether as an amendment to an existing will or part of a will drawn up for the first time, must not have been drafted before September 12, 1981. The only exception applies when the law of the testator's state treats the inclusion of the formula clause as provision, *ipso facto*, for the unlimited marital deduction. If you have not taken the necessary steps to qualify for the new deduction, your marital deduction will follow the pre-1982 formula—that is, $250,000 or one-half of adjusted gross estate, whichever is greater. If it were not for this rule, pre-1982 wills that mention the marital deduction, especially those designed to take full advantage of that deduction, could, now that the term denotes the new unlimited deduction, cause the survivor to inherit more of the decedent's estate than intended.

Apart from the loss of the new deduction, failure to change a will made before September 12, 1981, could operate to trigger liability for an estate tax where no tax would be due under the new marital deduction.

The Nonmarital Gift Exclusion

You can give up to $10,000 each year tax free to any person, with no limit on the number of recipients. If you give with your spouse's consent, that amount may be doubled. This exclusion also applies to trusts if the beneficiary receives a "present interest" (see "The Gift Tax" in this chapter) in the trust. Thus, if you have four adult children and four grandchildren, you and your spouse could give them a total of $160,000 annually, on a tax-free basis.

The Unified Credit for Estate and Gift Taxes.   In addition to these annual exclusions, you are entitled to a credit against amounts in excess of these exclusions. For 1982, the exemption equivalent of this credit is $225,000, or with the consent of your spouse $450,000. The credit will rise annually until 1987, when the exemption equivalent will stand at $600,000 and $1,200,000. On your death, the basis for assessing the estate tax will be the combination of the fair market value of the property you bequeath and the value of the taxable gifts you made since 1976—a combination termed the "transfer tax base." To the tax calculated on this base is applied the unified credit for estate and gift taxes.

This is how the credit works: assume that A gives away after 1976 $600,000, over and above the nonmarital exclusion, and dies in 1987, leaving an estate of $1,400,000. His estate's transfer tax base is $2,000,000, that is, the $600,000 in gifts added to the gross estate. The tax computed on this basis is $780,800, but this amount is reduced by the unified credit equivalent of $600,000, or $192,800, to produce a net estate tax of $588,000. Had the tax been computed on the gross estate alone, it would have been $512,800—$75,200 less than the actual tax.

Generally, the sooner you use the unified credit exemption the better, because the present value of the exemption is greater than the future value.

STRATEGIES FOR GIVING AND BEQUEATHING

To determine the optimal planning approach for disposing of your possessions, you will probably have to weigh a host of considerations: external, such as rules and economic trends, and internal, such as your age, means, and needs. In the following discussion we focus on some of the more important principles involved, illustrating with representative situations.

Utilizing the Marital Deduction

Because your spouse's estate will be subject to taxation without—unless he or she remarries—benefit of the marital deduction, it is advisable to withhold from your bequest to your spouse an amount equal to the unified credit exemption. This amount, at least, will be removed from all possibility of subsequent taxation as part of his or her estate. You can use the unified credit exemption currently, by gift, or ultimately, by bequest.

The marital bequests can be made either directly or through a trust on which your spouse would receive the income and, under certain conditions, the principal as well. The following example illustrates how forgoing the full permissible marital deduction can reduce the total tax on the combined value of both estates.

Assume that D dies in 1987, leaving an estate of $2 million entirely to his wife, who has no property of her own. On D's death, Mrs. D receives the $2 million free of estate taxes, due to the marital deduction. If Mrs. D never remarries and her estate is $2 million at her death, the estate tax will be $588,000, leaving $1,412,000 for her heirs, her two children. If, on the other hand, D left $600,000 directly to the children or in the form of a nonmarital trust with the children as remainder beneficiaries, the

$1,400,000 estate remaining to the widow would be liable on her death for a tax of $320,000. The $1,080,000 remaining in the widow's estate after taxes, added to the first $600,000, would give the children a total of $1,680,000—$268,000 more than they would have received under the first option.

Another way to reduce taxes is to equalize the total holdings of husband and wife. Thus, in the preceding example, if D left his wife $1 million the total estate taxes for husband and wife would be $306,000—$14,000 less than the $320,000 ultimately assessed on the $1,400,000 received by the wife in the bequest of the entire estate. On the other hand, half of the estate tax, $153,000, is paid on D's death, with the balance payable when the wife dies. The use of $153,000 might be worth more than the $14,000 saved. Nevertheless, the equal-estate arrangement is definitely advantageous when the spouses die simultaneously or the surviving spouse dies very shortly after the first spouse.

The Common Disaster Threat

If you or your spouse die as the result of the same occurrence, such as an airplane crash or a fire, it may not be possible to establish which of you succumbed first. The laws of many states provide that where there is any doubt about order of death, the wife is deemed to have predeceased. If this presumption is sustained, the marital deduction will be lost. To counter this presumption, it should be stipulated in your will that in the event of doubt the husband is deemed to have died first. The testamentary provision is standard in form and is known as the common disaster clause. Many wills with this clause also establish a formula for equalizing the two estates in the event of a common disaster.

If the wife dies after the husband, but not more than six months later, she would derive little benefit from the estate. To simplify administration and, in some cases, to save taxes as well, a couple should consider providing in their will for nullification of all or part of the bequest to the wife if she dies within the six-month period—not later, or the amount of the marital deduction will be taxed as part of the husband's estate. Of course, you and your spouse should consider this contingent cancellation provision when you draft your wills, to make sure that all of your beneficiaries are provided for according to your wishes.

Tax Reasons for Giving

If your net worth is greater than your needs, you should consider making gifts to your family or other beneficiaries during your lifetime. By this expedient, you can materially reduce taxes on your estate at the price of accelerating transfers to those who will ultimately receive the transfers. This can be accomplished, within limits, by taking advantage of the $10,000 annual exclusion and the marital deduction. (The reduction in the taxable value of your estate that you achieve by making a gift must be reckoned as the value of the property given *plus* any future appreciation realized on the property and/or income earned on it between the time you gave it and the time of your death.)

If everything, or nearly everything, is in your name, it is a good idea to utilize your spouse's lifetime credit as well as your own. If he or she predeceases you and you have been taking the exemption only for yourself, his or her exemption will be lost for lack of anything to which to apply the credit equivalent of that exemption. Because of inflation, the tax benefit of using up the gift-tax credit while you are alive may be greater than letting the credit shelter your estate from taxation after your death. On the other hand, appreciated property given by you during your lifetime will, when sold, generate taxable income to the recipient, because he or she must assume your cost basis, increased only to the extent of any gift tax you paid. If the property is transferred after your death, the recipient's basis will be its value at the time of death—presumably far higher than the cost basis. Of course, jointly held property received by your spouse is, as discussed earlier, a special case.

Vehicles for Bequests and Gifts

Bequests and gifts need not be outright; both may be accomplished by use of trusts. In addition, interest-free loans are an accepted method of gift giving.

Testamentary Trusts

If there is any doubt that your spouse can properly manage the property left to him or her, or that the property remaining at the time of his or her death will go to parties on which you both agreed, you should use the trust vehicle.

The General-Power-to-Appoint Trust.   With this kind of trust, the surviving spouse receives the income from the property during his or her lifetime but has no power over the trust assets except to dispose of them as he or she pleases under the terms of his or her will. If the spouse fails to exercise this right—that is, to provide for disposition in his or her will—the property will go to parties that you have designated in your will. The property used in funding this kind of trust must be either income producing or convertible to income producing at the behest of the survivor. For example, two types of assets that are not considered income producing are stock in a closely held corporation that is not paying a dividend and various types of tax shelters.

The Qualified-Terminable-Income Trust.   Under this arrangement, your spouse will receive the income currently, and on his or her death, the parties you have designated will receive the property. The same requirements that the property be income producing or convertible to income producing that apply to the general-power-to-appoint trust apply here as well. The main advantage of this trust is that your spouse cannot change your ultimate beneficiaries. (In many states, this type of trust does not qualify for the state marital deduction.)

The Estate Trust.   Here, the income need not be paid currently to the surviving spouse, but when he or she dies, any undistributed income, together with the remaining corpus, is distributed to his or her estate. The main advantage of this trust is that it can be funded with non-income producing property, whereas the main disadvantage is that the property passes under the surviving spouse's will.

In all three of the preceding trusts, the property qualifying for the marital deduction in the estate of the first spouse to die will be included in the surviving spouse's taxable estate.

Trusts for Gifts

Trusts are also extensively used in gift giving. As long as the trust, or the beneficiary of the trust, is in a lower income tax bracket than you are, you will save taxes on the trust income. Under the popular 10-year trust, the property or "corpus" reverts to the giver after the trust terminates. Of course, transfers to the trust are taxable gifts and, to the extent they exceed the allowable deduction, use up the lifetime credit.

Interest-Free Loans

You may also want to consider interest-free demand loans to family members. The courts have held, over IRS protests, that making an interest-free loan generally does not constitute a taxable gift if it is repayable on demand. The loan should be evidenced by a note; where the loan is for the benefit of a minor, the use of a trust should be considered.

Insurance

If you have life insurance policies, whether ordinary, group term, or any other type, providing for ownership of the policies and disposition of the proceeds on the death of the insured should be a major factor in your estate-tax planning. The general rule is that the proceeds of an insurance policy are included in the taxable estate of the insured if the insured owned the policy within three years of death. It is immaterial who took out the policy, paid the premium, or is the beneficiary, provided that it is not you or your estate. These proceeds are not taxable income to the beneficiary, so if you keep them out of your estate, they will escape taxation entirely.

The most obvious way to exclude the proceeds from your estate is to give the policy away during your lifetime, making the recipient the beneficiary of the policy as well as its owner. Except where a policy has a high cash surrender value, the tax cost of the gift is generally modest. For example, term insurance policies, even those with double-indemnity provisions or accidental death benefits, do not usually have much value during the life of the insured. (Company group term insurance has virtually no value.) If you give the policy directly (and through certain types of trust arrangements) the gift-tax exemption will apply not only to the value of the policy but also to payments of premiums you make after giving it. Finally, gifts of insurance policies normally involve no significant management or administrative problems until the death of the insured.

Requirements for Divestiture

In giving an insurance policy, you must divest youself of it completely and irrevocably. If you retain any control over the policy, the transfer will almost certainly be denied. The following rights or powers over the policy are criteria, or, in legalese, "incidents" of ownership:

The right to change the beneficiary.

The right to cancel or surrender the policy and receive its cash value, if any.

The right to assign or sell the policy or revoke an assignment.

The right to pledge the policy for a loan.

The right to borrow against the cash surrender value of the policy. If the borrowing takes place before the transfer and the payments of interest or principal are carried on after the transfer, there will be no incident of ownership, because the insured will derive no further economic benefits from the policy.

In construing ownership, the courts look beyond the forms of law to facts and circumstances. Thus, you may be considered to have retained control over the policy if you are the controlling shareholder in a corporation that formally owns the policy or are the trustee of a trust that holds the policy. To the Treasury, it is irrelevant who established the trust or donated the policy to it. On the other hand, a policy given pursuant to a divorce, and maintained by you solely for the benefit of your ex-spouse and that of the children will not be included in your estate. (The theory is that you do not have effective control over the insurance because the divorce decree gave your ex-spouse a vested interest in the policy.)

When Donee–Beneficiary Predeceases Donor–Insured.   If you act as the executor of an estate where the decedent was the owner–beneficiary of a policy on your life, you may be deemed to have an incident of ownership, unless the policy is in a trust (of which, naturally, you are not a trustee). Assume that the owner–beneficiary is your spouse and that you are his or her executor-designate. If there is no trust, the spouse should provide for another owner–beneficiary in the event that he or she predeceases you. Alternatively, your spouse can accomplish the same thing by specific bequest (not to you, of course).

If you, the insured, are found to have had an incident of ownership in the policy, the proceeds of the policy will be taxable as part of your estate when you die. If the owner–beneficiary predeceases the insured, the value of the policy—which is not the face amount of the policy—at the date of death will be included in the owner's estate. (The value of an insurance policy before the death of the insured will generally consist of the interpolated terminal reserve value—slightly more than cash surrender value—plus any unearned premiums.)

The Irrevocable Life Insurance Trust

The safest way to divest yourself of an insurance policy is to assign the policy to an irrevocable life insurance trust for the beneficiary, avoiding all incidents of ownership, including—but not limited to—acting as trustee.

The irrevocable life insurance trust may be the appropriate vehicle for gifts of insurance, not only for your spouse but also for other members of your family. With this kind of trust, you can achieve maximum flexibility by conferring discretionary powers on the trustee. For example, your trustee can be authorized to provide for the needs of the beneficiaries as they arise, by invading the corpus of the trust. The trustee can be empowered to use trust funds to lend money to your estate or buy assets from it to provide it with funds to pay taxes. To obtain the benefits of this assignment, however, you must live at least three years after the assignment.

The Gift Tax

An insurance policy, even it if has no cash value, is valued for gift-tax purposes at replacement value as of the time the gift is made. Although (as pointed out earlier) this value is usually no more than a fraction of the proceeds, with certain policies—notably, whole life—it can be significant. One way to reduce the gift on a policy tax is to borrow against its cash surrender value before assigning the policy; the loan will reduce the policy's net value. Another way is to split the policy into several parts and transfer one part at a time. Finally, you might be able to retain the cash surrender value of the policy and assign only the amount at risk, that is, the face amount less the cash surrender value.

In one set of circumstances, there is a hidden gift-tax trap to watch for. If your spouse receives a policy on your life as a gift and names his or her children as beneficiaries, the full proceeds of that policy on your death may be treated as a taxable gift from him or her to them. The standard way to prevent this from happening is to assign the policy to the children who are the beneficiaries.

Gifts to Trusts.   An outright gift of an insurance policy is, like the gift of almost any marketable item, treated as a transfer of present interest and therefore eligible for the $10,000 annual gift-tax exclusion. Payment of premiums by the donor after the transfer is treated in the same way if the beneficiary owns the policy. If, however, you place an insurance policy in a trust, the transfer will usually be deemed a gift of future interest, and the value of the policy as well as subsequent payments of premiums will not qualify for the exclusion. (With certain types of trusts, this can be prevented, as is explained later.) In either case, you can pay the premiums directly to the insurance company without risk of having an incident of ownership.

If you wish to put an insurance policy into a trust for the benefit of a minor—the usual practice, rather than to give full possession during minority—you can ensure that the gift will be one of present interest and therefore eligible for the gift-tax exclusion. The key is to stipulate that the beneficiary is to receive full ownership of the policy including proceeds, if any, plus any accumulated earnings at the age of 21. (In addition, it is advisable to give the trustee the power to dispose of the policy.) Another approach that should have the same result is to give the beneficiary the right to withdraw from the trust $5,000 or 5 percent of the value of the policy, whichever is greater.

Caveat

The estate-planning aspects of insurance are tricky, thanks to the variety and complexity of insurance policies and the vehicles for holding and transferring them. If you have given, or intend to give, insurance on your life, you should consider utilizing the services of a lawyer or an estate planner. That your death within three years of donating a policy would throw the proceeds into your estate argues for early action.

Estate Freezing

If your corporation is closely held, and a substantial part of your estate as well—both likely conditions—you should consider freezing the size of that asset and diverting future appreciation to your beneficiaries. It is much easier to do this at a reasonable tax cost now than it is to dispose of future accumulated wealth.

Recapitalization

The most common way to freeze the value of a closely held corporation is to recapitalize it so that you and your beneficiaries will hold a particular mix of voting and nonvoting common or preferred stock. If your beneficiaries are already shareholders, an exchange of their holdings may be necessary to achieve this end. If you are the sole shareholder, then you must make the beneficiaries shareholders, making sure their participation follows the pattern of holdings you want. If you are a joint equityholder with outsiders who are not to be beneficiaries, your exchange program will probably have to involve them. In any case, you should be able to accomplish the recapitalization without incurring any tax. The following examples illustrate several estate-freezing arrangements based on varying goals.

Example 1. A business man, the sole shareholder of a corporation, wishes to turn over his business, while living, to his two sons, who are active in the corporation. At the same time, he wishes to provide for his wife, who wants to be independent of the children. The first objective he accomplishes as follows: he recapitalizes the company and exchanges all of his common stock for a package of new common and preferred, with the par value of the nonvoting preferred comprising about 80 percent of the company's net worth. He then gives the common stock to his sons. (If the value of the common stock is less than $450,000, the father can use his credit and that of his wife to avoid all federal tax on the gift. By 1987, the total value of stock that could be given to the sons, tax exempt, would be as high as $1,200,000.) The effect of these moves is to freeze the value of the father's interest in the company so that all future appreciation will accrue to the common stock owned by the sons. For the second objective—providing for his wife—the dividend-paying preferred stock is ideally suited. If the dividend is fixed and cumulative, it is not at the discretion of the children.

If the second son were not active in the business but the father wanted to protect that son's interests, the father could create two classes of common stock (in addition to the preferred)—Class A common with full voting rights, and Class B with highly restricted voting rights—giving Class A to the active and Class B to the other. Alternatively, the father could make the common stock nonvoting, or he could put the gift to the second son in a trust of which the first son is trustee with the right to vote the stock.

If the father wished the active son to realize the entire future appreciation, he could give that son all the common stock and allow the second son only the preferred. Under this arrangement, the second son would be buffered against a decline in the value of the business under the first son's management.

If the father wished to retain control of the business, he could give the preferred stock full voting rights. Because there would be more preferred shares than common shares, he would retain voting control of the corporation. To ensure that the sons would have complete voting control over the corporation on his death, he would make them trustees of the marital trust.

Example 2. A businessman, A, is sole shareholder in a corporation with a fair market value of $3,000,000. None of A's children are active or interested in the enterprise, but several key employees would like to acquire significant equity holdings, although their combined capital is only $100,000. Our entrepreneur wants to protect his children's interests and to accommodate the employees.

He capitalizes his holdings into $2,500,000 of preferred stock and $500,000 of common and sells 20 percent of the common to the key employees. (He could have gone as high as 40 percent, if he were willing to let the corporation make an interest-free loan of $100,000 to them to buy an additional 20 percent interest. The loan could be repaid in future years with the aftertax proceeds of their bonuses.) The preferred stock he uses in an active program of gifts to his wife and children. He also enters into a buy–sell arrangement with the corporation whereby, on his death, all of his remaining stock and his family's stock will be redeemed. As a precaution against the possibility that the corporation will not have enough liquid assets to satisfy the claim, the redemption will be carried out in installments spread over a number of years. (When a closely held business comprises more than 35 percent of the adjusted gross value of an estate, the estate is not compelled to pay federal inheritance taxes on the value of that business for four years and has an additional 10 years to complete payment.)

Example 3. Two entrepreneurs, each owning 50 percent of a company, are concerned about continuity of control when one dies. They recapitalize, creating a package of nonvoting preferred and voting common. On the death of one, the company could redeem or the survivor could buy the nonvoting stock owned by the estate of the deceased. The equal division of the voting interests would continue.

Tainted Stock. One obstacle to estate freezing is that the preferred stock issued in a recapitalization will be "tainted"; that is, if the stock is sold during the lifetime of the recipient, the full proceeds of the sale will be taxed as ordinary income. If tainted stock is given to charity, the charitable deduction is limited to the taxpayer's cost basis. Although the taint is purged at death, it may limit the taxpayer's flexibility during his or her lifetime; the stock is less valuable for a gift program, for example. The common stock retained, however, need not be tainted, and if not, can be used for gift tax purposes.

Valuation Problems. A difficult problem you have to contend with when you recapitalize your company is what value to assign to the corporation and the securities to be issued. For example, in setting the dividend on preferred stock, you have to weigh the desirability of a low-dividend obligation against the fact that if the dividend rate is too low by current business standards, the IRS may value your preferred stock at far below par and assign the difference to the common stock. The higher value of the common stock would hardly be advantageous for gift-tax purposes. (If the preferred is noncumulative and the dividends are in arrears, any gap between par and true value will be greater than it would otherwise be.)

The IRS has taken the position that the fair market value of stock must be determined in accordance with the facts in each case. It is unrealistic to assume that the IRS will accept a valuation at par with a dividend of only 6 percent, when preferred stocks of quality listed corporations are yielding 10 percent or more. In a case involving a charitable gift of 6 percent noncumulative, nonvoting preferred stock, the Tax Court applied substantial discounts in valuing the stock for purposes of determining the amount of the charitable deduction.

In general, whenever a closely held company is recapitalized or reorganized and certain parties receive more than they gave up, the possibility exists that the difference will be taxed either as a gift from those who received less than they contributed or as compensation to those who received more. Thus, as in Example 2, if the key employees are deemed to have acquired the common stock in a bargain purchase, they may have received compensation to the extent of the bargain portion.

The valuation problem is the major reason why many proposed recapitalization plans are never completed. The taxpayer may be reluctant to load the corporation with a heavy dividend requirement, with its resulting drain on working capital. With adroit tax planning, however, the problem can be minimized, if not eliminated.

Redemptions.   After your spouse's death, it may be desirable for your company to repurchase some of the preferred stock from his or her estate. This must be planned carefully. The amount redeemed generally cannot exceed death taxes plus funeral and administrative expenses. Any additional amount may be taxed to the estate as a dividend.

Selling the Business

If you decide to sell your business rather than to keep it in the family, you will probably be faced with a capital-gains tax. One way to avoid the tax, which could go as high as 20 percent, is to be acquired by a publicly owned company via a tax-free exchange of stock. The disadvantage of this expedient is that it results in the family's losing control over a substantial portion of its net worth; that is, the family holdings would now consist of a minority interest in a company controlled by others.

The Personal Holding Company.   Another approach would be to have the corporation sell its assets and retain and reinvest the proceeds, thereby perpetuating itself as a family personal holding company. The corporation would probably realize only a small capital gain, and it is possible that it would realize none. From an estate-planning point of view, this arrangement can be very advantageous. The courts have been generous in allowing substantial discounts in valuing the stock of a personal holding company held by an estate. Discounts ranging from 20 percent to as high as 55 percent have been approved. Even the IRS has been willing to concede a substantial discount, and many cases have been settled at the appellate level with discounts of 25 percent or more. (For a discussion of personal holding companies, see Chapter 6.)

Conclusion

By now you should realize that the preparation and execution of an estate plan requires expert advice. For most taxpayers, the 1981 tax act has made the need for this assistance even more marked than it was. Although what is appropriate for one taxpayer may be inappropriate for another, the main objective of all tax planning is to fulfill the testator's wishes at a minimum tax cost, satisfy liquidity needs, and provide for capable management. With proper planning, which includes gift giving during your lifetime, you should be able to reduce the value of the estate while preserving a degree of control, minimize or avoid a present gift tax on the transfer, and pass on more "value" than meets the eye to your family.

CHAPTER
THIRTEEN

SELLING TO THE UNITED STATES GOVERNMENT

The U.S. government is the world's largest buyer of goods and services. In this chapter, we explain how the government buys and what it expects of sellers.

The first step in selling to the government is to find out what government agencies need the goods or services you have to offer. If your business can supply only a few products or services, you can generally rely on the Small Business Administration (SBA) field office serving your area to furnish this information. Specifically, the SBA local office should pinpoint the government agencies that are your potential customers. (Each regional office of the Administration lists all the products and services dispensed by the small businesses in that region by concern and category.) Be sure your request for information is accompanied by enough data about your facilities and products to enable the SBA to form an accurate idea of your capabilities. If your operation can supply a variety of products or services, you have several sources of information on government purchasing. Prominent among them are the General Services Administration (GSA) and the Department of Commerce publication, the *Commerce Business Daily*.

The GSA acts as purchasing agent for much of the equipment and supplies used by federal agencies, civil and military. For a list of the standard items bought, you can write the GSA or visit the nearest GSA Business Service Center. These centers are located in Atlanta, Boston, Chicago, Denver, Fort Worth, Houston, Kansas City (Missouri), Los Angeles, New York, Philadelphia, San Francisco, Seattle, and Washington, D.C.

The *Commerce Business Daily* is published Mondays through Fridays (except on federal legal holidays) by the U.S. Department of Commerce, in cooperation with government purchasing agencies. In this journal you will find a daily list of U.S. government procurement invitations for bids, subcontracting leads, contract awards, sales of surplus property, and foreign business opportunities. The publication is on file at SBA and Department of Commerce field offices and is available on a subscription basis via first-class mail from: Superintendent of Documents, *Commerce Business Daily*, Government Printing Office, Washington, D.C., 20402.

Other sources of information on the needs of government agencies are advertisements placed by the agencies in trade papers and even on post office bulletin boards.

Getting Listed with Government Agencies

After learning which agencies buy the products or services you can supply, you should ask the purchasing representatives of these agencies to send you the necessary forms to have your company placed on their lists of potential suppliers, usually termed bidder lists. These lists are made up of business concerns—manufacturers, regular dealers in a particular item, construction contractors, or other appropriate concerns—that have registered with the purchasing offices as suppliers of the item and have provided printed information on their operations to support that claim.

In answer to the request for bidder listing, the civilian purchasing agencies usually send a Standard Form 129 to fill out; military purchasing agencies may also send a Department of Defense Form 558–1. With Form 129 the purchasing agency may enclose a list of products and services it buys so that the concern can indicate those it wishes to supply. If, however, the purchasing office does not send a list, or if the list does not include the exact products or services the business can furnish, you should attach to the completed form a separate sheet showing the specific name of each product or service your business now produces, together with any other products or services you could provide the purchasing agency. In addition, if you are applying for a listing with a military agency, mention any defense items your enterprise has supplied in the past. Each product or service listed on this attached sheet should be carefully described. If possible, list by number the government specifications the product or service meets or can be made to meet.

Enclose with the completed form returned to the purchasing agency a covering letter referring to the attached list and asking that you be notified of placement lists and of which lists, if any, you are on.

Even before receiving assurance of placement on supplier lists, you should consider the possibility of selling to agencies that do not have your name and to which you have never applied. For this approach, the *Commerce Business Daily* and comparable commercial publications are helpful.

Advertised and Negotiated Purchase

Federal purchasing offices buy supplies and services in two ways: by advertising for bids and by negotiation. The former procedure is more formal and less flexible than the latter, but in both, the authorities are careful to preserve the element of competition.

Advertising for Bids

When making a purchase by this method, a purchasing office sends invitations for bids (IFB) to businesses. The basic source for potential bidders is the bidder list, but more often than not, the purchasing agency will want a greater number of bidders than it can get from its files. In that case, the agency will have recourse to the media to solicit qualified and interested bidders.

An invitation for bids will include, or will tell you how to get, a copy of the specifications for the needed item, describing in detail quality and other requirements. It will also include instructions for the preparation of bids and will state the conditions of purchase, delivery, and payment.

Bids submitted on a proposed purchase are opened in public in a formal procedure at the procurement office at a time designated in the invitation. Pertinent facts about each bid are read aloud and recorded on an abstract, a copy of which may be viewed by anyone for a specified period, usually six months.

The contract is awarded to the bidder whose bid is considered the most advantageous to the government in terms of price, delivery, and other factors, provided the bidder is considered competent to carry out the contract. A purchasing officer may reject all bids received on a purchase when he or she believes that prices are unreasonable or that there has been collusion or bad faith on the part of the bidders.

Buying by Negotiation

Under certain circumstances, which are prescribed by law and regulations, government agencies will purchase by negotiation with qualified suppliers (see "Procurement by Negotiation" in this chapter). As in standard bidding, the procurement office uses its bidder list for contact with suppliers. What under the standard procedure would be called a bid is here termed a price quotation or proposal, but the material requested covers much the same ground—that is, detailed analyses of estimated costs or other evidence of reasonable prices. These requests for proposals (RFP), or requests for quotation (RFQ), are sent to a number of suppliers, to ensure a reasonable range of choice. The fundamental distinction between buying by negotiation and standard bidding is that in the former there is no public disclosure of the submitted proposals or quotations. Instead, the contracting officer has the power to negotiate with the suppliers who have submitted acceptable proposals in order to select the final choice.

The Qualified Products List

With certain products, the invitation for bids or request for proposals will state that the item to be purchased is on a qualified products list. This means that only those bids or proposals offering products that have previously passed qualification tests will be considered. The qualification requirement is evoked with much greater frequency for some products than for others. Before you invest your time and money in qualifying a product, you should check with the government agency or activity responsible for qualification.

Types of Contracts

In formally advertised buying, the government generally uses the firm-fixed-price contract (FFP). Another type essentially derived from this one but with provision for escalation, the FPE, is also used in special circumstances (see "Types of Contracts" under "Procurement by Formal Advertising" in this chapter). In negotiated buying, the variety of contractual arrangements is far larger (see "Types of Contracts" under "Procurement by Negotiation" in this chapter). Cost-plus-percentage-of-cost contracts are prohibited for all procurements. Where there is a pressing need for speed, a type of provisional instrument may be issued to permit work to begin, pending the finalization of the negotiated contract. This instrument is called a letter contract.

Solicitation Content

Every government solicitation document, whether it is an invitation for bids under the formal advertising procedure or a request for proposals under negotiated procurement will contain the following information:

1. **Requirements for a Responsive and Sound Bid on Proposal.** These are usually presented in the form of a work statement or specification covering such points as delivery schedules, data to be furnished by both parties, and so on. This specification can be used by the applicant as the basis for his or her estimates. In the case of a negotiated purchase, agencies usually require proof of financial stability as well as of capacity to fulfill the contract requirements. You may be asked, therefore, to furnish with your proposal basic financial data such as a current profit and loss statement and your most recent balance sheet. Even if this information is not requested with your proposal, it may be asked for later.

2. **Terms and Conditions.** These cover the following points, among others:
   a. Funding and payment
   b. Performance monitoring
   c. Inspection and acceptance of finished products
   d. Subcontractors
   e. Use of government property
   f. Disputes
   g. Changes in the contract
   h. Termination (with and without prejudice to the contractor)
   Several of these provisions are discussed in "Implementing the Contract" in this chapter.

3. **Procedural Instructions.** Among the items of information essential for preparing bids or proposals are opening and closing dates, authorization for alternative bids, and instructions to the contractor regarding the format of a proposal and the criteria for evaluating proposals.

4. **Policy Provisions.** Most solicitations contain provisions reflecting the government's socioeconomic and financial policies. You may be

asked to certify or attest to compliance with these policies not only when you submit a bid or proposal but also at intervals during the life of the contract.

Government policies can be classified as business or public in nature. Business policies deal with such matters as contingent fee payments, use of current cost and price data, and independent price determination. Public policies are concerned with such matters as fostering small business and employment in general, improving wages and working conditions, equalizing employment opportunity, encouraging domestic purchasing—for example, the Buy American Act—and promoting a cleaner environment.

Nondiscrimination in employment and wages and working conditions are the subjects of two major policy provisions:

Equality of Employment Opportunity. This concept became law as a result of a series of presidential orders. Most contracts contain an equal opportunity clause forbidding discrimination against any job applicant or employee because of race, color, religion, sex, age, or national orgin. Both contractors and subcontractors have to file compliance reports in connection with this provision.

Adherence to Local Standards for Wages and Working Conditions. Under the Davis–Bacon Act of 1931, contractors and subcontractors working on public construction projects, including buildings, cannot pay lower wages than those prevailing in the municipality or other local jurisdiction in which the project is located. The secretary of labor has the power to determine what the prevailing wage is, and that determination is final and conclusive. The Services Contract Act of 1965 extended this concept to "service employees" and included fringe benefits in the wage computation. To fill some of the gaps in these laws, the Walsh–Healey Public Contracts Act requires contractors furnishing goods in excess of $10,000 to conform to "prevailing minimum wages," again as determined by the secretary of labor. Generally, the wages meant are the national minimums for similar work in the particular industry or similar industries. In some cases, however, the secretary has set higher minimums. In addition, the law forbids the contractor from using child or convict labor and also requires him or her to comply with occupational safety and health regulations.

Preparing Bids and Proposals

When you receive a solicitation, study the documents with the greatest of care before submitting your bid or proposal. Revision is virtually impossible after acceptance and, in the case of bids, very difficult even before acceptance. In this connection, remember that specifications, instructions to bidders, and conditions of purchase, delivery, and payment are part of the contract itself, as may also be special conditions relating to materials, packing, packaging, and delivery that may appear on a supplementary sheet accompanying the invitation and that may vary from the printed standard instructions. Any question you may have about specifications, methods of pricing, delivery, and similar matters should be taken up with the contracting officer prior to submittal.

If you decide, after reviewing the solicitation, that you cannot comply, be sure to write to the purchasing office to retain your listed status with it. Otherwise, you may be dropped. (You can ignore this recommendation when the solicitation absolved you from a "no bid" response.)

Once you have determined that you can physically fulfill the terms of the invitation, you must compute the price you will ask. This requires a very careful cost analysis covering materials, labor, overhead, packaging, freight, and many other items. Never substitute an item for one in the specifications no matter how objectively justifiable the substitution may appear, unless the specification contains an "or equal" provision. If you do, your bid and even your proposal may be rejected as being "nonresponsive" to the solicitation.

Submittal

When you submit your bid or proposal be sure to send the required number of copies and, in the case of a bid, to mail well before closing date. If the invitation called for a sample, be sure to tag and mark it carefully. Also make sure you have addressed it properly; the receiving point for samples may be different from that for the bids or proposals.

Proposals that arrive after the time set for opening but before the award is made will be given consideration if: (1) they were sent five days prior to the due date by registered mail or by certified mail, for which an official dated post office stamp (postmark) on the original receipt for certified mail has been obtained; (2) the government is satisfied that the late receipt was due solely to mishandling by the government after receipt at the government installation; or (3) the proposal is the only one received. You can modify or withdraw a submitted bid or proposal by writing or telegraphing the purchasing office. In the case of bids, however, notice of your action must be received by the office prior to the time set for opening.

Protest

If you believe that the government's evaluation of your bid or proposal has not been properly carried out, or if there is a defect in the procurement process, you have the right to protest. Protests can be registered before or after the award. You can file your protest with the contracting officer, who will forward it to a protest control officer, or you can protest directly to the comptroller general. The authorities are obliged to give a written protest full consideration and to reply specifically to each point raised. On the other hand, there is little use in protesting unless you have put together a convincing case supported by facts.

GOVERNMENT HELP IN SELLING TO THE GOVERNMENT

Government programs are an important source of assistance to businesses large and small. Of the programs applicable to small business, several are administered by the Small Business Administration, an agency of the government that works closely with government purchasers on behalf of small concerns.

The Small Business Administration

You should be thoroughly familiar with the functions of the Small Business Administration, which could be a valuable ally in competing for government business. The SBA has permanent representatives at major buying centers of the federal government and makes available representatives to smaller buying offices on a liaison basis.

Qualifying as a Small Business

The SBA has listed a number of criteria for qualifying an operation as a small business (under the Small Business Size Standards Regulation).

They include number of employees, annual receipts, and affiliates, among other factors. If you meet these criteria, you can certify yourself as a small business when bidding on a government contract. The SBA is not bound by these criteria alone, however. The administration reserves the right to deny you its special assistance if you are not independently owned and operated or if you are dominant in the field of operation in which you are bidding. In addition, your status as a small business can be reviewed at any time. (Businesses have the right to petition the SBA to initiate reviews of other enterprises.) For information on qualifying as a small business and on specific industry classifications—manufacturing, nonmanufacturing, construction, services, transportation, refined petroleum products, and research, development, and testing—contact the nearest SBA field office.

Small Business Administration Services

The SBA's essential function is to advise and assist small enterprises in doing business with the government. This function includes bringing government purchasers and small businesses together. In addition, as already noted, the SBA administers several government assistance programs applicable to small business.

Certificate of Competency. If you are a certified small business and a government purchaser determines that you are a bad risk in terms of technical or financial capacity, that agency must inform the SBA before awarding the contract. The SBA will carry out its own investigation, and if it decides in your favor, it will issue a certificate of competence, which will effectively reinstate you as a candidate.

Program for the Socially Disadvantaged. The SBA has the authority to assist small businesses owned or controlled by persons who belong to minority groups. Specifically, the administration is empowered under the Small Business Act, as amended, to contract with any government agency or department and to subcontract the work called for to any small business that qualifies under the act. To apply for this kind of assistance, you submit a certification that your business is owned or destined to be owned by a member of a disadvantaged minority group and include a proposed business development plan as well.

If you do business with the government on a recurring basis or if you stand a reasonable chance of getting, on your own, a contract equivalent in scope to the SBA subcontract, you are not eligible for this service. In addition, the SBA will not undertake this subcontract arrangement when the goods or services are already the subject of a public solicitation. Further information on this program is available at any SBA field office.

Set-Asides

When a contracting officer is satisfied that a particular purchase is within the capacity of a small business and that a sufficient number of small businesses would be interested in the contract, he or she may reserve the purchase entirely for applicants of this class. The contracting officer can also create a partial set-aside covering portions of a contract and leaving the rest of the contract for open bidding. Under this arrangement, the exclusivity implicit in the concept of set-asides is qualified by certain conditions too complicated to go into here. Nevertheless, partial set-asides can constitute an opportunity for small business. Partial set-asides are also available to *all* businesses operating or willing to operate in designated areas in which unemployment levels are higher than the national average.

PROCUREMENT BY FORMAL ADVERTISING

Purchasing or "procurement" by formal advertising is required of government agencies under the Federal Property and Administrative Services Act of 1949, as amended. Part 1–2 of the Federal Procurement Regulations issued under the act consitutes the primary source of guidance to government personnel for this method of contracting.

Prerequisites

Although formal advertising is the required method of procurement for use by government officers, it is not a system of procurement that can be used blindly. In order to have a successful formally advertised procurement, there are certain prerequisites with respect to the nature of the supplies or services to be procured that must be met. They are that:

1. There is adequate competition for the procurement.
2. There are adequate specifications describing the nature of the government requirement.
3. There is adequate time to carry out the procedures of formal advertising.
4. The price will be an adequate basis for determining the source to be awarded the contract.

Competition will ordinarily be deemed adequate if there are at least two organizations known to be able and willing to handle the contract. To establish this fact, agencies are prepared to undertake a certain amount of investigation. The absence of precise and accurate requirements is characteristic of research and development projects, and accordingly, conventional bidding on these projects is rare. In connection with the third prerquisite, do not assume that formal advertising always takes more time than negotiated procurement. With sensitive procurements, however, the latter procedure can be more easily expedited. The significance of the fourth circumstance is that when considerations other than price are critical to the awarding of a contract, these factors cannot always be specified in the invitation.

Processing of Bids

Advertised procurement is a highly proceduralized and formal process. All bids must arrive sealed and be opened publicly in a designated place at an appointed time, as set forth in the bid invitation. Of course, this procedure is designed so that no one can use your (or anyone else's) bid as a basis for his or hers.

At the public opening, the bids are abstracted; that is, the price offered by each bidder is publicly posted and revealed to all interested parties. After bid opening, all bidders must remain in the competition for the contract award during the time in which the government evaluates received bids and determines the winning bidder. This rule is known as the firm-bid rule. Exceptions to the rule may be made where a mistake has been discovered.

Constraints on Communication

Normally, during the formal advertising process you will not be permitted to communicate with an offering agency except on a formal, written basis. Whether you have bid at the time you make your inquiry is immaterial. The purpose of this policy is to prevent any party from extracting more information than any other. Government agencies sometimes hold prebid conferences at which questions may be asked, to facilitate equal and simultaneous disclosure of information to all parties. After bids have been submitted, do not expect officials to tell you the name and number of firms solicited, or to disclose the terms and conditions received from individual bidders, proprietary data included in bids, or anything that may prompt any party to raise a claim of prejudice or preference.

Factors in Evaluating Bids

Bids are evaluated on the basis of four criteria: responsiveness, price, nonprice factors, and bidder responsibility.

Responsiveness   Responsiveness means adherence to the precise terms set forth in the solicitation document, such as specifications, quantities to be delivered, schedules, and other stipulations, whether required by regulations or developed for purposes related to the particular purchase. If your bid is determined to be nonresponsive, you will be excluded from further consideration.

Price.   The price determined is the true or effective price, as opposed to the quoted price. A number of factors account for the distinction. For example, as a matter of principle, any discounts offered by the bidder, go to reducing the effective price. The terms on which the discounts are available, however, must be advantageous to the government. Thus, if you offer a discount for early payment, the maximum payment delay for which the discount is available must exceed the buyer's standard payment delay as stipulated in the invitation for bids.

Other adjustments that will be made in determining the effective price are for such factors as transportation, government inspection, use of government property, and possibly other elements set forth in the IFB. Note that any such adjustments in your bid price must be in accordance with the requirements specified in the invitation. Thus, you will have the opportunity to consider these factors when developing your bid.

Nonprice Factors.   Factors not related to price that may enter into the evaluation of bids include, among others, delivery schedules and the availability to the government of proprietary data. The IFB will identify these factors and also indicate the weight to be given them in the evaluation process. In addition, certain priorities may apply in the event that the low bids of two or more competitors are equal and the bids are otherwise equal in all respects. Under these conditions, the award decision may be governed by the small business or the labor surplus area set-aside program (FPR 1–2.407–6).

Bidder Responsibility.   Under government policy, a contractor who cannot be classified by the contracting officer as a responsible contractor cannot be awarded a government contract. There are several bases upon which the contracting officer must evaluate the responsibility of potential sources. Two of the most important are, first, the capacity of the contractor to perform the work, including his or her ability to comply with the government's specified delivery schedule, and second, his or her ability to finance the costs of work until payment by the government is received. These two elements are known as *capacity* and *credit*.

Acceptance, Rejection, and Award

Ordinarily, the contract will be awarded during the acceptance period specified in the IFB. If this is impossible, the contracting officer will obtain an extension from each bidder. The award is made by furnishing to the successful bidder a properly executed award document or a notice of award in a format as determined by the procuring agency.

A government agency may terminate bidding at any stage without awarding the contract. Naturally, this action penalizes bidders in proportion to the time and money they invested in preparing their bids. There are many reasons for cancelling an advertised procurement. The commonest are:

Indications of collusion among the bidders

Ambiguities or defects in the specifications

Cessation of need for the supplies or services

If this should happen, you will be notified and told why the action was taken. The government assumes no liability for your bidding costs however.

Mistakes in Bids

As in any formal offer, mistakes in bids can range in potential consequence from trivial to catastrophic.

Disposition before Award.   A contract officer has two ways in which to handle a mistake in a bid: he or she can allow a correction or a withdrawal of the bid. In practice, the officer may be reluctant to let you withdraw if he or she considers that it is feasible to correct the error.

In general, the officer will deem correction feasible if *both* of the following conditions are present:

The change would not alter the relative standing of the bidders.

The error is of the kind whose existence and scope can be demonstrated without recourse to any document not part of the original bid. (In practice, nearly all errors of this sort are clerical in nature).

Do not assume, however, that any claim of error you make will be uncritically accepted. The officer may decide that there was no error and that you are merely looking for a chance to get in a last-minute change or to back out of the bidding. In that case, he or she may refuse you the right either to make the change or to withdraw.

Disposition after Award.   If you have accepted the contract on the basis of a bid that contains an error, you will, of course, have more difficulty in getting an adjustment than you would have had adjusting the bid before acceptance. If, however, you can show that the error was obvious—either because it created a conflict with other features of the bid or because it produced an estimate clearly out of proportion to the whole procurement—you can have the contract rescinded. Otherwise, your contract will stand unless the change would favor the government.

Types of Contracts

There are two types of contracts used in formal advertising procurement, the firm-fixed-price contract (FFP) and the fixed-price contract with escalation (FPE). Under the first type, the contractor assumes 100 percent of the monetary risk of performance; under the second, the government accepts some of the risk (FPR 1–2.104–1).

PROCUREMENT BY NEGOTIATION

Negotiated procurement is authorized only when formal advertising is not feasible. As the term *negotiated* implies, this kind of government buying involves a discussion between the government agency and the potential supplier. Virtually all facets of the proposed relationship may be covered, not only price, performance, and quality requirements but also such factors as the contractor's managerial structure and the availability to the contractor of government facilities.

Usually, negotiated purchase is competitive. In certain circumstances, however, the government recognizes that "sole source" or noncompetitive procurement is essential. The commonest reason for noncompetitive negotiated procurement is that one organization or individual is believed to stand out far above the rest in the capacity to supply the needed goods or services within the required time. Even here, however, there is an element of competition, because if, as a result of the discussions, it appears that the agency's confidence is misplaced, another contractor will be solicited.

In contrast to the situation under bidding, you are not expected to confine your communications to formalized written inquiries. The very nature of the procedure precludes this kind of restriction. Nevertheless, the same restrictions apply to sensitive information as apply under bidding (see "Procurement by Formal Advertising" in this chapter).

Legal Background

The authority to negotiate nonmilitary procurement is granted government agencies in 15 situations that are set out in the Federal Property and Administrative Services Act. The authority to negotiate military procurement is granted in 17 situations that are set out in 10 U.S.C. 2304.

The Federal Property and Administrative Services Act

This enactment allows for purchases by negotiation in such areas as medical sevices and research and development. It also provides for negotiated procurement when purchases are small or competition is not feasible. (Usually, the request for a proposal will contain a declaration, or "determination and finding," asserting the legality of the procedure in that instance.)

The "Truth in Negotiations" Act

The central requirement of this statute is that where there is reasonable expectation that a negotiated procurement will exceed $500,000 the contractor must submit cost and pricing data in support of the proposal. The requirement, which is subject to certain exceptions, applies not only to new procurement actions but also to any negotiated contract modification that exceeds $500,000, even though the original procurement action may have been formally advertised and therefore exempt from the requirement. The law also allows the contracting officer to apply this requirement where the original contract or the modification totals less than $500,000.

The law stipulates that the submitted cost and pricing data must be current, complete, and accurate at the time of the negotiation agreement and that the contractor must so certify to the contracting officer. In addition, the contractor is held responsible for obtaining this same type of information from any subcontractors.

To implement these provisions, the standard negotiated contract provides for an audit of performance records. If the cost and pricing data previously submitted and certified are discovered to be overstated at the time of submission and certification, the government has the right to reduce the agreed-on price by the amount of the overstatement. Finally, the 1962 statute requires the contracting officer to negotiate with all offerors "in competitive range"—that is, those that have passed a preliminary scrutiny.

The Negotiating Process

Negotiations may be carried out in writing or orally. The contracting officer will point out apparent ambiguities, uncertainties, or deficiencies in your proposal and will give you a reasonable opportunity to clarify, correct, or otherwise strengthen it. The officer may conclude the negotiation process by asking all offerors for a best and final offer and advising them of a cutoff date.

Criteria for Choice

The selection decision is based upon the contracting officer's judgment as to which offeror or which proposal offers the greatest advantage to the government, "price and other factors considered." This means that a higher-priced offer may be selected over lower-priced offers if other factors, especially technical superiority, are found to overweigh the price factor. The process of evaluation is least subjective in the case of research and development procurement, where systems have been established for quantifying technical and managerial capabilities.

Debriefings

If your proposal is one of those turned down, and you wish to know the reason why, the offering agency will grant you an explanatory or debriefing conference. At this session, you can learn in general terms the factors that weighed against you and for your competitor. If you plan to do business with the government on a regular basis, you should take advantage of the opportunity to improve your bargaining skills that these sessions offer.

Types of Contracts

In the Federal Procurement Regulations (Sections 1–3.404 through 1–3.409), the following types of contracts are delineated for use by federal civilian agencies in negotiated purchasing:

Firm fixed price (FFP)

Fixed price with escalation (FPE)

Fixed price incentive (FPI)

Fixed price redeterminable prospective (FPRP)

Fixed price redeterminable retroactive (FPRR)

Cost reimbursement (CR)

Cost sharing (CS)

Cost plus incentive fee (CPIF)

Cost plus a fixed fee (CPFF)

Time and materials (T&M)

Labor hour (LH)

Letter (LC)

Indefinite delivery (IDC)

These contracts range from the stringent fixed-price type, under which price is predetermined when the contract is awarded, to the cost type, under which the ultimate price to be paid for the procurement is determined in an audit of performance costs undertaken after the completion of the work. Between·these extremes is a spectrum of pricing arrangements varying in flexibility. One of the commonest is the fixed price redeterminable, which allows for recomputing initial costs that are likely to vary later, such as production runs.

IMPLEMENTING THE CONTRACT

When you accept a contract you begin a relationship with the government agency that will last the life of the contract. Implementation of the terms and conditions of that contract will involve administrative procedures of varying complexity. Some of these are discussed in the following subsections.

Administrative Considerations

Among the points covered in the terms and conditions of the contract (some of which are listed in the overview section), four merit a closer look. These are funding and payment, inspection and acceptance, changes in the contract, and termination.

Funding and Payment

If your contract is of the fixed-price type, you will be paid either in a lump sum at the completion of the work or—and this is the commoner arrangement—in a series of partial payments based on partial delivery and acceptance. If your contract is terminated for default in performance, you may be required to return these payments, that is, to write off the expenses you incurred. Under a cost-reimbursement contract, you will receive the funds on presentation of an invoice and verification of the cost incurred during contract performance.

Inspection and Acceptance

Basically, the inspection and acceptance clause gives the contracting officer the right to inspect your production process at reasonable intervals during the life of the contract. The clause also entitles the officer to inspect your finished product before accepting it and to refuse acceptance for cause. If your product is the kind for which qualitative factors can be expressed by specifications, the purchaser may be satisfied with simple proof of conformity to agreed-on numbers. In that case, you should set up an efficient quality-control system. If the contracting officer is satisfied that you have such a system, you may be subjected to little or no surveillance.

Ordinarily, once the government accepts your product, it has no recourse, at least for that particular run or batch, unless it can prove fraud or demonstrate that the defects are of a kind that defy ordinary inspection techniques. Some contracts, however, require the contractor to grant the purchaser an extended warranty, valid after acceptance.

Changes

All government contracts contain a clause giving the purchaser broad authority to make changes affecting the work contracted for. If you incur any additional costs because of these changes, you have the right to demand additional compensation—even with a fixed-price contract. You must submit a written request for the adjustment within 30 days after receiving written notice of the intended change.

Sometimes contract provisions are altered informally at the instigation of the contractor or at the request of the government agency. With this practice, there is always the possibility that later, when you request compensation for expenses resulting from the change, the official who made the commitment is no longer around or has lost all record of it.

Termination

Your contract with a government agency will contain a provision for termination either at the convenience of the government or for default of the contractor. Termination at convenience is usually the result of a change in the government's needs or a cutoff of essential funds. In any case, you are entitled to compensation, but you should be prepared for some delay and considerable red tape.

When you are terminated for default you are held responsible for the nonperformance of your contract. The government will contend that you either failed to make a delivery of acceptable quality on schedule or were not making adequate progress toward fulfilling the contract. In the latter case, you must be given notice of the government's intention to terminate and an opportunity to show why this action should not be taken. Normally, a default relieves the government of the obligation to pay you anything, even amounts to cover costs previously incurred. Furthermore, the government may recover from you any excess in the costs called for under your contract over the costs of obtaining the needed goods or services elsewhere.

Delays.   Delays in meeting delivery schedules are a major cause of termination by default. Often a government agency will accept a later delivery, thereby prompting the contractor to believe that the lateness will be ignored. Unfortunately, the acceptance of your late delivery does not constitute a waiver of the government's right to declare you in default because of that lateness. Therefore, if anything happens that could impede your ability to meet delivery schedules and you are not at fault, it is very important that you demand an immediate adjustment in the schedules, including, if necessary, an extension in the life of the contract. Once the machinery of termination has been set in motion, you may be able to save yourself from being sued—by proving you were not to blame—but you may have a difficult time reversing the termination decision.

CHAPTER
FOURTEEN

GOING PUBLIC

The expression *going public* describes the process by which the securities—generally, common or preferred stock or bonds—of a privately owned company are, for the first time, offered for sale to and purchased by the general public. When the securities offered are in fact purchased by the public, the offering is called successful, and the company is then "publicly owned."

Shareholders of growth-oriented closely held companies may begin to have visions of the company's name appearing in the New York Stock Exchange listings when they find that the capital needed to meet short- and long-term goals has outpaced traditional sources. Additional capital from the public is very attractive. After all, the purchasers of a company's common stock are paid no interest on their investment; the corporate officers do not guarantee its repayment, marketability, or value; and, so far as the corporation is concerned, the investment is permanent.

A company may sell its previously unissued securities to raise additional capital, in which case the company will receive all of the proceeds—a "primary offering." Alternatively, securities that belonged to the owners of the company may be sold, whereby the owners receive the proceeds—a "secondary distribution." Sometimes the offering may be a combination, partly for the account of shareholders and partly for the account of the company.

An investor is generally motivated to purchase a new stock issue only if he or she thinks it is a better investment than an insured certificate of deposit, Treasury bill, or the like. The value of the investment will increase only if, over time, the public places a higher value on the security than at the date he or she purchased it. Although many factors affect the market value of a company's stock, the company's performance is a major one. In turn, the company's performance may be dependent on its access to capital for expansion, equipment, acquisitions, advertising, and so on. Therefore, investors want all or a major portion of the proceeds of an offering to be available to the company. An initial offering is much less attractive when a substantial amount of the proceeds is intended for the present owners. Consequently, initial public offerings are almost always primary offerings or offerings in which only a small number of shares held by owners are included in the offering.

In this chapter we discuss the positives and negatives of "going public." We cover the team members needed for the undertaking, the types of offerings, and the process of registering securities for sale under the various securities laws. We also discuss the company's ongoing reporting obligations. For purposes of this chapter, we assume that the management of a privately held company is considering a sale to the public of only its common stock.

PROS AND CONS OF GOING PUBLIC

The ultimate decision to go public should not be treated lightly. Although it offers many attractive advantages, it also has many disadvantages that must be weighed carefully. Once a company takes the step, it is difficult to retreat to nonpublic status.

Why Go Public?

The more important reasons that companies go public are discussed in the following subsections.

Owner Diversification and Liquidity

If you have all or most of your wealth invested in your business, going public is one means by which you can sell part of your holdings for cash and diversify by using the cash to invest in Treasury bills, other common stocks, bonds, real estate, or blue delft china. Most owners would like to limit the number of shares sold so that sufficient cash is raised yet control of the business is retained.

Estate-Tax Planning

In the event of your death, your shares in the company you own must be valued to determine the taxable value of your estate. If, as a result, substantial estate taxes are due, your executors could be forced to sell the company in order to raise the cash needed to pay the estate taxes. When a company's shares are widely owned by the public and the stock is actively traded on an exchange or in the over-the-counter market, the value and marketability of the securities for estate-tax purposes can be more clearly established.

Marketability of Investments

You may want to dispose of a portion of your holdings during your lifetime in order to be in a more liquid position. This disposition would, of course, be easier if there were an established market for the securities of your company. If would also be easier for you or any other shareholder to borrow money with collateral consisting of securities that have an established market than with securities having no market.

Access to Long-Term Capital

During the time it is privately owned, a company may be severely restricted in its sources of capital. For the most part, a company expands by reinvesting its undistributed earnings and by looking to its owners, banks, or institutional lenders for additional capital funds. Without additional capital, the company's earning capacity may be restricted, the ability of the owners to provide capital may be limited, and borrowings must be repaid with interest. Sale of the company's stock, however, provides permanent non-interest-bearing capital. Furthermore, once the company and its securities are known to the investing public, future offerings of additional stock of the company, assuming no adverse change in its affairs, may be easier to sell. Lending institutions often prefer borrowers that are publicly owned, since the market represents a potential source of additional equity capital through future offerings.

Subsequent Capital Needs

When securities are offered for sale to the public, they must first be registered with the Securities and Exchange Commission (SEC). Once the company has gone through the SEC's registration process, succeeding issues will ordinarily take less time to process. Registered companies may, under certain circumstances, also qualify to use simplified registration forms when offering additional securities.

Expansion through Business Combinations

When a company's securities have an established market, it is easier to negotiate mergers or acquisitions using the company's own securities.

When privately owned companies want to acquire another business, it is difficult to trade their stock for the acquired entity since it is not possible to measure clearly the market value of the stock being given up. With publicly held shares, however, there is less room for argument about the value of those shares, since the newspaper listings of quotations show the value that the investing public places on the shares. All other things being equal, the owners of a private company are often more interested in merging with a public company than with another private company because the shareholders may prefer to exchange their private holdings for a readily marketable security.

Employee Benefit Plans and Incentives

When a company is publicly owned, it is possible to establish stock compensation arrangements that will serve as an inducement to attract and keep key personnel. Stock option plans, for example, may be more attractive to officers and other key personnel than are generous salary arrangements, since these plans provide the employee with a sense of ownership and the opportunity to share in any appreciation in the price of the stock while offering tax advantages as well.

Public Awareness of Business

Every shareholder is a potential customer. The company often benefits when its shares are owned by the public, especially if the company sells a product or service that the public buys. The more widespread the distribution of shares, the greater the benefits.

Reasons Not to Go Public

There are some significant disadvantages associated with going public, and you should consider them carefully before making your decision.

Accounting and Tax Practices

Owner–managers are typically more concerned with tax savings than with earnings per share. Their historical accounting practices may be designed solely for the purpose of minimizing taxes on income. Their financial statements may not have been audited or even prepared in accordance with generally accepted accounting principles (GAAP). If this applies to you, you must be prepared to put your "accounting house" in order before going public. Conformity of financial statements to prescribed rules and GAAP is a condition of filing with the SEC. The cost and other implications of the changes you might have to make to meet the SEC standards could conceivably be a significant hurdle to the big step.

Lack of Operating Confidentiality

The registration statement and subsequent reports to shareholders will require disclosure of many facets of your company's business, operations, and finances that may never before have been known outside the company. Some particularly sensitive areas of disclosure will be the remuneration of officers and directors; the security holdings of officers, directors, and major stockholders ("insiders"); details regarding stock option plans and deferred compensation plans; and extensive financial information, including sales, costs of sales, gross profits, net income, borrowings, sales to major customers, and much more.

Lack of Business Flexibility

Prior to going public, you can operate your business independently. You can take whatever risks you wish to take, secure in the knowledge that it is only your own money (or the bank's) that is at stake. Once the company becomes publicly owned, you acquire as many partners as you have shareholders, and you will be accountable to them.

In a closely held company, management has the flexibility to focus attention on long-term goals, even if earnings in the near term will suffer. In a public company, the investor's return is dependent on the company's performance. Shareholders expect steady growth in sales, profits, market share, product innovation, and so on. Management must always weigh short-term strategies to achieve growth with long-term goals. For example, management may believe that a substantial advertising and marketing campaign will result in the development of a profitable product line within a year or two. In the interim, however, the cost of the campaign will depress earnings. Management must weigh the potential long-term benefits against shareholder reaction, the effect on the market value of the stock, and the risk that the long-term sales goal may not be achieved. Finally, business flexibility may be limited in certain actions, such as sale of the company and election of officers, which require the vote of the shareholders. The ability to act quickly is lost if management must wait for the vote to take place.

Initial Cost of Offering

The process of going public is expensive and time-consuming. The preparation of the registration document is a complicated process that occupies the time of many people within the organization and several outside experts. Ordinarily, the documents must pass critical review by two sets of lawyers, those of the company and those of the underwriter, and the financial information must be audited by an independent public accountant. The printing bill alone in an undertaking of this kind is often quite substantial.

Ongoing Costs

After going public, most companies become subject to the SEC's periodic reporting requirements, which are designed to keep the information in the registration statement up to date. This will require the maintenance of adequate financial staff and outside experts, adding to the company's cost of doing business.

Demand for Dividends

As owner of a private company, you may have declared dividends sporadically, depending on your needs and in consideration of the sections of the Internal Revenue Code dealing with unreasonable compensation or accumulations of earnings (see Chapter 11). As publicly owned, however, the company may have to adopt a more regular dividend policy because the shareholders may demand it. Generally, however, investors in companies that have "gone public" do not expect a dividend during the first several years of its public life. They expect earnings to be reinvested to ensure long-term viability.

Restrictions on Management

After the public offering, the officers, directors, and principal holders of the company's equity securities will, in all probability, become subject to the insider trading provisions under SEC regulations. Because they have access to information before the public does, such persons (officers, directors, and certain large shareholders) must exercise caution in trading in the company's equity securities. For example, gains they realize in closed transactions (purchase and sale or sale and purchase) within a six-month period may be recoverable by the company if these parties are found to have obtained an advantage from insider information.

Possible Loss of Management Control

If more than 50 percent of the company's shares are sold to the public, the original owners could eventually lose control of the company. This is especially likely to happen if most of the shares sold to the public become concentrated in the hands of a few individuals who could challenge management and possibly obtain control of the company by voting themselves on the board of directors at the annual stockholder meeting. If, however, the shares held by the public are widely distributed, control over the company could be exercised by management even though less than 50 percent of the shares are owned.

Obtaining and Paying the Underwriter

The company must generally obtain the services of an underwriter, who will sell the stock and perform ongoing investment banking services. In addition to their commission upon a successful offering of generally up to 10 percent, underwriters generally require a nonrefundable fee at the time they are engaged to cover their initial expenses.

WHEN TO GO PUBLIC

After giving careful consideration to the pros and cons of going public, you may conclude that the advantages are sufficiently attractive and that the disadvantages can, at the very least, be tolerated. The next question to answer is when to do it.

Clearly, the objective is to sell the company's stock at the highest possible price. After all, the higher the price is, the less the dilution of ownership suffered by existing shareholders. That is, the higher the price, the fewer shares that need be issued to others to raise a given amount of capital. In addition, the higher the value placed on shares being sold, the higher the value of the shares owned by existing shareholders.

The Importance of Timing

Timing plays as important a part as any other factor in determining the final price of the shares. Almost any company that went public during the late 1960s (a great bull market) would have done so at a higher offering price than the same company could have gotten in the mid-1970s (the worst bear market since the 1940s). In addition to cyclical market factors, particular industries become "hot" and "cold." In today's environment, the hot industries are those involving computers, genetic engineering, and energy. Unlike the private sale of stock, where negotiations can be carried on in the form of face-to-face meetings, stock sold through the public markets is basically priced by market psychology. Hence, the importance of timing in pricing a public stock issue.

Other Factors

Other pertinent factors are the company's historical growth rate of revenue and earnings and, in general, how the company compares to its competitors. If the company is a leader in its industry and the industry is hot, the company will be valued at a higher price that it would if the circumstances were reversed.

The following are some of the other factors to consider in deciding when to go public.

Are additional capital funds from financial institutions, venture capitalists, or current shareholders either no longer available or available only at a greater cost than a public offering?

Has the company demonstrated a sustained or increasing rate of growth high enough to attract investors? Generally, a company that outpaces the industry average in growth will have a better chance of attracting prospective investors than will one with either marginal or inconsistent growth.

Has the company reached the point at which the prospects for maintaining a strong sales and earnings growth trend in the future are reasonably good?

Do the company's products or services have a high degree of visibility and interest to the investing public?

Is management at a stage where it believes it can cope with the costs of the transition and meet the disclosure and financial reporting requirements and other associated demands that will be made by the newly acquired "business partners" and the regulatory authorities?

Are new security issues faring well in the market?

Is the economic situation favorable, and is there reasonable expectation that it will remain so in the near term?

Has the stock market been strong and generally rising, and is it reasonable to expect that it will remain so at least in the near term?

A good underwriter helps identify the right time—the "window"—for the offering, that is, when it can be sold for the highest price. (The underwriter has a vested interest in selling the stock for as high a price as possible since his or her compensation is based on the selling price.) The underwriter will also try to isolate the positive and unique characteristics of its client. Quantitatively, this is done through the preparation of "spread" sheets that compare the important financial characteristics of the company to other businesses in its industry. The underwriter's impression of you and your managers, particularly in the way you make oral presentations to groups of the underwriter's stockbrokers, could affect the price of the stock.

THE TEAM

Once you have decided to go forward with the public offering, your next most important task is to assemble the "registration team" to get the offering accomplished. The team will consist of, in addition to management, the company's legal counsel, the underwriter, the underwriter's legal counsel, and independent accountants.

The Underwriter

The principal role of the underwriter is to sell the securities to the public. Prior to that time, however, the underwriter also plays a significant role in advising the company on the opportunities for financing, structuring the transaction, and assisting in determining the proper timing of the offering. The choice of underwriter is not a decision to be taken lightly since the investment bankers who perform these services vary widely in quality, cost, and types of services. Some of the factors to be considered in selecting the underwriter are:

Reputation.   The firm should have a good reputation in the investment community and among others who have used its services.

Experience.   The underwriter should have experience and success with the underwritings that are similar in number of shares and dollar amount to your contemplated offering.

Market-Making Capabilities.   The underwriter should have the ability to attract a large number of investors in the sale of the initial offering and to generate sufficient interest in the stock so as to maintain a good market for the stock after the initial offering is sold.

Ability to Provide Other Investment Banking Services after the Offering.   The underwriter should be prepared to provide such services as assisting in locating additional sources of public or private capital, advising potential acquisitions, and general financial counseling.

Fees to be Charged.   The underwriter's commissions and expenses for performing the brokering function should be competitive.

The best way to gather information on the capabilities of the underwriter is to ask the officers of other companies who have used its services. The company's accountant and lawyer, both of whom have frequent contact with underwriters on a regular basis, should also be reliable sources of recommendations. Ultimately, it is necessary for management to interview several underwriting firms and ask for proposals from each before selecting the underwriter.

Other Team Members

Many of the factors that should be considered in the selection of the underwriter, such as reputation, experience, service, and fee, are for the most part equally applicable in the selection of the other team members. The other team members and their roles are discussed in the following subsections.

Counsel for the Company

The competence of company legal counsel and his or her familiarity with SEC rules and regulations and the registration process are critical to the timely and effective coordination of this undertaking. His or her principal role is to advise the company with respect to compliance with the provisions of the securities acts and the various state and other federal laws to which the company and the offering will become subject. Counsel will also oversee the progress of the various members of the registration team and ensure the timeliness and completeness of the process. He or she also coordinates the resolution of any questions arising from the SEC review and the filing of the necessary amendments, and should any conferences with the SEC be necessary, counsel would be expected to attend them together with the company's representative.

Counsel for the Underwriter

Counsel for the underwriter is generally responsible for drafting the underwriting agreement. He or she also reviews the entire registration statement and any related agreements and contracts that are filed as exhibits thereto. His or her principal objective in reviewing the registration statement is to ascertain on behalf of the underwriter that the registration statement is complete and not misleading.

The Independent Accountant

The independent accountant's principal responsibilities in connection with the preparation of a registration statement are:

Examining and expressing an opinion on the various financial statements that are required to be included in the document

Reading, in depth, the textual portion of the registration statement in
order to ascertain any inconsistencies that may necessitate changes or
corrections to the text or the financial statements

Issuing a letter—referred to as a "comfort letter"—to the underwriters,
covering, in general, compliance of the financial statements, in both
form and content, with the applicable SEC regulations and describing
any adverse changes in the company's financial position since the
date of the last audited balance sheet

TYPES OF OFFERINGS

When the underwriter is selected, a "letter of intent" should be signed
that outlines the proposed terms of the offering and in effect acknowl-
edges the intent of the underwriter to execute an underwriting agreement before the conclusion of the registration process. The letter of intent is not a binding agreement to underwrite the offering but rather a
preliminary understanding as to the terms of the offering. It outlines the
underwriter's compensation and any reimbursement for his or her expenses and defines the type of underwriting. The following types of underwriting may be entered into:

Best Efforts.   The underwriter agrees to use his or her best efforts to
sell as many shares as possible and is not obligated to purchase any
unsold securities.

Best Efforts, All or None.   The offering is cancelled if the underwriter
is unable to sell the entire issue.

Firm Commitment.   The underwriter agrees to buy all of the stock
being offered for sale and thereby assumes the risk for any unsold securities.

The Underwriting Agreement

Regardless of the type of underwriting, the signing of the actual underwriting agreement will generally not take place until the registration

statement is expected to be effective. Thus, even though your company may incur considerable expenses in anticipation of an offering, there is no advance assurance that the offering will actually take place. A reputable underwriter, however, will generally not turn away from the underwriting without having a valid and significant reason.

Normally, the underwriting agreement is a document of 10–15 printed pages and will cover matters including:

Agreement by the company to sell and the underwriter to purchase a certain number of shares at a designated price (depending on the type of offering)

Warranties by the company as to the completeness and accuracy of the information included in the registration statement

Indemnification of the underwriter against liabilities arising under the federal securities laws

Conditions or events that must occur before the underwriter is obligated to pay for the securities, such as receipt of a representation letter from the company's counsel that the company has met all legal requirements to complete the offering and of an acceptable comfort letter from the company's independent accountants

Time and location of the closing

THE PROCESS

Once you have selected the underwriter and the other members of the registration team are in place, you can proceed in orderly fashion to move the public offering forward. The process generally commences with an organizational conference attended by all the members of the registration team, including:

The chief executive and financial officers of the company

Counsel for the company

A representative of the underwriters

Counsel for the underwriters

The independent accountant

Matters usually discussed at the organizational conference include the nature of the offering, the SEC registration form to use, the anticipated filing date, and a detailed timetable (see Appendix to this chapter) for the registration by each member of the team and indicating the dates on which the steps are to be completed. The entire process generally requires several months and in capsule form consists of the following steps:

Preparation of the initial registration statement

Filing the initial registration statement with the SEC

Obtaining the SEC's review comments and resolving them

Preparing the amended registration statement including additional disclosures required by the SEC

Distribution of the preliminary ("red herring") prospectus

Holding the due diligence meeting

Finalizing the underwriting agreement and determining the number of shares to be offered

Setting of the final price for the shares

Closing

The Initial Registration Statement

The form and content of the registration statement are prescribed by the SEC. The type of information included in the statement will vary to a certain extent depending on the particular registration form called for in the filing.

Generally, the responsibility for the preparation of the nonfinancial portions of the registration statement falls upon counsel for the company. Preparation of the financial portions usually rests with the company's financial management in consultation with outside accountants. The registration statement is in two parts: part one normally goes to the prospective (or public) buyers of the securities; part two contains supplemental data and is available for public inspection at the offices of the SEC.

Part One.

Part one of the registration statement, also known as the prospectus, contains basic business information covering:

The company's business and its properties

The underwriter's compensation (in detail)

Any significant legal proceedings in which the company is involved

The extent of the company's competition

The securities being offered

Names of directors and officers and their remuneration

Any options outstanding to purchase securities

The company's financial history, as follows:

> Detailed financial statements for three years that have been audited by an independent public accountant, and, in some instances, interim unaudited financial data as well
>
> Selected financial data, including such items as revenues, net income, earnings per share, total assets, and long-term debt, all for a period of five years
>
> Management's description of the company's financial condition in terms of liquidity and capital resources and its explanation of any factors that significantly affected the company's operating results

The prospectus generally serves two purposes. The first is as a selling document to prospective buyers of the securities. The second is as a form of legal protection for the issuing company and its officers. It ensures that a prospective purchaser has been provided with relevant information about the company so he or she can make an informed judgment with respect to his or her investment.

The dual functions that the prospectus serves may, however, be in conflict with each other. Management naturally wishes to tell the prospective investors about the company's past achievements and to predict successful operations. At the same time, to guard against possible litigation from purchasers of the securities who may claim they were misled, management must make sure that it adequately discloses the risks. The members of the team preparing the registration statement must use their professional judgment to balance these two objectives.

Part Two

Part two of the registration statement contains supplemental data, which are not required to be provided to each prospective investor. The statement includes such items as:

A listing of subsidiaries of the registrant

Certain data with respect to recent sales of unregistered securities

Listings of financial statements and copies of certain documents filed as exhibits

Descriptions of marketing arrangements

Details of the expenses of the offering

Schedules of pertinent financial data

Filing and Securities and Exchange Commission Review

Registration statements filed by first-time issuers are subjected to review by staff specialists at the SEC, generally consisting of a lawyer, accountant, and financial analyst. The group may also consult with other staff experts, such as mining or petroleum engineers. The staff reviews the documents filed to determine whether there has been full and fair disclosure, particularly whether the document contains any untrue or misleading material statements of fact or whether there are omissions of material facts. The SEC review cannot be relied on by anyone, however, for assurance of the accuracy of the data, and no comfort should be derived from the fact that such a review has been performed.

The review of the financial data is performed by a staff accountant, who reads the entire prospectus and the remainder of the registration statement to become familiar with the company and its business. The staff accountant may also refer to published annual and interim reports and newspaper articles for information regarding the company and its industry. The accountant's review is primarily directed at the financial statements and other financial data and the independent accountants' report, to determine whether they comply with the requirements of the SEC and the applicable pronouncements of the American Institute of Certified Public Accountants and the Financial Accounting Standards Board, as well as with the various SEC staff interpretations and policies dealing with accounting and auditing issues.

Although the securities laws contemplate a review of registration statements filed with the SEC, they do not specify the review procedures to be followed by the SEC in connection with the processing of these documents. The "informal" procedures followed have been developed by the SEC to make the comments resulting from the review available to registrants and to permit necessary revisions of a registration statement without formal proceedings. The informal-comment technique has proved to be an effective method of communicating and resolving defects before permitting a registration statement to become effective.

In connection with the review of a registration statement, the SEC generally issues a letter that sets forth the deficiencies and suggested revisions noted in its review. The letter, referred to as a letter of comment, is generally mailed to the company's counsel.

To save time in the registration process, company counsel generally maintains close contact with the staff of the SEC during the period when the registration statement is being reviewed. Counsel often arranges to receive staff comments by telephone in order to expedite preparation of the required amendment and/or response. (In certain situations, a formal letter of comment is not even issued.) Telephone contact is often used in connection with the review of an amendment to a registration statement that has been prepared in response to comments raised by the SEC on the previous filing. Oral communication of comments by the SEC is generally welcomed by registrants and their underwriters as a time-saving measure.

In the case of a carefully prepared document, the comments of the staff are usually relatively few in number and minor in character. Whether the comments are few or many, however, each must be addressed and resolved before the registration statement can become effective. If the comments are well founded and significant, the registration statement must be appropriately amended. Although differences of opinion sometimes exist as to the propriety of a particular comment or request, comments and suggestions made by the SEC often prove to be constructive and appropriate.

The Amended Registration Statement

After the necessary revisions to the registration statement arising from the comments by the SEC staff have been identified, the preparation of a revised statement begins. Amendments to the initial registration statement may also be necessary as a result of significant developments that occur subsequent to the original filing date. For example, there might be a material change in the business or financial condition of the company. (If the change is a material adverse one, the underwriting could cease, inasmuch as such a disclosure could render the stock unsalable.) Similarly, a major pending lawsuit could be settled favorably, which one would want to disclose since it removes any uncertainty about the company and its future. Generally, the changes that go into the revised registration statement will necessitate reprinting the statement.

The Preliminary ("Red Herring") Prospectus

Even before the amended registration is filed, a preliminary prospectus is sent to brokers and prospective purchasers. Circulation of the preliminary prospectus is important in connection with the formation of an underwriting group, that is, the various brokerage companies that the underwriter assembles to distribute the stock. SEC rules require that this prospectus substantially conform with the requirements of the Securities Act and that the cover page bear, in red ink—hence the term *red herring*—the caption "Preliminary Prospectus" and the following statement printed in type as large as that generally used in the body of the prospectus:

> A registration statement relating to these securities has been filed with the Securities and Exchange Commission but has not yet become effective. Information contained herein is subject to completion or amendment. These securities may not be sold nor may offers to buy be accepted prior to the time the registration statement becomes effective. This prospectus shall not constitute an offer to sell or the solicitation of an offer to buy, nor shall there be any sale of these securities in any State in which such offer, solicitation or sale would be unlawful prior to registration or qualification under the securities laws of any such State.

The SEC rules also stipulate that the preliminary prospectus may omit the offering price, underwriting discounts or commissions, discounts or commissions to dealers, amount of proceeds, or other matters dependent on the offering price.

The Due Diligence Meeting

After the registration statement is filed, but before it becomes effective, the principal underwriter holds what is known as a due diligence meeting. The reason for the meeting can be found in a provision of the SEC rules that states that, except for the company and its principals, no person will be held civilly liable in connection with untrue statements or material omissions in SEC filings if he or she can prove that

> he had, after reasonable investigation, reasonable ground to believe and did believe, at the time such part of the registration statement became effective, that the statements therein were true and that there was no omission to state a material fact required to be stated therein or necessary to make the statements therein not misleading.

The meeting is attended not only by the principal underwriter and often by members of the underwriting group but also by the company's principal officers, counsel for the company, counsel for the underwriter, and the independent accountant. The usual procedure is for the underwriters to question the company representatives concerning the company and its business; products; competitive position; recent developments in finance, marketing, operations, and other areas; and future prospects.

The Price Amendment and the Underwriting Agreement

When a registration statement has been filed, the registrant and the underwriter have generally reached agreement as to securities to be sold. In almost all cases, however, the issuer and the underwriter have not yet determined the final price at which the securities are to be offered to the public, the exact amount of underwriter's discount or commission, and the net proceeds to the registrant. The negotiation and final determination of these amounts depends on a number of factors, as discussed earlier, including past and present performance of the company and conditions in the securities markets, the prices of other similar issues of the registrant's securities, and the prices of securities of companies in similar industries at the time the registration statement becomes effective. The basic objective is to set the price at the highest that the underwriter can use and yet not so high that he or she will be unable to sell the shares being offered.

Upon completion of negotiations with the underwriter (which usually happens about the time the registration statement is ready to become effective), the agreement is signed by authorized representatives of the registrant and the underwriter. At this time, the final amendment to the registration statement is prepared, including, as applicable, the agreed-on offering price, underwriter's discount or commission, and the net proceeds to the company. This amendment is called the price amendment. If the staff of the SEC's Division of Corporation Finance has no important reservations with respect to the registration statement (i.e., any questions previously raised have been properly disposed of), the registrant and underwriter will customarily request that the offering be declared effective immediately—referred to as requesting "acceleration." If acceleration is granted, the underwriter may proceed with the sale of securities to the public.

Closing Date

The closing date, which is generally specified in the underwriting agreement, is usually within 10 days to two weeks after the effective date of the registration statement. At the closing, the company delivers the registered securities to the underwriter and receives payment for the issue. Various legal documents are also exchanged at the closing, as well as an updated comfort letter prepared by the independent accountant.

REPORTING REQUIREMENTS AFTER BECOMING PUBLIC

No discussion on the subject of going public would be complete without giving consideration to the continuing obligations of the now-public company to provide information to its shareholders.

The question of when a company is obligated to file a particular report with the SEC or the type of report to be filed is a legal one, and competent counsel should be consulted. The following subsections, however, are provided as an overview of the general filing requirements and various types of common reports.

What Companies Are Subject

Generally, a company is subject to the SEC reporting requirements if the company's securities: (1) are registered on a national securities exchange; or (2) are traded interstate—that is, over the counter—*and* as of the last day of the fiscal year, the company's assets exceed $1 million *and* a class of the company's equity securities are held by 500 or more persons.

Summary of Forms

The following list summarizes the principal information forms that must be filed and the character of each.

Form	Description
10–K	Annual report to the SEC. It discloses in detail information about the company's activities, financial condition, and results of operations and also contains the company's annual financial statements.
10–Q	Quarterly report required for each of the first three quarters of the fiscal year. It includes condensed financial data and information on significant events.
8–K	Report filed upon the occurrence of certain significant events, such as a change in control, bankruptcy, or a change in independent accountants.
Proxy or information statements	Data furnished to shareholders to provide them with information that they need to decide how to assign their proxies (votes).

In addition to the foregoing, public companies must provide annual reports to shareholders with much the same financial information as is included in Form 10–K.

To meet the various reporting requirements imposed on them, public companies must maintain an adequate financial staff, supported by both competent legal counsel and independent accountants.

APPENDIX: TIMETABLE FOR REGISTRATION PROCEDURES

The following is a sample timetable for accomplishing a registration of securities.

Date	Description of Procedure	General Responsibility
April 20	Hold board of directors meeting to authorize: Issuance of additional amount of stock to be offered Preparation of registration statement for filing with SEC Negotiation of underwriting agreement	Registrant
April 25	Hold organizational meeting to discuss preparation of registration statement	All parties
April 26	Begin drafting registration statement	Registrant
April 30	Complete and distribute timetable for registration process.	Registrant's counsel
May 10	Distribute first draft of underwriting for review	Underwriters' counsel
May 15	Distribute questionnaires to directors and officers covering matters relating to registration requirements	Registrant's counsel
May 20	Distribute first draft of textual portion of registration statement for review	Registrant and counsel
May 25	Submit draft of financial statements to be included in registration statement	Registrant and independent accountant
May 27	Review draft of registration statement.	All parties
June 1	Send complete draft of registration statement to printer	Registrant or counsel
June 10	Approve and submit final audited financial statements and related report for inclusion in registration statement	Independent accountant

Date	Description of Procedure	General Responsibility
June 12–22	Receive and correct first printed proofs of registration statement	All parties
	Distribute proof of registration statement to directors and officers	Registrant or counsel
	Send revised draft of registration statement to printer	Registrant or counsel
June 23	Hold board of directors meeting to approve and sign registration statements	Registrant
June 24	File registration statement with SEC	Registrant's counsel
	Distribute preliminary ("red herring") prospectus	Underwriters
July 15	Receive letter of comment from SEC regarding registration statement.	Registrant and counsel
July 16	Hold meeting to discuss letter of comment	All parties
July 19	Complete draft of registration statement amendments resulting from the SEC's comment letter and send to printer	Registrant and counsel
July 20–21	Review printer's proof of amendment to registration statement	All parties
	Send corrected proof to printer	Registrant's counsel
July 22	File amendments to registration statement to cover SEC comments and to reflect any material developments since initial filing on June 24	Registrant and counsel

Date	Description of Procedure	General Responsibility
	Notify SEC in writing that a final (price) amendment will be filed on August 1 and that the company requests "acceleration" in order that the registration statement may become effective as of the close of business on that date	Registrant or counsel
July 27	Resolve any final comments and changes with SEC by telephone	Registrant and counsel
July 29	Hold due diligence meeting to determine that no events have taken place that are not disclosed in the registration statement or that do not require disclosure and that all parties are satisfied that the registration statement is not misleading	All parties
August 1	Finalize offering price	Registrant and underwriter
August 2	Deliver first comfort letter to underwriters	Independent accountant
	Sign underwriting agreement	Registrant and underwriter
	File amendment to registration statement identifying price	Registrant and counsel
	Receive notification that registration statement has become effective	Registrant and counsel
	Notify stock exchange of effectiveness	Registrant's counsel
August 7	Deliver second comfort letter to underwriters	Independent accountant

Date	Description of Procedure	General Responsibility
	Complete settlement with underwriters: issue stock, collect proceeds from offering, sign all final documents, and so on	Registrant and counsel; underwriters and counsel

CHAPTER
FIFTEEN

EVALUATING BUSINESS PERFORMANCE

S ooner or later almost every entrepreneur recognizes the need to evaluate his or her business's health, that is, to measure its performance. The entrepreneur's interest in performance evaluation may be sparked by a cocktail party comment about how well a similar business is doing or by an article in a business periodical that suggests how well his or her business *should* be doing.

When trade creditors, lenders, or shareholders ask for financial statements, they are often performing their own evaluation, formal or informal, of your business. The trade creditor or lender is concerned with the company's viability—its ability to pay its obligations. Their interest is often short term, focused on whether you can pay back a loan or pay for goods and services. Your own interest must be for both the short and long term.

Performance evaluation, if done properly and regularly, will give you the opportunity to identify areas for improvement. The process can highlight departments that are operating below expectations, procedures that are inefficient, and emphases that should be shifted, for example, from production to sales. As a result of the review you may find a need to bring in experts who will assess your conclusions and evaluate your proposed solutions before they are tested in the real world.

In this chapter we will discuss various approaches to this self-evaluation process and present a diagnostic questionnaire organized by business functions and management processes that can be used to identify weaknesses and, by the form of the questions, remedies. We also include a list of over 80 ideas to increase revenues and operating efficiency and decrease expenses.

METHODS OF EVALUATION

Performance may be evaluated objectively or subjectively. An objective evaluation is based on quantifiable measures; sales and net income for a period are examples. A subjective evaluation is qualitative and therefore judgmental; it is concerned with how the business is being managed. To evaluate the effectiveness of a marketing program is essentially a subjective exercise. The objective and subjective approaches can also be differentiated in terms of ends and means. Objective measures of performance focus on the accomplishment or the end result. Subjective measures focus on the process or means by which the end result is achieved.

You do not have to choose between the advantages and disadvantages of each type of performance measurement. By incorporating both objective and subjective measures of performance into the evaluation process, you will be able to benefit from the advantages of each.

Objective Measures of Performance

For many entrepreneurs, the most appropriate objective measure of performance is the personal financial benefit derived from owning a business. These benefits include not only salary and direct fringe benefits, such as medical and life insurance and perhaps a retirement plan, but also indirect benefits, such as travel and entertainment, use of an automobile, a country club membership, and other items of value the owner can extract from his or her business. Although these latter items may be ordinary and necessary in the course of pursuing the business, they nonetheless permit the owner to live better because the cost of the meal, entertainment, or club dues is tax deductible to the corporation but is not taxable to him or her.

These benefits, however, are not a measure of the viability of your business. That viability is determined in the light of a broad spectrum of criteria, which in turn are best expressed by ratios.

Ratio Analysis

Indiscriminate use of a multitude of ratios as a means of measuring performance can be confusing. How, for example, should you react when half of the ratios indicate good performance and the other half indicate poor performance? Clearly, some ratios are more significant than others, and proper ratio analysis requires identifying and giving weight to the more significant ones.

We suggest that your identification of meaningful ratios begin with the appropriate analytical focus, or performance area. Among the most frequently used analytical focuses are:

Revenue or sales

Net income

Cash flow

Return on investment

Return on equity

Table 15.1 explains how to evaluate these focuses and summarizes the advantages and disadvantages of each as parameters of performance.

Table 15.1
ALTERNATIVE ANALYTICAL FOCUSES:
SUMMARY OF ADVANTAGES AND DISADVANTAGES

Analytical focus	Advantages	Disadvantages
Revenue or sales	Easy to calculate	Ignores the cost of generating revenues
	Measurable for short periods of time (daily)	Ignores amount of assets needed to generate revenues
Net income	Reflects expenses that accompany generation of revenues	Greatly impacted by noncash charges such as depreciation and amortization
	Relatively easy to understand and calculate	Ignores amount of assets needed to generate revenues
Cash flow[a]	Theoretically measures cash-generating capability of the entity	Ignores amount of assets needed to generate revenues
Return on investment[b]	Measures net results of operations in comparison with assets utilized	Does not differentiate between effects of equity and debt financing
Return on equity[c]	Measures efficiency with which shareholders' investment is utilized	Sometimes of limited meaning where shareholder investment is minimal
	Easily related to the factors of profitability, asset turnover, and financial leverage	

[a]Cash flow is frequently calculated by adding back "noncash" charges such as depreciation and amortization to net income.
[b]There are many variations in the calculation of ROI. A frequently used one is as follows: net income plus interest expense, depreciation, and amortization divided by stockholders' equity plus long-term debt.
[c]ROE is frequently calculated by dividing net income (for the period) by average shareholders' equity (during the period).

Return on Equity.   We believe that for analytical purposes return on equity (ROE) is generally the best measure of performance. When using this measure, you should increase net income by the excess of your salary and benefits, less the income tax benefits derived, over what you would otherwise expect to be earning as an employee elsewhere. This measure is appropriate because each investor has alternatives for his or her investable funds, ranging from a relatively risk-free investment in government debt obligations to the comparatively risky investment of the business itself. Conceptually, a business must earn over time a rate of return greater than what the owner could have earned by investing in a relatively safe debt obligation. Otherwise, existing shareholders would be better served by liquidating their investment in the business and simply buying a Treasury bill.

An advantage of using ROE as the primary focus is that such return can be explained, with mathematical precision, by performance with regard to profitability, asset turnover, and financial leverage. The formula is:

$$\text{ROE} = \frac{\text{net income}}{\text{shareholders' equity}} = \frac{\text{net income}}{\text{revenues}} \times \frac{\text{revenues}}{\text{assets}} \times \frac{\text{assets}}{\text{shareholders' equity}}$$

Shareholder's equity and assets are average balances for the period. Each of the three components of ROE can in turn be viewed as:

measures of profitability

$$\left(\frac{\text{net income}}{\text{revenues}}\right)$$

asset turnover

$$\left(\frac{\text{revenues}}{\text{assets}}\right)$$

financial leverage

$$\left(\frac{\text{assets}}{\text{shareholders' equity}}\right)$$

Profitability refers to the amount of profits generated compared with the sales for the period. Asset turnover measures how efficiently assets such as receivables, inventory, and plant and equipment are being used in generating sales. Financial leverage measures the value of assets being financed by shareholders' money rather than by money provided by creditors. These three ratios constitute what may be thought of as second-level performance indicators. Third-level performance indicators are ratios that explain these three terms, as shown in Figure 15.1.

The list in Figure 15.1 shows how each level of ratios can in turn be explained by a lower-level set of ratios. Thus, not only can return on equity be explained by profitability, asset turnover, and leverage, but asset turnover can also be explained by receivables turnover, inventory turnover, and fixed-asset turnover. This presentation creates an analytical framework through which one can understand the effect of changes in any one ratio.

The framework also can be used to determine which of the ratios provide the most meaningful indication of how your particular business *is* doing as compared with how well it *should* be doing. For most businesses, sales in a given day, month, or even year may be subject to wide fluctuations and therefore have a significant impact on both profitability and turnover. Hence for most companies, sales constitute a key performance indicator. Some companies, however, are able to correlate closely sales to salesperson contacts, and for them these contacts may be more useful in indicating performance than sales. Salesperson contacts in turn are a function of the number of salespersons and the average contacts per salesperson. If average contacts are relatively constant, at least over the short term, the number of salespersons may be the more appropriate indicator.

In a manufacturing company, significant ratios would generally include inventory turnover, receivables turnover, and gross margin. If gross margin, for example, can be reliably related to the ratio of labor hours to sales, then labor hours becomes a meaningful performance indicator.

No matter which indicators are identified as key, in and of themselves they all have limited value. Thus a calculated ROE must be interpreted in conjunction with such data as yields on alternative investments, the return generated by the entity in past years and projected for future years, and the return generated by similar businesses.

Performance Indicator	Formula
Return on equity	$\dfrac{\text{net income}}{\text{shareholders' equity}}$
Profitability	$\dfrac{\text{net income}}{\text{revenues}}$
Gross margin	$\dfrac{\text{revenue less cost of goods sold}}{\text{sales}}$
Production–purchasing efficiency	$\dfrac{\text{cost of goods sold}}{\text{revenues}}$
Selling efficiency	$\dfrac{\text{selling expense}}{\text{revenues}}$
Administrative efficiency	$\dfrac{\text{general and administrative expenses}}{\text{revenues}}$
Effective tax rate	$\dfrac{\text{income taxes}}{\text{pretax profit}}$
Asset turnover	$\dfrac{\text{revenues}}{\text{assets}}$
Receivables turnover	$\dfrac{\text{revenues}}{\text{average receivables}}$
Inventory turnover	$\dfrac{\text{cost of goods sold}}{\text{average inventory}}$
Fixed-asset turnover	$\dfrac{\text{revenues}}{\text{average fixed assets}}$
Leverage	$\dfrac{\text{assets}}{\text{shareholders' equity}}$ or $\dfrac{\text{total debt}}{\text{shareholders' equity}}$
Current ratio	$\dfrac{\text{current assets}}{\text{current liabilities}}$
Quick ratio	$\dfrac{\text{cash and receivables}}{\text{current liabilities}}$

FIGURE 15.1 Hierarchy of Ratios.

Developing a Base of Comparative Information

There are numerous sources of information that can be utilized to help evaluate an entity's performance. The most readily available, and hence probably most frequently used, is historical data.

Historical Comparisons. Knowing that XYZ Inc.'s return on equity for the last six years was 6, 8, 10, 11, 11.5, and 12 percent (with the most recent year last) adds meaning to the evaluation. This historical information demonstrates that performance has been improving steadily. Historical data has some limitations, however. For one thing, it may not be available, especially in a start-up situation. Even if it is available, overreliance on comparisons with historical data may lead to mediocre performance. Management may strive, only to improve upon the poor results of prior periods.

Comparisons with Plan or Budget Data. An alternative basis for comparison is the plan or budget for the entity. Thus if the ROE for the year is 12 percent, this figure takes on added meaning when compared with a budgeted return of 14 percent. The value of comparing the actual ROE to budget is, of course, dependent on the quality of the budget. To some, the budget is little more than an extrapolation of past performance, reflective of a "We will do it the same way we did it last year" mentality. In such cases, using the budget as a comparative source has the same limitation as using historical performance—that is, the comparison may not get to the root of mediocre performance.

Similarly, to the extent that planned or budgeted data is based on unrealistically formulated objectives, the value of the comparison is weakened if the ROE is set too high; for example, comparison with the year's results may show a less favorable performance than the facts warrant. Assuming performance standards in the budgeting process have been set objectively, however, comparison of actual results with budgeted results can be a worthwhile process.

Industry Comparison. Comparisons with historical and budgeted data can be supplemented by comparisons with industry data. Industry data on performance of companies in a given industry may be available from three important sources:

Trade and industry groups

Government, primarily federal, especially the Department of Commerce

Private compilers of data for public use, such as Robert Morris Associates, Standard & Poor's, and Dun & Bradstreet

An enhancement of the comparison with industry groups is a comparison with specific companies *in* the industry group. Because industry data covers both good and poor performers, overall industrial comparisons seldom provide the kind of insights that can be applied in improving performance. On the other hand, the equivalent data on a company that is similar in size and scope of operations to your own may be very useful in this respect. The identification of these similar companies, which may be thought of as peers to your entity, and subsequent comparative analysis can be quite worthwhile. (Unfortunately, developing an appropriate peer group and gaining access to information on the peers is difficult in that many of the peers may be privately held companies for which performance information is not available.)

When you make industry comparisons, be sure that the data is accurate, timely, and essentially comparable. Comparing a gasoline retailer to a gasoline wholesaler is of little value to the wholesaler looking to evaluate the performance of his or her business. In regard to comparability, "essential" is sufficient, because the impact of differences—for example, in accounting for inventory costs—can be factored into any analysis.

Tabular Analysis of ROE.   Table 15.2 depicts what an analysis of Company XYZ's ROE might look like using the following four comparative bases: intercompany, peer group, industry, and yields on long-term government bonds. The table indicates that XYZ's ROE performance, although improving in absolute terms over the last five years, has been mediocre relative to the performances of its peer group, especially Companies A and D. Company A has been a consistently high-ranking performer, although its performance has not shown the dramatic progress of Company D, which over the last five years has progressed from the worst performer to the best performer in the peer group. The strong showing of these two companies has raised the peer group performance average over XYZ's performance, even though Companies B and C have not performed well.

Table 15.2
COMPARATIVE ANALYSIS OF RETURN ON EQUITY

Company	19X5 Projected %	19X5 Actual %	19X5 Actual Rank	19X4 Actual %	19X4 Actual Rank	19X3 Actual %	19X3 Actual Rank	19X2 Actual %	19X2 Actual Rank	19X1 Actual %	19X1 Actual Rank
A	NA	14.8	2	14.2	1	14.1	1	14.2	2	14.4	2
XYZ	14.0	12.0	3	11.5	3	11.0	4	10.0	4	8.0	4
B	NA	11.9	4	11.2	4	13.2	2	14.3	1	14.6	1
C	NA	8.2	5	8.0	5	8.1	5	7.9	5	8.1	3
D	NA	14.9	1	13.5	2	12.0	3	10.4	3	7.9	5
Peer group average		12.4		11.7		11.7		11.4		10.6	
Industry average		11.9		11.3		11.6		11.2		10.5	
Long-term government bond yield		12.1		11.2		8.9		7.9		7.4	

Although XYZ's improvement in ROE in the latest year was notable, it was still less than that achieved by the peer group and the industry as a whole. The performance of all companies, except A and D, and of the industry as a whole was poor in the last year in comparison with the yield on the less risky government bonds.

The effect of the table is to demonstrate the power of comparative analysis. Suddenly XYZ's performance, which without comparative analysis had seemed to be good because of the consistent progress in increasing ROE, appears to be relatively poor. To begin to understand why XYZ is not performing as well as Companies A or D would require comparative analysis of other factors in the ratio hierarchy or analytical framework.

Timing the Objective Evaluation

Utilizing the ROE analytical framework and the full comparative analysis requires information regarding performance of peer companies and the industry. Information on your company's performance should be available on a timely basis, but unfortunately, the other information will often be available only on an annual basis. If the peer group is composed of public companies, limited quarterly data may be available. Companies operating in regulated industries may publish data monthly and in some cases even weekly or daily. In general, a full comparative analysis can be done only once a year. This is probably just as well, given the limited resources you may have for this kind of activity. By itself, the ROE analytical focus and framework does not require data from outside the company. Therefore, it should be calculated more often than the comparative analysis is undertaken. As with any data gathering project, you should assign responsibility and prepare a timetable for development of the analysis.

Determining *why* something has occurred may take additional time, but therein lies the larger payoff of identifying opportunities for improving performance.

Delaying this evaluation of critical variables subject to significant change exposes your business to the risk of poor performance continuing undetected. Utilizing a monthly key indicator report (as more fully described in Chapter 8) summarizing performance will reduce this risk.

Because of the objective nature of these measures, the calculation can be easily done by you or one of your employees. The real challenge is in analyzing the results to identify how performance improvements can be made. Remember that mere generalization of data without such analysis is almost certainly a waste of time.

Subjective Measures of Performance

You are probably involved to some extent in subjective evaluation every working day. When you walk out to the shop floor to see how production is running, you are engaging in subjective evaluation. But such evaluations are seldom systematically performed; rather, they occur "ad hoc," squeezed between other activities or in response to a crisis. To be effective, subjective evaluation must be systematic and planned in such a manner that every activity is regularly covered. This is not to say that periodic systematic evaluation should replace ad hoc evaluation; rather, it should supplement it. Through ad hoc evaluation, you can pick up obvious performance deficiencies and act quickly to correct them.

The Management Process

The activities of any manager can be classified into five major categories: planning, organizing, staffing, directing, and controlling. Planning is the process of comparing alternative objectives, selecting the optimal ones, and determining the methodology and schedule for achieving them. Organizing is the establishment of a formal structure of roles that defines the duties of people working together to accomplish the objectives established in the planning process. Staffing provides an inflow of capable and experienced personnel in sufficient numbers to meet organizational needs. Directing is concerned with leadership and the effective management of people through guiding and monitoring their efforts. Finally, controlling can be defined as the process of reviewing activities and correcting deviations from planned results.

Functions of a Business

Almost every business is involved in the functions of marketing, or determining what product will be sold, where, at what price, and with what promotion; purchasing, or obtaining the goods that will be sold or used in production; production, or conversion of purchased material into finished goods; and distribution, or transporting the finished goods to market. These primary functions need to be coupled with effective support functions such as accounting, finance, legal, personnel, and EDP.

When the management processes and functions are combined, we have a summary of all management activities. This summary can be depicted as a matrix, as is shown in Figure 15.2.

The matrix can be read either across rows or down columns. Reading across the first row, we see that to perform the function of marketing properly one needs to be involved in all five of the management processes: planning, organizing, staffing, directing, and controlling. Reading down the first column shows that planning should be done in connection with each of the business functions of marketing, purchasing, production, distribution, and support. Keep in mind that the number of boxes is not necessarily indicative of the number of managers or even employees, for in smaller companies one person may handle several of these activities.

By providing an overview of all management activities, the matrix identifies those that must be subjectively evaluated as to specifically how

Functions	Processes				
	Planning	Organization	Staffing	Directing	Controlling
Marketing					
Purchasing					
Production					
Distribution					
Support					

FIGURE 15.2   Matrix of business functions and management processes.

each is being performed and how performance might be improved. This evaluation, as pointed out earlier, lacks the mathematical precision inherent in the objective evaluation process.

Conducting the Subjective Evaluation

Using the matrix in Figure 15.2 as a guide, you should develop a schedule for reviewing each activity on a cycle of no more than six months. Ideally, the focus of the analysis should alternate between functions—that is, first the management processes involved in marketing, then in purchasing, then in the production, and so on—and processes—that is, first planning in all five functions, then organizing in all five functions, and so on.

For each activity, there must be a comparison between how the activity is performed and how it should be performed. But how do you derive a standard for how an activity should be performed? The answer is primarily from your experience and past observations of how your company performed the activity or how some other company performs it. To a lesser extent, your standard can be based on the ideas of qualified authorities as expressed in business periodicals, books, and lectures.

In making a subjective evaluation, you can, of course, make use of second opinions. For example, the accountant's review of controls or the consultant's evaluation of a firm's planning process can provide useful input into the evaluation process. Naturally, you must be sure of the qualifications of anyone you consult.

The Diagnostic Questionnaire.   The diagnostic questionnaire in the Appendix to this chapter (Exhibit 15.1) highlights some of the many questions for you to ask as part of your analysis.

PERFORMANCE IMPROVEMENT

In general, performance improvement is brought about in one or more of the following ways:

Increasing the volume of profitable business

Decreasing the expenses associated with generating the business

Using assets more efficiently

The Appendix to this chapter (Exhibit 15.2) contains an "idea" list of potential opportunities in each of these three areas.

The Procedure

Merely identifying opportunities for improving performance is not enough. Action must be taken to implement the findings. A logical procedure for accomplishing this would involve the following steps:

Determining alternative means of operating in the area under analysis
Evaluating the impact of operating by alternative means
Selecting the appropriate alternative
Blueprinting the implementation of selected alternatives
Determining priority of alternatives selected for implementation
Assigning responsibility and timetable for implementation
Monitoring implementation
Monitoring results periodically after implementation, reevaluating as necessary

Performance improvement need not be a formal or cumbersome process. Some opportunities for improvement will be obvious. On the other hand, some possibilities, because of their scope and implications, cannot be properly weighed without a written analysis. For example, deciding whether to purchase a machine that will replace five laborers requires the projection of expenses under the alternatives of purchase and no purchase. The factors in the decision include projected sales volume, machine capacity, product profitability, machine reliability, financing costs, peripheral equipment needs, projected wage scales, payroll taxes, tax credits, and utility costs. Anyone other than a mathematical genius could hardly handle all this in his or her head.

Summary

This chapter has cited detailed techniques for measuring performance, identifying opportunities for improvements, and making improvements. The real key to improving performance lies not with these techniques, however, but rather with you. Improvement can occur only if you want it to occur and if you are open-minded about the changes that may be necessary.

APPENDIX

Exhibit 15.1   Diagnostic Questionnaire for Performance Evaluation

Management Processes

(Applicable to the entire business, including all business functions)

Planning:

Is there a long-range plan that sets out objectives and a course of action for each of the business functions?

Is there a long-range financial forecast?

Is there a detailed budget against which actual performance is compared and significant variances analyzed?

Do all personnel understand who reports to whom?

How is morale and the general work environment?

Is there a backup for key personnel?

Staffing:

What is being done to identify and attract qualified personnel in keeping with projected needs?

How are potential employees and existing employees evaluated?

Has a benefits package been designed that will facilitate hiring and retention of personnel?

What means for improving motivation of personnel have been identified?

Have training programs been developed?

Are there career plans for key personnel?

Directing:

Is there a clear description of each employee's responsibilities and duties?

Does each employee know his or her objectives?

Is there periodic feedback on progress against objectives and means for improving performance where it is deficient?

Controlling:

Have you put in place a system for timely reporting of activity in such major functions as:

Marketing?
Purchasing?
Production?
Distribution?

Is there a system for timely reporting of financial results with comparison to budgeted results?

Has a cost system for identifying product costs been developed?

Are results of operations promptly analyzed and appropriate corrective action identified?

Is corrective action promptly implemented?

Business Functions

Marketing:

Have marketing objectives and strategies been clearly defined?

Has the market been identified and analyzed—where it is, who the customer is, who the noncustomer is, and why; decrease or increase in market size, anticipated changes and their impact?

Is there a long-term sales forecast by broad product category or dollar volume for use in planning production facilities, manpower, or long-range procurement?

Is a product-by-product review of profitability, continuance, composition, and obsolescence conducted to answer such questions as:

Do a few products account for a large percentage of sales? Should low-volume items be trimmed?

Is any product line threatened by social or technological changes?

Are sales and profitability results regularly analyzed, and compared with budget, by product line, customer, market, territory, salesperson, outside agent, and distribution channels?

Are short-term sales forecasts prepared for successive periods showing type of product, number of units, unit sales, and price?

Are short-term sales forecasts supplied to production management for developing manufacturing plans and to financial management for developing a profit plan?

Have active programs in market research, new markets, and new product development been established?

Is there a formal mechanism for new-product review and approval?

Are marketing responsibilities clearly assigned?

Is compensation of salespersons structured to promote sales of high gross-margin items?

Is there periodic performance evaluation of brokers, distributors, and manufacturers?

Is there periodic review of advertising effectiveness?

Do you regularly prepare reports on bids submitted versus invitations to bid, sales commitments received versus bids submitted, and analysis of reasons for lost bids?

Are periodic returns and claims reports listed by customer?

Have you established periodic reports on variations from established prices and significant terms listed by customer, product, or salesperson?

Has budget control of advertising effectiveness been implemented?

Has an expense budget been prepared, with estimated cost for each sales segment (product, customer type, territory, and so on) and expense classification?

Do you bill back unusual customer-caused costs, such as excessive handling and special packaging?

Are customer invoices and credit memoranda being issued promptly?

Purchasing:

Have purchase authorizations on repetitively used articles been reduced via a systematic stocking program?

Are purchase authorizations for repetitively used articles under a
stocking program based on lead time plus safety-stock considerations,
or is periodic planning being used?

Do purchase authorizations designate the date materials are required?

Do purchase authorizations for specialized components or equipment
include technical and performance specifications?

Have statements of purchasing policies been issued covering:
  Corporate relationships, particularly buying responsibilities?
  Competitive buying, source selection, and bidding?
  Maintenance of multiple buying sources to protect continuity of
  supply?
  Rules on commitments and contracts?
  Reciprocity?
  Conflict of interest?

Is the purchasing function centralized so that locations do not com-
pete with one another, thereby maximizing purchasing power?

Is full use being made of nationwide buying contracts and blanket
purchase commitments as a means of maximizing purchasing power?

Have purchasing personnel been supplied with summaries of commodity buying and supplier buying volumes to facilitate negotiations
with suppliers?

Does the purchasing agent participate in decisions relating to stand-
ardization, value analysis, and lease-versus-buy options to purchase
equipment under lease?

Is there a plan to ensure that materials are delivered within the time
specified on purchase commitments?

Are there up-to-date procedures to foster use of accurate weights and
weighing routines (that is, periodic testing of scales or use of statistical
sampling techniques)?

Is there a policy on acceptance or nonacceptance of overshipments or
undershipments?

Is the purchasing agent informed quickly when shipments are received or when they are overdue, as well as of the quantity and quality of each?

Are payments deferred until due date?

Is purchasing tied in closely with inventory analysis and control?

Are perpetual inventory records maintained on all important items?

Have there been significant book-to-physical-inventory adjustments? If so, why?

Has the rate of back-order change been analyzed?

Have there been interruptions in production schedules due to lack of materials? If so, why?

Is the customer-service measurement system functioning properly?

Have machine setup costs increased significantly? If so, why?

Are product delivery schedules being met?

Are work-in-process increases disproportionate to sales?

Are scrap costs rising faster than they should?

Production:

Has short-term production and inventory forecasting been developed?

Has plant productivity improved?

Is labor utilization continually reassessed to determine how it can be improved?

Are seasonal peaks and lows in plant operations minimized to the fullest degree possible?

Do supply sources offer the optimal combination of reliability and competitive price?

Do you minimize production costs through efficiencies in material, handling, materials management, plant layout, shop scheduling, maintenance programs, quality control, control over labor usage, product design, and research and development programs?

Is overtime authorized before it is actually incurred?

Do records indicate whether production schedules are met and the reasons for any deviations?

Does the system ensure periodic identification, review, and disposal of slow-moving or obsolete stock?

Is the cost accounting system using the same basic data and/or records as the production system?

Is there in effect a standard cost system, developed by element or expense for each significant operation, each important cost center, and each product.?

Does the cost system identify and facilitate control over direct (variable) product costs?

Are you utilizing production management that includes organization charts, job descriptions, and clear-cut assignments of responsibility?

Are production and production changes initiated only upon written request?

Does preparation of time cards, time sheets, and attendance records distinguish between direct and indirect costs and facilitate control over those costs?

Is production management furnished with "bills of material" or route sheets listing parts and quality of each required to produce one unit of a particular product or subassembly?

Do production management route sheets specify what must be produced, how, where, and in what sequence?

Are labor assignments based on route documents specifying operations to be performed, time allowed, sequence of operations, machines to be used, and alternative routings when feasible?

Is preventive maintenance utilized to curb machine downtime?

Is there an up-to-date system of inventory control?

Distribution:

Are distribution costs including demurrage reviewed?

Do you determine means of distribution by evaluating such items as:

Truck?

Common carrier?

Contract carrier?

Rail?

Are opportunities to back-haul identified?

Do you monitor the condition of goods upon delivery?

Support—Finance:

Have you identified opportunities to increase earnings from surplus cash by maintaining minimum bank balances in demand accounts?

Have you identified opportunities to improve collection of receivables through:

Generating bills more promptly?
Designing appropriate incentives for customer prompt payment?
Reducing mail and processing time through utilization of a lockbox?

Are opportunities to reduce inventories through proper purchasing and production procedures identified (see "Purchasing" in this questionnaire)?

Do you identify and dispose of assets not needed for operations?

Have all asset acquisitions been evaluated as to the merits of leasing versus buying?

Is insurance coverage reviewed to keep programs in line with needs and changing conditions?

Has a plan been developed for enhancing your relationships with financial institutions to reduce your interest rates on borrowing?

Support—EDP:

Have the costs and capabilities of service bureaus versus a company-operated facility been evaluated?

Have systems development plans of various departments been ranked for priority of implementation?

Are EDP systems and procedures documented?

Have adequate security measures been implemented for protection from loss due to errors, fraud, embezzlement, sabotage, malicious mischief, and accidental destruction?

Exhibit 15.2   Techniques for Improving Efficiency

The following is a list of ideas for increasing revenues, decreasing expenses, and operating more efficiently.

Techniques	Objectives							
	Cut Purchase Costs	Cut Freight Costs	Maximize Working Capital	Cut Scrap	Reduce Downtime	Cut Labor Costs	Cut Administrative Overhead	Increase Revenues
Reduce numbers of different types of articles in stock	X		X				X	
Standardize preferred items	X				X		X	
Define roles of purchasing personnel at different levels of large organization	X		X				X	
Evaluate vendor quality, delivery, and cost performances	X		X		X			
Provide enough time to shop the market	X							
Centralize negotiations for major items, including freight	X	X						
Use traveling requisitions							X	
Give purchasing personnel a free hand in vendor selection, based on operating specifications	X				X			
Issue complete purchase orders for significant transactions	X							
Reduce rush procurement	X	X			X		X	
Prescribe preferred routing for incoming bulk items		X			X			
Seek competitive bids for significant transactions	X							
Establish floor below which bids will not be obtained							X	

	(1)	(2)	(3)	(4)	(5)	(6)
Subject all buying contracts to periodic review	X					
Develop approved vendor list for highly technical purchases	X			X		
Combine related items on purchase orders	X					X
Conduct make-or-buy studies						
Use purchase order copy as receiving report	X					X
Test-weight bulk commodities						
Authorize telephone releases for minor items bought on contract	X	X				X
Eliminate useless copies made by receiving clerks						X
Stagger incoming loads to eliminate demurrage and shipping overtime	X	X		X	X	
Speed up invoice processing to avoid discount losses						
Set up plant delivery system						
Signal vendor overshipments to buyers for bargaining purposes	X					
Negotiate terms with suppliers affecting packaging, pallets, and so on					X	
Reduce distance between receiving and storage facilities					X	
Set up inspection schedule for incoming goods to curb acceptance of damaged items	X		X	X		
Step up billing to vendors of rework	X		X			

Techniques	Objectives							
	Cut Purchase Costs	Cut Freight Costs	Maximize Working Capital	Cut Scrap	Reduce Downtime	Cut Labor Costs	Cut Administrative Overhead	Increase Revenues
Bill freight to vendors on rejected shipments		X						
Pass minor invoice discrepancies							X	
Control slow-moving inventories and initiate time for disposal actions	X		X	X				
Establish reorder points and economic ordering or production quantities	X		X		X		X	
Plan use of inventory space						X		
Maintain current locator files in storerooms						X		
Establish technologically significant materials codes	X				X	X		
Shift burden of carrying inventory to suppliers	X		X				X	
Introduce self-help storeroom bins for inexpensive items							X	
Install storeroom facilities to cut metals on site	X							
Determine optimum buying sizes for metals	X			X				
Recharge flashlight batteries instead of buying new ones	X							
Clean gloves instead of buying new ones	X							

Technique	1	2	3	4	5	6	7
Use rebuilding services for valves, instruments, and so on	X						
Use nonoriginal equipment sources for spares	X						
Circumscribe addition of new articles to stock	X					X	
Correlate forecasting data for marketing and production	X		X		X		
Control off-sheet discounts							X
Control application of freight terms to customers							X
Consider freight factor in setting selling prices							X
Develop standard routing guides for outgoing shipments		X					
Signal premium freight for investigation		X					
Establish prompt control over freight claims		X					
Negotiate favorable terms with freight audit agency		X					
Highlight unprofitable territories, products, customers, warehouses							X
Act as self-insurer on rental cars			X				
Negotiate hotel rates on guaranteed basis			X				
Use compacts rather than big cars			X				
Use coach class on planes			X				
Stratify salespersons' calls on basis of customer needs			X				

Techniques	Cut Purchase Costs	Cut Freight Costs	Maximize Working Capital	Cut Scrap	Reduce Downtime	Cut Labor Costs	Cut Administrative Overhead	Increase Revenues
Capture order information near source					X		X	
Use self-checking capabilities of computers							X	
Check new customer credit *before* shipment							X	
Train order-input clerks to reduce need for editing							X	
Signal costly piecemeal order releases by customers								X
Invoice special warehousing or packaging services								X
Invoice cancellation charges where practical								X
Report physical percentage-of-contract completion versus dollar percentage								X
Reduce delays before production order reaches floor					X	X		
Avoid emergency inventory transfers from plant to plant		X						
Eliminate duplications on operating and accounting records							X	
Take inventory cycle counts at low of stocks							X	

Consider adaptability of current stocks when planning engineering changes	X	
Substitute second shift for overtime		X
Avoid split labor assignments of high-rate persons to lower-rate jobs		X
Monitor machine running speeds to avoid breakdowns	X	
Stabilize labor force by level loading		X
Plan maintenance jobs		X
Reduce fire insurance premiums by complying with inspection reports	X	
Sell used EDP cards to scrap-paper dealers	X	
Invest excess cash	X	
Monitor unemployment insurance claims where experience rating is a factor	X	
Negotiate interruptible rates with utilities where practical	X	